Shamming sick.

VICTORIAN CHINA
FAIRINGS
THE COLLECTORS' GUIDE

To Pamela,

Welcome back to collecting

Kindest Regards

Derek Forbes

Velocipeding on a rainy day.

By about 1867 there were fourteen Fairings depicting velocipedes, bone-shakers or bicycles. They are all fairly rare, very desirable and command top prices if they come on the market (see also the Fairing on page 34).

VICTORIAN CHINA
FAIRINGS
THE COLLECTORS' GUIDE

By Derek H. Jordan

ANTIQUE COLLECTORS' CLUB

British Library Cataloguing-in-Publication Data
A catalogue record for this book is available from the British Library

Printed in England
Published by the Antique Collectors' Club Ltd., Woodbridge, Suffolk, IP12 4SD

Antique Collectors' Club

THE ANTIQUE COLLECTORS' CLUB was formed in 1966 and quickly grew to a five figure membership spread throughout the world. It publishes the only independently run monthly antiques magazine, *Antique Collecting*, which caters for those collectors who are interested in widening their knowledge of antiques, both by greater awareness of quality and by discussion of the factors which influence the price that is likely to be asked. The Antique Collectors' Club pioneered the provision of information on prices for collectors and the magazine still leads in the provision of detailed articles on a variety of subjects.

It was in response to the enormous demand for information on 'what to pay' that the price guide series was introduced in 1968 with the first edition of *The Price Guide to Antique Furniture* (completely revised 1978 and 1989), a book which broke new ground by illustrating the more common types of antique furniture, the sort that collectors could buy in shops and at auctions rather than the rare museum pieces which had previously been used (and still to a large extent are used) to make up the limited amount of illustrations in books published by commercial publishers. Many other price guides have followed, all copiously illustrated, and greatly appreciated by collectors for the valuable information they contain, quite apart from prices. The Price Guide Series heralded the publication of many standard works of reference on art and antiques. *The Dictionary of British Art* (now in six volumes), *The Pictorial Dictionary of British 19th Century Furniture Design*, *Oak Furniture* and *Early English Clocks* were followed by many deeply researched reference works such as *The Directory of Gold and Silversmiths*, providing new information. Many of these books are now accepted as the standard work of reference on their subject.

The Antique Collectors' Club has widened its list to include books on gardens, garden design, garden history and architecture. All the Club's publications are available through bookshops world wide and a full catalogue of all these titles is available free of charge from the addresses below.

Club membership, open to all collectors, costs little. Members receive free of charge *Antique Collecting*, the Club's magazine (published ten times a year), which contains well-illustrated articles dealing with the practical aspects of collecting not normally dealt with by magazines. Prices, features of value, investment potential, fakes and forgeries are all given prominence in the magazine.

Among other facilities available to members are private buying and selling facilities and the opportunity to meet other collectors at their local antique collectors' club. There are over eighty in Britain and more than a dozen overseas. Members may also buy the Club's publications at special pre-publication prices.

As its motto implies, the Club is an organisation designed to help collectors get the most out of their hobby: it is informal and friendly and gives enormous enjoyment to all concerned.

For Collectors — By Collectors — About Collecting
ANTIQUE COLLECTORS' CLUB
www.antique-acc.com

Sandy Lane, Old Martlesham, Woodbridge, Suffolk, IP12 4SD, UK
Tel: 01394 389950 Fax: 01394 389999
e-mail: sales@antique-acc.com
or
Market Street Industrial Park, Wappingers' Falls, NY 12590, USA
Tel: (845) 297 0003 Fax: (845) 297 0068 Orders: (800) 252 5231
e-mail: info@antiquecc.com

Dedication

This book is dedicated to all my non-collecting friends
who I have bored silly over the years.

Contents

Acknowledgements

A book does not write itself. I have many people to thank who contributed to the writing, editing, proofreading, fact-checking, photography of some of the pieces in their wonderful collections and the myriad of jobs that have to be performed before you see the result which is in your hands. To these people, and any that I may have missed, a heartfelt thank you:

Richard Boughner
Ruth and Ron Bragman
Trixie and Brian Currie
Gerald Fearnley
Barbara Gair
Freddie James
Wynne and Rhiannon Jones
Stuart Katz
Novello Morgan
June and Don Murfet
Kate and Stuart Piepenstock
Lizia Renna
Dave Twitchett
Tricia West

My wife Sally, without whose words of encouragement and infinite patience, this book would not have been written.

My brother Alan, for technical assistance.

Foreword

I was fifty-seven years old when I was first introduced to Fairings. My wife, Sally, joined an Antiques Appreciation class at our local Adult Education Centre and we started to buy a small piece of anything we could find that she had learned something about: Clarice Cliffe, Moorcroft, Lalique, Susie Cooper, Shelley, Sylvac, Carlton Ware, and Fairings.

I came across my first Fairings at the Folkestone Antiques Fair where a knowledgeable dealer sold me three in very good condition: *Shall we sleep first or how? Twelve months after marriage* and *The last in bed to put out the light.*

From that moment, I was hooked. I wanted to know more about them and own more of them. I started off slowly, unable to get any books on the subject. Most of my information came from friendly dealers. Then my daughter, Sara, found 'Victorian Fairings' by M. Anderson, in a second-hand book shop and bought it for sixty pence. It is an excellent book but well worn and in need of replacement. However, I have never been able to buy another.

It was about time to publish an up-to-date reference book that is readily available. This Guide is intended to offer the largest pictorial record of Fairings to date.

I have also included some match-strikers and a few pin boxes, especially if they are captioned, but pin boxes are numerous and have been catalogued recently. I have not detailed any series numbers which may be found on the bottom of most pieces. These are covered well in W. S. Bristow's 'Victorian China Fairings' which though long out of print, can be obtained from dealers or at auctions for about £40. However, a collector does not need these numbers to make a start.

I hope this book will encourage you to collect Fairings and that they will bring the immense enjoyment to you that I have obtained over the years in looking for them, talking about them and learning about them from other enthusiasts.

Good hunting!

The last in bed to put out the light. Three examples of the most common and popular Fairing of them all showing variations in size and detail.

Introduction

Fairings - What are they? Briefly, they are small Victorian china ornaments usually captioned, making a social, political, or humorous comment on English life from about 1850 to 1914 when the First World War brought to an end this trade.

Ironically Fairings were not made in England, but in Germany by Conta & Boehme of Pössneck. Founded in 1800, this company had perfected the skill of mass production to such an extent that English manufacturers could not compete with them. Other German factories attempted to compete with Conta & Boehme but most of the works were not as well-crafted; they were thinner and not so well modelled, though still quite collectable.

The original ideas and designs must have come from England; it would seem that no foreigner could know us so well. However, some of the clothes depicted on Fairings are of German origin and some captions just miss the mark of their intended meanings, for example, *Shall we sleep first or how?* "what" would have been more colloquially used in place of "how". Some were made for the European market and from time to time, they surface in England, complete with inscriptions in German or French.

Fairings were definitely made for the huge English Fair market. The word "fair" comes from the Latin *feria* meaning holiday, a great day for the masses, a chance to catch up on gossip, fashions, new ideas and generally to have a good time and perhaps buy or win a small china ornament. Today, we call these small German ornaments of the Victorian/Edwardian period, Fairings.

Some Fairings have two or three different captions while some captions are found on two or three different Fairings, but this is rare and the illustrations will note any differences you are likely to encounter. It may sound complicated, but bear in mind, that though they were assembled and painted by hand, most Fairings are similar, within the same caption.

I have listed alphabetically all Fairings by caption omitting "A" and "The", so that each can be found easily.

The four pieces above are from a group of Fairings which are much sought
after by serious collectors (see Frontispiece).

How were Fairings Made?

The best Fairings were made in Germany by Conta & Boehme between 1850 and 1890. After this date, other unknown German factories and one in Japan, took over the craft until 1914. These latter manufacturers used lighter weight materials that sold at cheaper prices, producing pieces that were not as good but still very collectable.

About 1850, Conta & Boehme discovered an inexpensive and easy way of painting and gilding that would stand the heat of the kilns. This allowed a white, heavy porcelain paste to be moulded in several parts. While still pliable, the parts were then fitted together by hand, the craftsmen adding the small items such as bottles, glasses, pots, lamps, and so on. The whole piece would then be fired at a very high temperature, cooled slowly, and then dipped in a liquid glaze to be fired a second time. The colours and gilt were painted by hand and fired for the last time at a lower temperature. Occasionally, when a figure had been joined, for example to a chair, one would find fire cracks. These are heat expansion cracks such as those found in bread. They are short and jagged and although not desirable, they are quite acceptable in a piece.

The first Fairings of 1850-1860 were larger than those that followed with no markings under the base. From circa 1860, manufacturers started to scratch serial numbers onto the Fairing prior to the firing process primarily for identification and recording purposes. They then started to impress the number into the base along with their trade mark of a bent arm holding a dagger inside a shield, as shown above.

About 1890, the inferior factories took over most of the trade. Conta & Boehme continued in business until 1931 but turned away from captioned Fairings to produce posy holders, match-strikers, candlesticks, and other ornaments, many depicting children at play or with animals. These are numerous but not "accepted" Fairings. The names of the factories that produced inferior Fairings are unknown, but one of their marks, when applied, was as the illustration shown on the left.

From 1891, "Made in Germany" was used as all china had to state its place of origin. This is a useful date to remember when dating any china especially if it states, "Made in England", it cannot be earlier than 1891. "Made in Japan" also appeared on a few Fairings which were copies of German pieces, particularly those made for the Welsh market, but these are really not worth collecting when one has so many finer quality Fairings to find.

Walk in Please – a rare piece which would command a high price if it came on the market (page 159).

The Price Guide

While *"Let us do business together"* is the correct approach, proceed only if the price is right. How does one arrive at the correct price? Most Fairings enthusiasts use the alphabetical system of grading by rarity and demand and thus arrive at a price ranging from the fairly common group "A" Fairings to the extremely rare group "X" types.

The prices quoted below are what one would expect to pay at an auction with a margin of 20% either way. This seems a big difference, but there are many factors that affect the price on the day. Firstly is the auction well attended? Are there two bidders who really want it? Does the item depict animals? Non-Fairings collectors go for these. On the down side, is the piece damaged or repaired? Can the caption be read easily? Buying at auction is a case of *caveat emptor* (buyer beware).

A dealer will generally have an asking price above the Guide Average Price which is to cover his/her expenses and profit. One should try to negotiate a reduction, especially if the piece is damaged or repaired. If it is in good condition, and truly desirable, then you must decide if the price is reasonable above the guide average price. The market is finite and will only increase in value as more people collect or good Fairings are lost, broken or sold abroad. Purchasing from a dealer will considerably reduce the risk of buying a reproduction, which I deal with later.

In the Price Guide below, no letters go beyond F with the exception of X. These seven levels of value are sufficient and should remain relative to each other in the future. Group X Fairings rarely come onto the market and are the most difficult to price as the range is so great.

	PRICE GUIDE		
	20% OFF	**AVERAGE PRICE**	**20% ON**
A	£40	£50	£60
B	£80	£100	£120
C	£120	£150	£180
D	£160	£200	£240
E	£200	£250	£300
F	£320	£400	£480
X	From £400 to £3,000		

If old age could! Again, a rare piece and highly desirable to the serious collector.

About Fairings

It is quite possible that the first Fairing that one will come across is the most common Fairing of all, *The last in bed to put out the light*, Group A. £50 is the average price for a good old one although the candle may be broken on the table at the bottom of the bed. It is said that this was snapped off deliberately as a sign of good luck when first received. Size: height of three inches (76mm), a base of approximately three and half inches by two inches (89mm x 51mm), and a base height of five-eighths of an inch (11mm). Roughly scratched number under the base 2851. Circa 1860. Simple – not quite! This is the most common Fairing and was produced with many small differences in each until well after 1870. The tablecloth, candle holder, bedhead and bedfoot can all have different designs. The man's or woman's limbs can be found to have slightly different positions. Pieces become lighter in weight until hollow with no canopy over the bed. A collector should aim for the first one described above and pay less for the later ones. Larger, four inch (105mm) high models with no numbers are rarer, 1850-1860, and will cost an average £65. Smaller than standard Fairings will also command this higher price. This Fairing comes from the most popular themes: bedroom and marriage scenes. Listed below are examples of the many differences and variations in Group A and B that one may find. Rarer ones than these may be found in the Pictorial Guide.

GROUP A

The last in bed to put out the light
The most popular.

Shall we sleep first or how
Man and woman sitting in bed.
The larger 1850 version extends into Group B.

When a man's married his troubles begin
Husband holding the baby.
Light in weight made in other factories about 1890.

Twelve months after marriage
Husband, again, is looking after the baby.
This Fairing is prone to hand damage.
Check it before you agree upon a price.
Larger 1850 versions are all different.
Only the captions are the same. All belong to Group B.

Three o'clock in the morning
Husband is looking after the baby again.
Larger 1850 version is slightly different and rarer.
Its range extends into Group B.

Reception at three o'clock in the morning
Wife hitting husband with slipper.
Light in weight, made in other factories about 1890.

Returning at one o'clock in the morning (small)
Wife hitting husband with slipper.
Heavy in weight. Made by Conta & Boehme.

Group B

Returning at one o'clock in the morning (large)
Wife is hitting husband with slipper.
This is heavier in weight.
It is early Conta & Boehme.

When a man's married his troubles begin
Same caption as in Group A but depicts
an entirely different scene with no bed.
The man is holding the baby. This is a
heavy Conta & Boehme.

One o'clock in the morning
Husband is being reprimanded.
The piece is heavy in weight and made
by Conta & Boehme.

A cat, A cat
A cat jumps onto the man's shoulder as
he retires. There are several versions of this
as well as two different captions,

Come pussie, come and *An awkward interruption.*

I am not going further than Group B as I have now covered most of them. All of the above bedroom/marriage scenes will show up again and again so endeavour to get a good one, hopefully at a fair price.

Fairings depicted a "slice of the life" of their times so what more appropriate theme was there than popular music? In the top ten song sheets of the 1860s there was George Leybourne singing *Champagne Charlie is My Name*. Look under section C and there he is sitting on a barrel. Two more pieces emerged from song sheets, *Come away do*, a super Group X of that name and *On the Rink*, the reverse side of the same song sheet. Another song sheet, *Full Cry Gallop* inspired two Fairings, *Pluck* and *The decided smash*. Here again, the language barrier may be at work – 'Plucky' and 'The Inevitable Smash' would make more sense. The popular song *Where are you going to, my pretty maid?* is answered by her *I'm going a milking, sir, she said.*

Another song by Charles A. Gardiner called, *Shut Your Eyes Tightly And Open Your Mouth* is responsible for *Open your mouth and shut your eyes*, a Group X Fairing. People think this has to do with taking medicine, but it does not. I have a Fairing that had been repaired with the addition of a spoon when in fact the original object was a candle. The candle that is being put into the lad's mouth is put there by the joker, who is pretending that he is giving him cherries which he swings over his head. (See page 19.) The words of the song that inspired this Fairing are. . .

Open your mouth and shut your eyes.
Ripe as the fruits are they for fun, while he not dreaming of a trick,
Bites in good faith, and stead of fruit, his sharp teeth in a candle stick.

Children were amused by Fairings which often had the themes of nursery rhymes and stories: Old Mother Hubbard, Little Bo Peep, Little Red Riding Hood, Rip Van Winkle, Dick Whittington and his Cat. All these are light in weight which means they were produced by another German factory from about 1890

This illustration with its words for a popular song of the 1860s inspired the Fairing *Open your mouth and shut your eyes* on page 121.

and onwards. At least two were derived from postcards, *Now they'll blame me for this*, a dog looking at a wet, puddling umbrella, and *The last match*, a man tying to light his pipe in the wind, sometimes captioned *Pat's last match*. Both are light in weight and were made about 1900.

Politics were not left out as a Fairing theme. In 1881, the Corrupt Practices Bill was submitted to Parliament, so the Fairing's comment to this was, *Free and independent elector*, Group F, showing a politician slipping a bribe to someone or vice versa. Sounds familiar? *Petticoat government* is not political. It simply shows the wife ruling over her husband. *In chancery*, Group F, was based on running disputes between the farmers and huntsmen in the 1870s. I have one of the Victorian coloured drawings, in a cartoon from which this Fairing was derived. According to the drawing, the clothes and colours of the Fairing are not accurate for the huntsman, but the message is clear; the huntsman is pulling the tail of a cow, whilst the farmer pulls the horns. Who is milking the cow? Why, a lawyer, of course wearing his wig!

Throughout history, there has always been a war going on somewhere. In 1870, it was the Franco-Prussian war. The British were neutral, but a little propaganda did appear in Fairings with their depictions of English doctors and nurses tending the wounded of both sides in, *English neutrality 1870, attending the sick*, Group F.

There are two others, completely different from each other, but with similar captions. (See photographs on page 60.) Three pocket watch holders represent the main antagonists of this war in *Gravelotte*, Group X, showing the King of Prussia, and Prince Bismarck, in *Sedan*, Group X, the King of Prussia and Prince Napoleon III, and *Unser Fritz*, Group X.

The Crimean War 1854-6, was represented by *Our soldiers* and *Our Sisters of Charity*. From America we have *Union for ever*. *Radetsky*, an unusual and rare Fairing depicting Field Marshall, Josef Radetsky of the Austrian Army, 1766-1858, one of the few Fairings I have seen with a three-dimensional horse, much like a tin soldier. All these are rare and come under Group X.

Moving on from war scenes, there are several Fairings that I find amusing, although a famous person from *The Antiques Road Show* said, "disgusting" when I showed him *Come along these flowers don't smell very good*, Group C, showing a little boy squatting behind the bush. Then there is, *How's your poor feet*, Group X, showing a sailor with two wooden legs. Another favourite is *By appointment the first of April*, Group F, in which two children peep over a fence having arranged for a gentleman to meet a donkey. *Lor' three legs I'll charge 2d*, Group C, depicts a young lad cleaning the shoes of a three-legged man. *Married for money*, Group B, shows a bored wife who reads her book in bed. *Naughty words*, Group C, shows a rude parrot talking to the vicar. *Necessity knows no law*, Group B, has a girl peeing into a top hat. *Home from the club he fears the storm*, Group D, portrays a man sitting in bed with his wife and he has his umbrella up. There are many more but everyone's sense of fun is different so I'll leave it to you to decide if *That's funny, very funny, very, very funny!* or just disgusting.

Quite a few Fairings are regarded as pairs. Here are some of them.

GROUP A

Grandma	Young girl dressed up as Grandma.
Grandpa	Young boy dressed up as Grandpa.
Mr. Moody	Famous evangelist of the time.
Mr. Sankey	Famous evangelist of the time.
I am starting on a long journey	Man with bag (Matchstriker).
I am off with him	Woman with bag and umbrella (Matchstriker).

All these pairs look different from other Fairings as they are single figures rather than the usual group scene. There are different varieties and sizes and good ones might fall into the Group B price range for a pair. If you find only one of any pair, buy it and have fun looking for the other one. It will turn up.

Group B

Morning prayer	Child and mother sitting on bed.
Evening prayer	Child and mother sitting on bed facing in opposite directions.
Before marriage	Shows a thin couple, now Group C.
After marriage	They are both overweight.

All these are of a thin consistency in their making unlike those made by Conta & Boehme. Although a pair, the Fairing, *Before marriage* is rarer than *After marriage* and, therefore, falls under Group C.

Group C

Tug of war	Child pulling a croissant from a dog.
Spoils of war	Child crying, having lost.
Tug of war	Child pulling a doll from a dog.
Spoils of war	The doll rips.

These come in two sizes the larger pair usually fetches a higher price. Both sets can be found captioned in the French *La bataille* and *La victoire*. Carefully check the back fencing which is often damaged or repaired.

Attack	Children are trying to get a tin container from a cupboard.
Defeat	They fail and are about to fall. This one is rarer than *Attack*.
Pluck	Children in a dog cart are chasing a rabbit.
The decided smash	The children and cart crash as the dog catches the rabbit.

These originate from the song *Full Cry Gallop*. They can suffer from damage, especially on the fencing and on the little girl whose arm is in the air.

Group D

How's business	Two boys asking the question.
Slack	Same boys sitting looking idle.

These two originate from the pictures on a much earlier china drinking mug. Although I show them both in Group D, *How's business* is so rare its value must be considered as a Group F.

Group E

Before marriage	Man and a woman embracing on a couch.
After marriage	Man and a woman looking away from each other.

These are small, heavy Conta & Boehme, both are rare.

GROUP F

A long pull and a strong pull   Boy holding a patient's head while
the dentist pulls out a tooth.

GROUP X

Out by jingo   They all collapse with the dentist holding
the tooth.

Dentists appreciate this pair for obvious reasons. *Out by jingo* is in Group X because it is rarer. I have obtained four *Long Pulls*, but only managed to find one *Out by jingo* in good condition. Sometimes *Long pull* is captioned with the French, *Sans douleur*, without pain.

Under the 'P' section you will find, *A present from. . .*, Group A. I have included three as a representative of a whole series, impressed with numbers around 4,000+ under a round base, all Group A. I once thought I would like to collect them, but never did, so I leave it to someone else. I think they are fun to collect. The most frequently found are:

A present from Aberdeen	*A present from Criccieth*
A present from Abergavenny	*A present from Ely*
A present from Canterbury	*A present from Skegness*

Velocipedes, boneshakers or bicycles, were introduced by the French in the early 1860s. Most show French women riding them; no English lady would show an ankle like that. By about 1867, there were fourteen Fairings depicting them. They are attractive and sought after by all serious collectors. Their desirability has now put all of them into Group X. *Velocipede for stout travellers*, sold recently at auction for £1,200 + £200 commission. *To Epsom* has just sold for £2,400 plus commission, a record price. However, do not lose heart. I picked up a Group F in 1997 for £63 and I know a dealer who purchased one for £26. What a bargain! It pays to know your subject.

Beware of a collision	Group X
A dangerous encounter	Group X ⎫ *Same Fairing*
Girls of the period	Group X ⎭
Dangerous	Group X
Every vehicle driven by a horse, mule or ass 2d	Group X (Large and Small)
Kiss me quick	Group X (Large and Small)
To Epsom	Group X (Two Figures)
To Epsom	Group X (Four Figures)
Velocipeding on a rainy day	Group X
Velocipede for stout travellers	Group X
Who is the fastest of the three?	Group X
Uncaptioned man on bicycle with wife behind him and baby on the crossbar	Group X

It is a lot of fun, but expensive to seek out the rarer Fairings. Most are self-explanatory like *Returning from a journey*, Group X, with the lover hiding under the bed, and *Two different views*, Group E, with one man looking through his telescope while the other looks down the lady's dress. The Group X, *Two different views* is rude.

I should mention that *The Vienna Series* is not comprised of true Fairings but is every collector's dream. There are five pieces made by the Royal Vienna Factory circa 1850 and all fall under Group X. They have no captions, but are generally regarded as the inspiration for the Fairings that followed. One can see in them *The Landlord in love, A Mouse, A Mouse!* and, of course, *The bedroom romp*. Under the base, one will see a shield with two lines across it and the letter R in blue.

No one knows for sure how many Fairings there are because new ones keep showing up every now and then. The Fairing on the front cover of this book, bought in 1999, *More free than welcome*, Group X, is new to anyone I show it to. It does not appear in any reference book. Undiscovered Fairings are out there, somewhere and it is great fun trying to find and collect them. I sincerely hope this guide encourages you to look for them and helps you to recognize the genuine ones if you choose to buy them. You may then be as enthusiastic as I am.

Happy Collecting!

PS.
While publishing this book a new Fairing has been found *Pray do me the favour*. It sold at auction for £1,200 + commission, and the highest price now paid at auction for a Fairing has risen to £3,200 + commission, for *Come away do*.

AUTHOR'S NOTE

Readers wishing to start their own collection may find it helpful to refer to my website on **www.chinafairings.co.uk** or email me at **chinafairings@aol.com**

Genuine

Reproduction

The Dreaded Reproduction

With a little experience you will have no trouble in spotting the dreaded reproduction. Most reproductions are dreadful; they have bright or garish colours, are badly modelled with captions printed instead of script and sometimes may even be printed lopsidedly. Some are artificial captions such as *Loose pins* and *Father's joy*. Everything about them indicates cheapness. New ones cost about £4.

One can get a list of them from: The Fairings Collectors Society, P.O. Box 27, Furneux Pellham, Huntingford, Hertfordshire, SG9 0TW, England.

Other reproductions are harder to recognize but again, one can get to know them firstly by comparing them to those that are authentic. Those that are genuine are softer in colour and slightly better modelled. Initially, one ought to buy from a good antiques dealer and ask if the Fairing is genuine. If one is in any doubt, do not buy, especially if they are inexpensive. One does not buy a real Fairing for £20 or less.

A better reproduction, but still a fake is, *The Welsh tea party*, for spills or posy, (see opposite). The caption gives it away because it is in black printing and it should be in black script. It is also a little larger than the authentic Fairing although this is hard to tell unless one has both pieces in hand. Earlier copies of Fairings, circa 1980, are those that are light in weight with two half inch holes under the base on each side and a bar or ridge across the middle. These are of a better quality and acceptable to some as long as one does not pay more than £20. Keep in mind that they will not appreciate in value. Frankly, it is more fun to recognize them and leave them where they are.

I always gently wash the Fairings I want for my collection in warm water; dealers never do. They like to see a hundred years of grime on them and the collector must look for it, too. Watch out for newly applied dirt. Uncleaned Fairings do have a nice mellow appearance to them and some collectors prefer it. Sometimes you

Genuine

A 1980s reproduction.

see small brown flecks in the china. This is normal and is due, in part, to poor china or sand picked up in the production process and should reduce the price. I often give friends two Fairings to handle, one genuine, one fake. Most can identify the genuine one the first time, even the difficult ones. The more one handles them, the easier it is to tell. Remember to use your eyes. Does it fall into a category with overly bright colours, bad modelling, poor printing, or does it look old, slightly chipped, grimy in the corners, black script, good modelling, and muted colours? What is underneath? If in doubt, ask and ask again. If still in doubt, leave it.

Modern fake.

Look at the caption, bright new colours, poor gilding with scrolls. Modelling not as bad as some encountered. Marks under the base are also fake. The numbers start at 18★★ on most fakes, so anything starting with 18★★ leave alone. New £4.

Under the base "Made in Germany" can be seen. The two large holes give this away as a 1980s reproduction. Valued at under £20.

(Above) On the left is a 1980s reproduction.
Caption poor, no scrolling, turn it over and look at the bottom
. . . two holes.

On the right is the genuine Fairing.
Detailed modelling and better painting.

(Opposite page. Top) On the left is a modern fake. This piece is
so poorly reproduced, even the caption is incorrect, "*OR 1
HOUR*". New £4.

On the right is the genuine article with the correct caption,
"or how?"

(Opposite page. Bottom) On the left is a modern fake.
Compare the dog's face, bottles and the caption, gilding is thin
and poor.

On the right is the genuine Fairing. The dog's face has
character, the articles on the table are bottles not birds. The
caption is faded but genuine.
The gilding is properly worn.

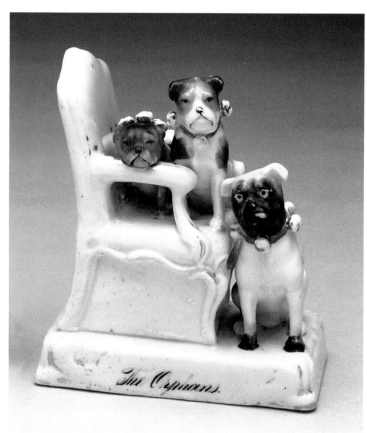

A modern fake. Colours too new and the caption is printed.

A genuine Fairing. This piece is always very pale.

A modern fake. Can you discern the errors?

Genuine. The details of the cats are so much better.

A modern fake. This Fairing is truly awful. Bad modelling, new colours, caption badly printed, gilding very poor. About £4 new.

An early reproduction. This is a very good copy. The gold printing is almost correct, the modelling good, the base is flat with one small hole in the corner and the gilding is good. The head of the boy on the left should be facing into the centre, not out. No others are as good as this. Value up to £40.

Which is which? Although the piece on the right has the brighter colours, is it the genuine Fairing? Look at the captions. Which has the better modelling? Is one bottle finer? Can you eat the lobsters?
I am sure you will have fun spotting fakes at the antique fairs.

ANSWER:
The right hand
Fairing
is genuine

Before Restoration

After Restoration

Repairs

Fairings that have been repaired or restored should not command the prices shown in the Price Guide, unless they are very rare in Groups F and X. The price of a Fairing also depends on how well the restoration has been carried out and how extensively it has been done. If a whole figure has been replaced this is bad news in any Fairing and it should be avoided. However, if the price is reduced sufficiently, buy it until a better one becomes available. I bought, at Auction, a rare Group X, *How Bridget served the tomatoes undressed*, for £40 plus commission. Two of the three figure's heads had been poorly restored, but at that price I thought it acceptable as I will probably never see a good one for sale in my lifetime. In Groups A, B and C, extensive restoration is not acceptable. It is far better to wait for a good one. These turn up all the time as they are not rare.

Small repairs like restored hands, cups, fences, bottles are acceptable as long as they are well done. Purists may disagree with this, but one has to be realistic about the Fairings that are available, moreover the flaw should be reflected in the price. If buying from a dealer, always point out any defects and discuss the price. If the dealer has already discounted it, then one must decide on its value independently.

HOW DO I TELL IF IT HAS BEEN REPAIRED?

First examine the Fairing in detail, utilizing a loop or magnifying glass if necessary. Look at parts that stick out or up: hands, teapots, bottles, anything that is vulnerable to being broken off. Look at colour. Do they match? Is the piece out of shape or missing altogether? Look for cracks, joins, or uneven surfaces. Then give it the "kiss test". Place your lips on a suspect area and feel if it is warmer than the main object. A few tries on a known repair will give one the feel. Replacements are always warmer; it has to do with the density of the materials used to restore the Fairing. Another test, although dealers do not like it for obvious reasons, is to tap your teeth on a piece. The repair will feel softer to the teeth and will produce a lower note of tap from the main body. I do not do this. I like my teeth and I think the "kiss test" is better.

Compare this Fairing with the example shown in the Frontispiece which
carries the same inscription.

Collecting on the Internet

Since I began writing this book, many established auction houses have acquired an online presence. One may now view auction catalogues and leave a bid online prior to the auction date. Reports on the condition of the piece or photographs may also be reviewed online. It only costs the price of a phone call. If your bid is successful, your added costs are the bid, the usual house commission and postage. In the future we may be able to bid live just as if we were in the auction room.

Another type of auction called, "Person to Person online Trading", is available on the Internet. Worldwide, eBay is the largest, based in the U.S.A., this company acts as an agent and only charges a commission to the seller.

To locate Fairings online www.ebay.co.uk is a good starting point and works like this. Type the word FAIRING in the eBay search space. The result will be about 200 listings for motorbike fairings. Hidden amongst these will be listings for china Fairings. By being more selective with one's searches, i.e. click on, "antiques" in the eBay home page, you will narrow down considerably the hunt for china Fairings.

Once you find an item on which to make an offer, follow the web site's bidding instructions. You will be asked for a user I.D., which is your identity concealed via a nickname. It is fun thinking up a good one, but keep it short. Bidding requires a password, use one that you can remember easily. Each item on eBay is on offer for about three to ten days. The bidding ends on the last second of the deadline, therefore, I would advise you to place your best and final bid as late as possible. Bidding early will give someone a chance to overbid you. Due to differing time zones I have been known to bid at three o'clock in the morning!

A credit card is required to pay for items bought on eBay. This can be done securely through bidpay.com or paypal.com online.

Buying online is the way of the future and will enable more people to bid on Fairings causing an increase in their price. It will also bring Fairings to the market from all parts of the world, especially from countries where British families have settled in the last 150 years.

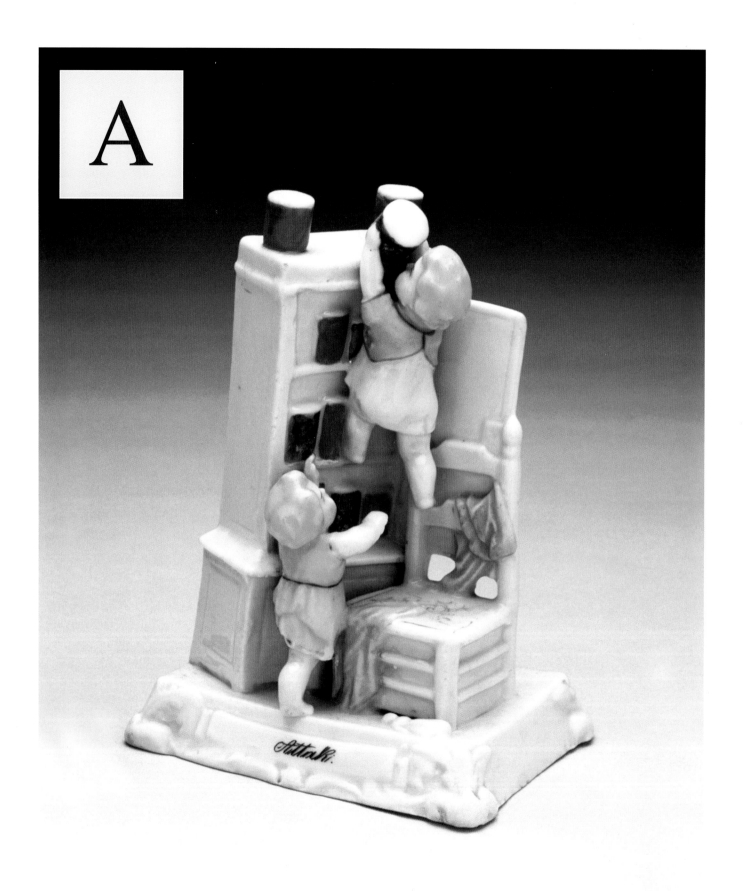

According to the rule 1876-77
Group C
Pinbox

Adolphus won't tell Papa
Group X

After
Group D

After marriage
Group B

After marriage
Group B
Pinbox

After marriage
Group E

After the ball
Group B

After the race 1875
Group C
Pinbox

After you my dear Alphonso
Group E

All over
Group X

Alone at last
Group B
Also captioned: Enfin Seule

Am I Right, or any other Man
Group X

PICTURE DUPLICATED
An awkward interruption
Group B
See: Cat! A Cat! A.

An awkward interruption
Group C

An Awkward interruption
Group C

Angels whisper, The
Group B

Animated spirits
Group X

Animated spirits
Group X

Announcement
Group A
Matchstriker

Anti vivisectors
Group B
Pinbox

Anxious to study
Group B

Any flags Ma'am
Group C
Matchstriker

Any lights Sir?
Group C
Also captioned: Match sir?
Matchstriker

Attack
Group C

Attentive Maid, The
Group E

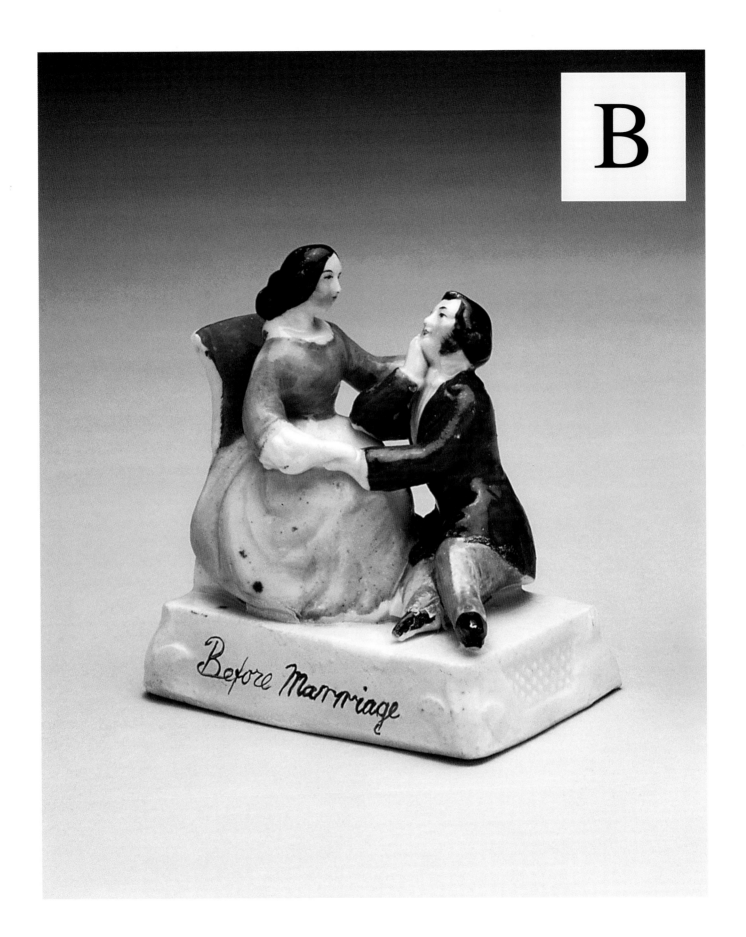

Before Marriage

Babes in the Wood, The
Group X

Baby Rock me to Sleep Mother
Group C
Pinbox

Baby's first step
Group C

Baby's first step
Group C

PICTURE NOT AVAILABLE
Ba_dervergnugen
Group X
Depicts a lady in a mud bath assisted by her maid

Bataille, La
Group C
See: Tug of war

Baumwolle oder Seide
Group X
(Cotton or silk)

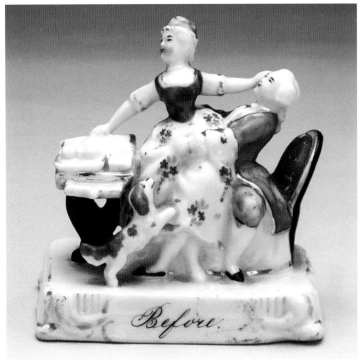

Before
Group E

Before marriage
Group C

Before marriage
Group E

**Be good and if you can't
be good, be careful**
Group C

Benoni and Leila
Group F

**Between two stools you
fall to the ground**
Group E

Beware of a collision
Group X

PICTURE DUPLICATED
Bitte mein fraulein
Group D
See: Favourable opportunity

PICTURE NOT AVAILABLE
Broken bottle, A
Group E
Two Scotsmen lamenting over broken whisky bottle

Birkenhead to Liverpool
Group B
Pinbox
Also captioned: Carnarvon to Liverpool
Also captioned: Liverpool to Menai Bridge

Broken Hoop, The
Group E

Buttonhole Sir
Group C
Matchstriker

By appointment the first of April
Group F

PICTURE DUPLICATED
By golly I am in luck
Group C
See: It's a shame to take the money

Checkmate.

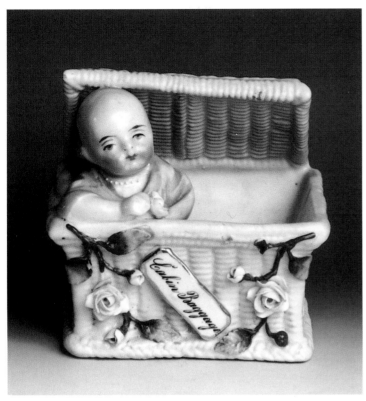

Cabin Baggage
Group B

Campbell and Havelock
Group A

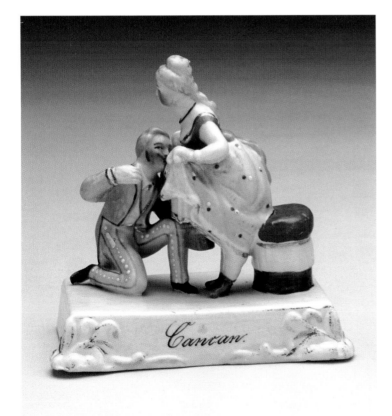

Cancan No. 2897
Group X

Cancan No. 3300
Group F

Cancan No. 2898
Group F

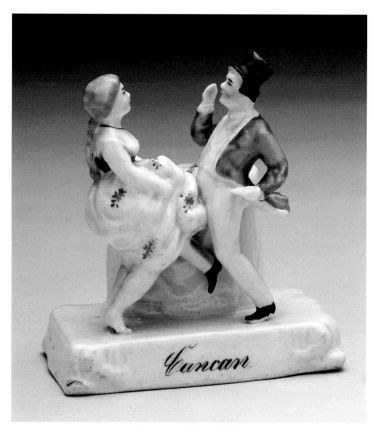

Cancan No. 3301
Group F

Can you do this grandma?
Group D

PICTURE DUPLICATED
Carnarvon to Liverpool
Group B
See: Birkenhead to Liverpool

Cat! A Cat! A
Group B
Also captioned: Come pussie come
Also captioned: An awkward interruption

Cat! A Cat! A
Group B

Caught!
Group B
Matchstriker

Caught in the act – No caption
Group E
Matchstriker

PICTURE DUPLICATED
Coming from the ball
Group D
See: Return from the ball

Champagne Charlie is my name
Group F
Pinbox

Champagne Charlie is my name
Group E
Pinbox

Chaste Joseph, The
Group X

Checkmate
Group E

Children's meeting
Group C

Child's prayer, The
Group B
Pinbox

Cold hands – Cold feet
Group B
Uncaptioned Matchstriker

**Come along, these flowers
don't smell very good**
Group C
Front Side

**Come along, these flowers
don't smell very good**
Group C
Reverse Side

PICTURE DUPLICATED
Come at once
Group X
See: Just in time

Come away do
Group X

Come along old fellow you will not get anything
Group X

PICTURE DUPLICATED
Come pussie, come
Group B
See: Cat! A cat! A

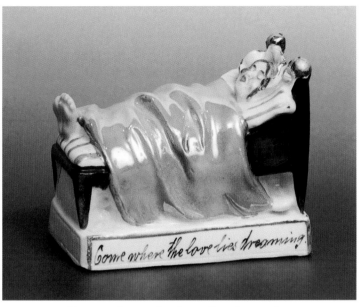

Come where the love lies dreaming
Group D

Coming home from the Sea Side
Group X

Consomation
Group X

PICTURE NOT AVAILABLE
Constitutional
Group C
Depicts man reading newspaper, perhaps on the toilet

Convenience of married life, The
Group X

Copper Sir, A
Group B
Matchstriker

Courtship
Group X

Cousin and Cousine
Group F
Pinbox

Cousin and Cousine
Group F

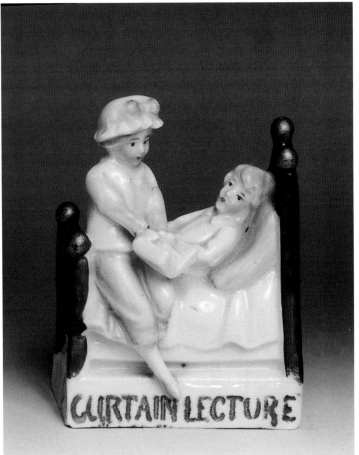

Curtain lecture
Group B

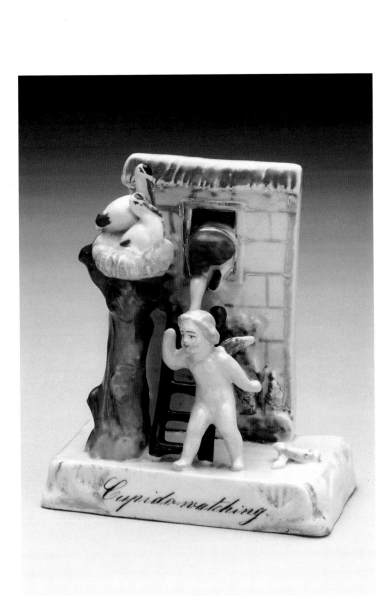

Cupid's watching
Group F

Dandy of 1863
Lady of 1863
Group A

Daily News, The
Group C
Matchstriker
Also captioned: Daily Telegraph, The
Also captioned: Le Figaro

PICTURE DUPLICATED
Dangerous encounter
Group X
See: Girls of the period

Dangerous
Group X

Decided Smash, The
Group C

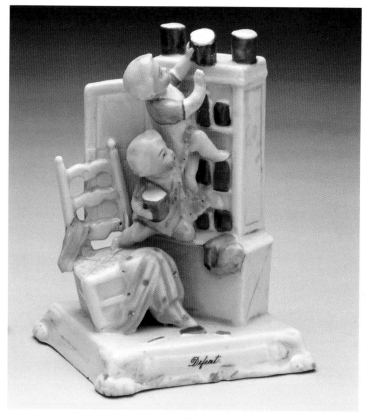

Defeat
Group C

Delights of Matrimony, The
Group B

PICTURE DUPLICATED
Der Letze Löscht Das Licht Aus
Group A
See: Last in Bed to Put Out the Light, The

Der Ubertretue Fasttag
Group X
(Fast Day Misdemeanour)

Dick Whittington and his Cat
Group B

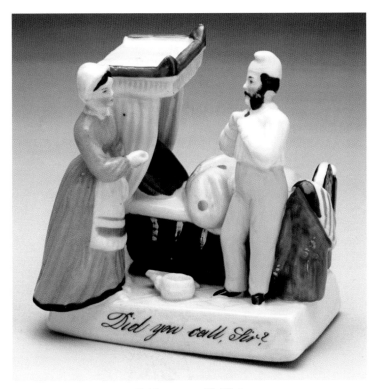

Did you call Sir?
Group X

Did you ring Sir?
Group D

PICTURE NOT AVAILABLE
Difficult problem, A
Group E
Depicts a girl and boy sitting on a bench with a slate

PICTURE DUPLICATED
Die folgen später heimkehr
Group B
See: Returning at one o'clock in the morning

PICTURE DUPLICATED
Disagreeable surprise
Group F
See: Wet reception, The

Difficult problem, A
Group B
Paired with: Happily solved

Doctor, The
Group B

Don't wake the baby
Group E

Don't you like the change?
Group X

Don't you wish you may get it?
Group D

Doubtful case, A
Group F

Drummer Boy - Baker Boy
Group C
Uncaptioned Matchstriker

English neutrality 1870
attending the wounded.

E

Early bird catches the worm, The
Group D

Eighty strokes of the pulse in the minute
Group X

PICTURE DUPLICATED
Enfin seule
Group B
See: Alone at last

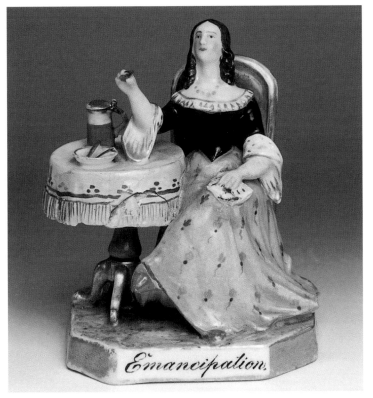

Emancipation
Group F

Engaged
Group A

English neutrality 1870
Attending the sick and the wounded
Group F

English neutrality 1870
Attending the sick
Group F

English neutrality 1871
Attending the wounded
Group F

Evening Prayer
Group B

Every vehicle driven by a horse, mule or ass 2d
Group X - large

Every vehicle driven by a horse, mule or ass 2d
Group X - small

F

Fair Play Boys
Group F

Family cares
Group A

Fast asleep
Group A Single - Group B Pair

Favourable opportunity
Group D
Also captioned: Bitte Mein Fraulein

Fine hairs
Group C
Doubtful Caption

First caresses
Group X

First Temptation
Group B

First pray
Group C

Fishwives
Group A

Five o'clock Tea
Group C

Five o'clock Tea
Group B

Flower seller, The
Group C

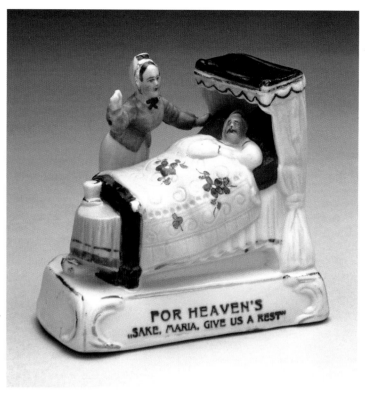

For heaven's sake Maria, give us a rest
Group C

Free and Independent Elector
Group F

Fresh Chestnuts Sir?
Group A
Matchstriker

Fresh morning, A
Group C
Matchstriker

Funny Story, A
Group C

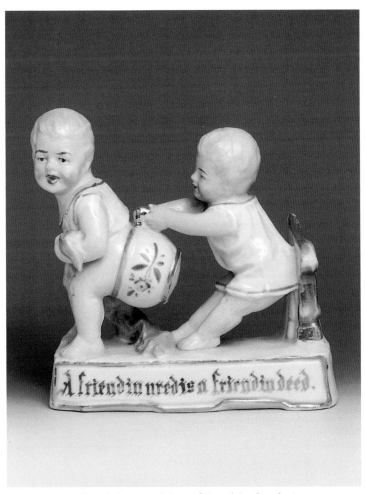

Friend in need is a friend indeed, A
Group C

Going to the ball.

Game of patience, A
Group F

Gentlemen of the jury
Group C

Girls of the period, The
Group X
Also captioned: A dangerous encounter

Go away Mamma I am busy
Group D

God bless our home
Group B

God save the Queen
Group D

Going, Going, Gone
Group C

Going to the ball
Group D

Good friends
Group F

Good night
Group A

Good Templars
Group C

Good Templars
Group C
Pinbox

Grandma – Grandpa
Group A for a single
Group B for a pair
Numerous varieties, large and small

Grandpapa – Grandma
Group B
Pinboxes

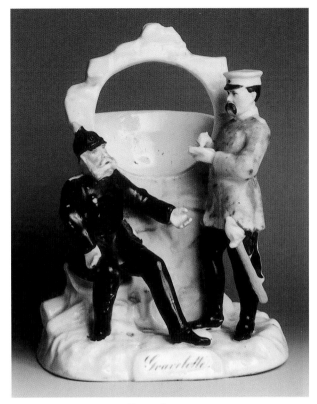

Gravelotte
Group X
Watch Holder

Great Nord of Scotland Railway
Group B
Also captioned: Swansea to Bristol
Pinbox

Guardian Angel, The
Group C
Also captioned: Our first efforts are not in vain

HUNTING THE SLIPPER

PICTURE DUPLICATED
Happily solved
Group B
See: Difficult problem, A

PICTURE DUPLICATED
(Happy Father) What two? Yes Sir, two little beauties
Group C
See: Looking down upon his luck

Happy father! What two?
Yes Sir, two little beauties
Group C

(Happy father!) What two?
Yes Sir, two little beauties
Group C

Happy Father! What two?
Yes Sir, two little beauties
Group E

Happy Father! What two?
Yes Sir, two little beauties
Group E

Happy Father! What two?
Yes Sir, two little beauties
Group F

PICTURE DUPLICATED
Havelock
Group A
See: Campbell

Happy pair, A
Group X
Similar to: What have these met for?

Hark Jo somebody's coming
Group D
Also captioned: Hark Tom somebody's coming
Also captioned: Good templars

He don't like his Pants
Group X

Her first ball
Group C

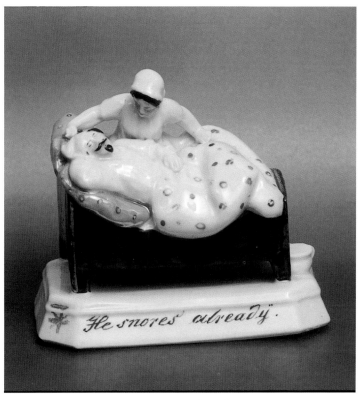

He snores already
Group F

He will be a fine man if he lives
Group X

Highland fling, A
Group B

PICTURE NOT AVAILABLE

His first love letter
Group C Matchstriker
Depicts a boy reading a letter

His first pair
Group C

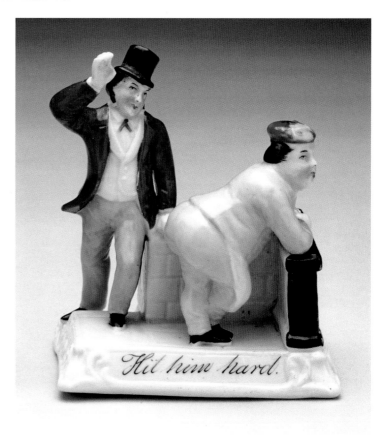

Hit him hard
Group X

Home from the club he fears the storm
Group D

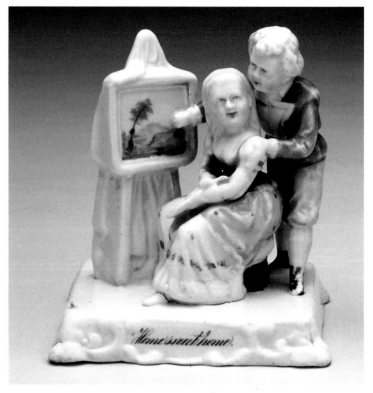

Home sweet home
Group X

How Bridget Served the Tomatoes Undressed
Group X

How curious it must feel to have those moustaches on my lips, Charlie!
Group X

How happy could I be with either
Group D

How quietly they repose
Group D
Also captioned: Soft repose

How's business?
Group F

How's your poor feet?
Group X

Hst! My dolls sleep
Group X

Hunting the slipper
Group B

If youth knew.

I am going a-milking Sir, she said
Group C

I am off with him
I am starting on a long journey
Group A for single. Group B for a pair
Matchstrikers - 4 varieties

I beg your pardon
Group F

I beg your pardon
Group F

Ich bin ein sweiter Salome
Group F
(I am a second Salome)

If old age could!
Group E small
Group F large

If you please, Sir
Group E

If you please, Sir
Group C
Matchstriker

If youth knew!
Group X

If youth knew
Group F

I have had my bath, now it's your turn
Group B single
Group C pair
Matchstrikers

I have had my bath, now it's your turn
Group B single
Group C pair

I'm first Sir
Group D

In chancery
Group F
Also captioned: The lawsuit

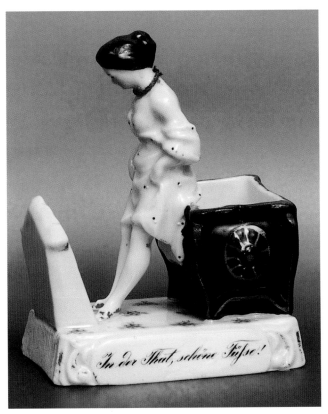

In der Tat, schöne Füfse!
Group X
(For sure beautiful feet)

Infallible
Group F

It's a shame to take the Money
Group C
Also captioned: By golly I am in luck

It's only mustache
Group X

PICTURE DUPLICATED
I will warm you
Group X
See: Quiet interruption

I will never take you again
Group C

I wish I were a fish
Group C
Pinbox

J

Jenny Jones and Ned Morgan
Group A
Also figures reversed

Just as it should be
Group F

Just in time
Group X
Also captioned: Come at once

Kiss me quick
Group X large and small

King John
Group C

Kiss me quick
Group C small

Kiss me quick
Group C large

Knight of labour, A
Group C

Lady of 1863
Group A
See: Dandy of 1863

Ladies of Llangollen
Group B

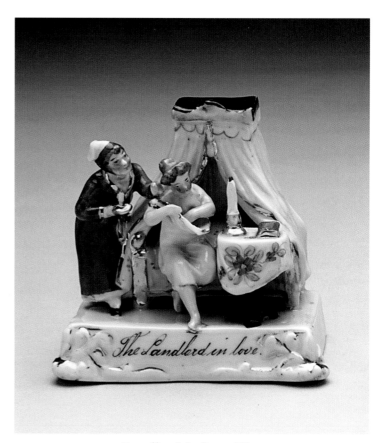

Landlord in love, The
Group E

Landlord in love, The
Group F

Last in bed to put out the light, The
Group A

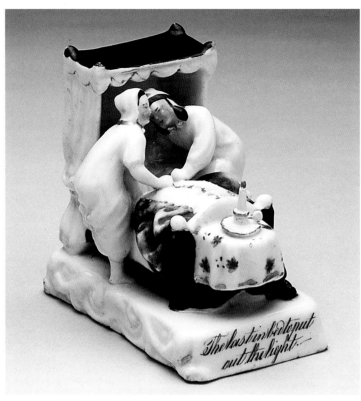

Last in bed to put out the light, The
Group A
(numerous varieties)

Let us be friends
Group C

PICTURE DUPLICATED
Last match, The
Group B
See: Pat's last match

PICTURE DUPLICATED
Lawsuit, The
Group F
See: In chancery

Let us do business together
Group B

Let us speak of a man as we find him
Group X

Little Bo Peep
Group B

Little Boy Blue
Group B

Little John in trouble
Group C
Pinbox

Little Red Riding Hood
Group B

Little shoemaker, The
Group X

PICTURE DUPLICATED
Liverpool to Menai Bridge
Group B
See: Birkenhead to Liverpool

Little Turk, A
Group B

Long and short of it, The
Group D

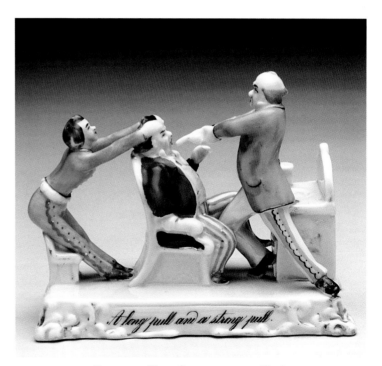

Long pull and a strong pull, A
Group F
Also captioned: Sans delours

Looking down on his luck
Group C

Looking down upon his luck
Group C
Also captioned: Happy father, what two?
Yes sir two little beauties

Looking out
Group B
Also utilizing different figures

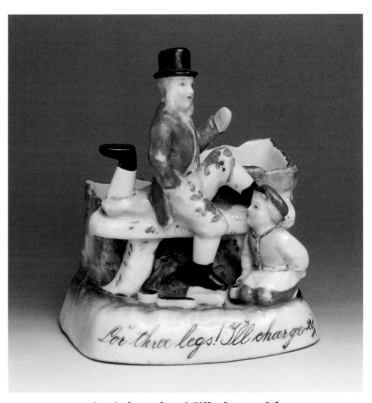

Lor' three legs! I'll charge 2d
Group E
Matchstriker

Lor' three legs! I'll charge 2d
Group D

Lor' three legs! I'll charge 2d
Group C
Also in a Pinbox

Lor' three legs! I'll charge 2d
Group B

Lost
Group E

Love in winter
Group X

Lovers disturbed, The
Group F

Love's first lesson
Group D

Love's old sweet song
Group D

PICTURE DUPLICATED
Lucky dog, A
Group B
See: Privileged pet, A

Midnights holy hour.

Mama – Papa
Group A single
Group B pair

Manx Cat
Group E

Marriage
Group X

Married Blessedness
Group C

Married for money
Group B

Master's winning ways
Group X

PICTURE DUPLICATED
Match Sir?
Group C
See: Any lights Sir?

Matches
Group C

Matrimonial Bliss
Group E

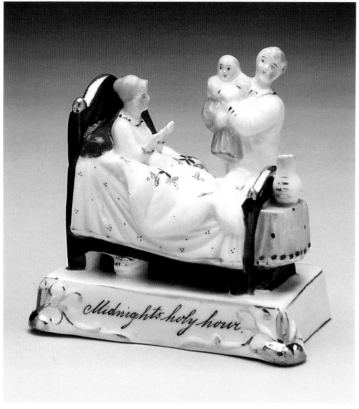

Midnight's holy hour
Group B

Might is Right
Group B

Misfortune
Group E

Missus is Master
Group B
Also in a pinbox

Model of Laxey, The
Group B
Pin Box

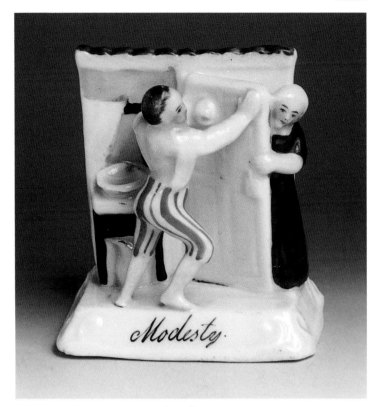

Modesty
Group D
Early model

Modesty
Group C
Late model, captioned in gold

More Free than Welcome
Group X

Morning Prayer
Group B

Mother Hubbard
Group B
See: Old Mother Hubbard

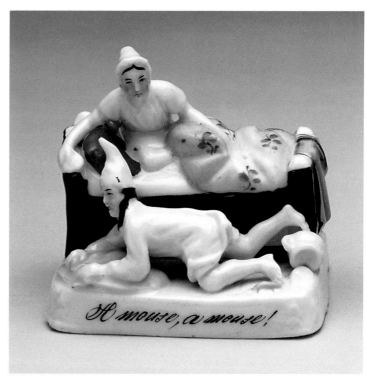

Mouse, a mouse! A
Group D
This Fairing is rare

Mouse! a mouse! A
Group B

Mr. Jones, remove your hat
Group C

Mr. Jones, take off your hat
Group C

Much ado about nothing
Group C

Mr. Moody – Mr. Sankey
Group A

Murder, The
Group C

Music hath charms
Group B

Music hath charms
Group B
Pinbox

Mylord and Milady
Group C
Matchstriker

Naughty words
Group C
Also captioned: Rude words

Necessity knows no law
Group B

New woman, The
Group C

New woman, The
Group B
Pinbox

Nice views
Group X

Night before Christmas, The
Group E

Night cap, The
Group C

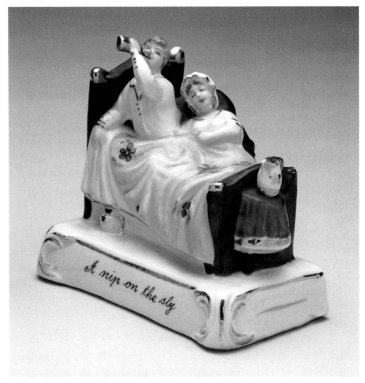

Nip on the sly, A
Group C

No Followers Allowed
Group F

Nothing venture, nothing have
Group X

Now dogs jump!
Group D

Now Ma–am, say when?
Group C

Now they'll blame me for this
Group D

Grandmama

Grandpapa

Now I'm Grandmama and Grandpapa
Group A single
Group B pair

Nuts to you!
Group E

O

Our sisters of charity.

118

Off to the Seaside
Group B pair
Matchstriker

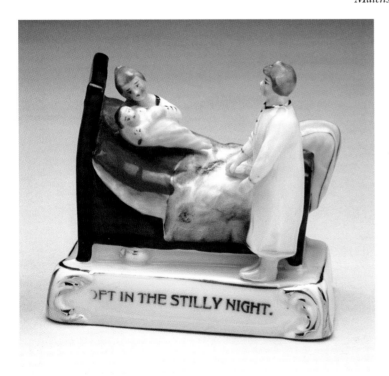

Oft in the stilly night!
Group C

O' do leave me a drop!
Group D

Oh! What a difference in the morning!
Group C

Old Mother Hubbard
Group B
Also captioned: Mother Hubbard

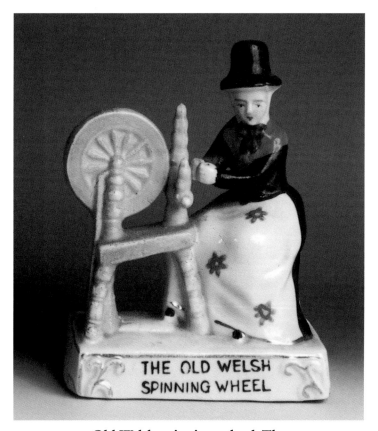

Old Welsh spinning wheel, The
Group A

One o'clock in the morning
Group B

On the rink
Group F
One of several

Open your mouth and shut your eyes
Group X

Opportunity creates Thieves
Group D

Organ boy, The
Group F

Ornament fire stove
Group C
Matchstriker

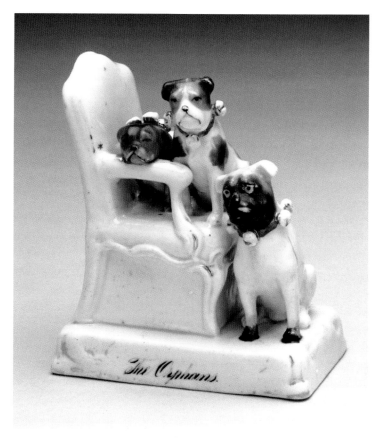

Orphans, The
Group C

Our best wishes
Group X

PICTURE DUPLICATED
Our best wishes
Group X
See: Repentance

PICTURE DUPLICATED
Our first efforts are not in vain
Group C
See: Guardian angel, The

Our Lodger's such a nice young man
Group D

Our sisters of charity
Group X

Our snappish Mother-in-law
Group C

Our soldiers
Group X

PICTURE DUPLICATED
Où sont les rats?
Group C
See: Who said rats?

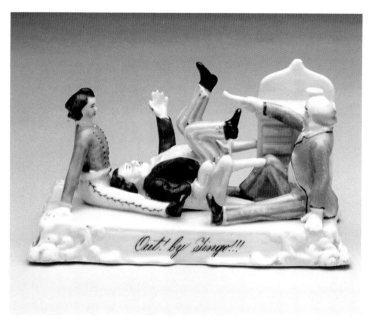

Out! by jingo!
Group X

Over the garden wall
Group B
Pinbox

Oyster Day
Group C

Oysters, Sir?
Group B
Also captioned: Oesters mynheer

Papa
Group A
See: Mama

Paddling his own canoe
Group B
Pinbox

Pastoral visit by Rev. John Jones, A
Group A

Pat's last match
Group B
Also captioned: Last match, The

Peau d'lapin chiffons
Group C
Matchstriker

Peep through a telescope, A
Group D

Penny please Sir, A
Group B
Matchstriker

Pins madame?
Group F
Pinbox

Pleasant termination to a happy evening, A
Group F

**Please Sir, what would you charge
to christen my doll?**
Group E

Pluck
Group C

Polen Abschied
Group D
(Pole Goodbye)

Polly and Scotch
Group A
Several varieties

Power of love, The
Group B

Pray do me the favour
Group X

PICTURE NOT AVAILABLE
Precious luggage
Group D
Depicts two old men carrying a bottle

Precious baggage
Group B

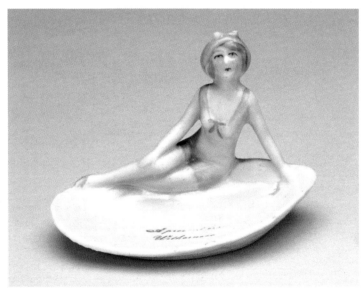

Present from Withernsea, A
Group A

Present from Great Yarmouth, A
Group A
Matchstriker

Present from Pebles, A
Group A
Also captioned: Present from Canterbury, A
Matchstriker

Privileged pet, A
Group B
Also captioned: Lucky dog, A

PICTURES NOT AVAILABLE
**Many Fairings were captioned
"A present from" various towns**
All Group A

Quelle est la plus
Group B
See: Which is prettiest?

Quiet interruption
Group X
Also captioned: I will warm you

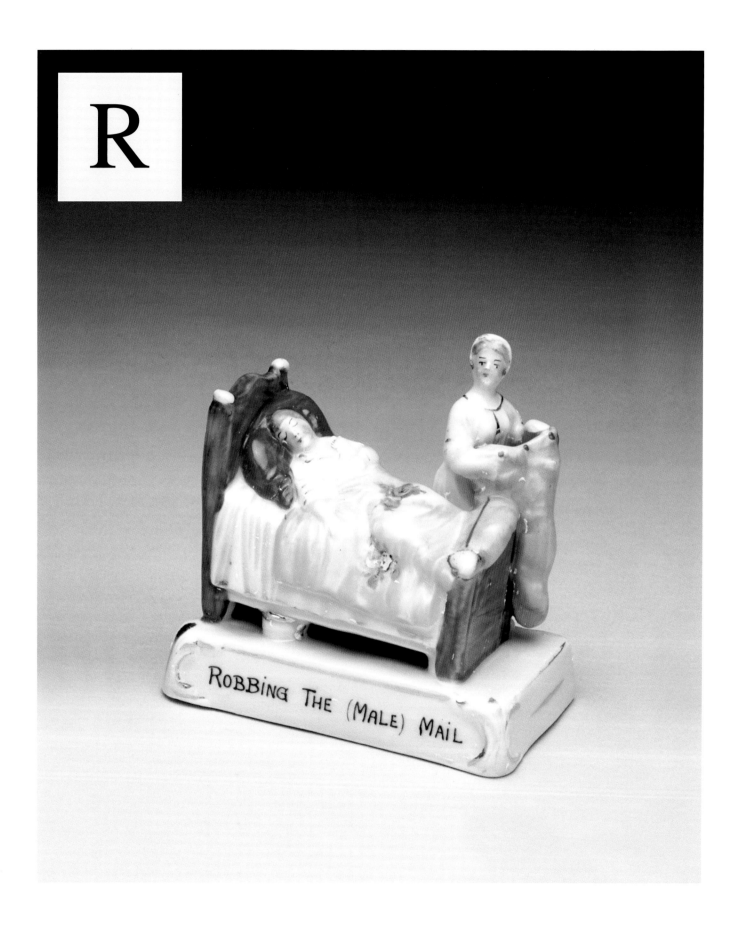

ROBBING THE (MALE) MAIL

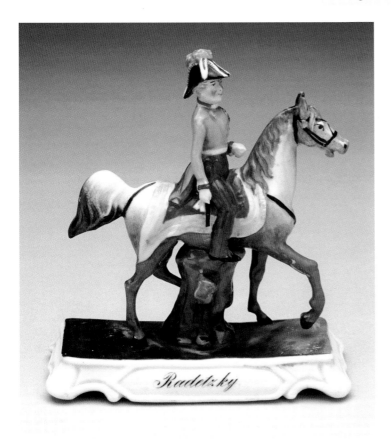

Radetsky
Group X

Ready to start
Group A single
Group B pair

Reception at 3 o'clock in the morning
Group A

Rent in arrear
Group C
Also captioned: Rent settled

Repentance
Group X
Also captioned: Our best wishes

Return, The
Group X

Return from the ball
Group D
Also captioned: Coming from the ball

Returning at one o'clock in the morning
Group C

Returning at one o'clock in the morning
Group A
Also captioned: Die folgen später heimkehr

Returning from working
Group B
Matchstriker

Returning from journey
Group X
Also captioned: Retour de voyage

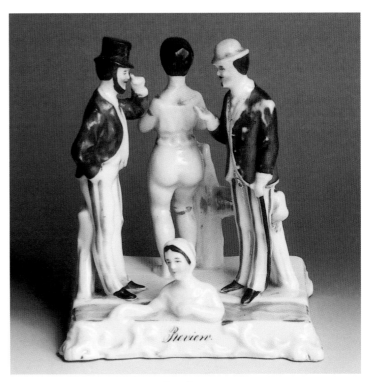

Review
Group X

Rip Van Winkle
Group B

Robbing the (male) mail
Group C

Rough on boys
Group C

Royal Manchester Exchange
Group B
Pinbox

Shall we sleep first,
or how?

Safe messenger, A
Group B
Matchstriker

Sailing our Ships
Group C

Sans douleur
Group F
(Without pain)
Also captioned: A long pull and a strong pull

Sarah's young man
Group B

Sedan
Group X
Watch holder

Seeing him home
Group E

Shall we sleep first or how?
Group A standard size

Shall we sleep first or how?
Group B large size

Shall we sleep first or how?
Group A - standard size

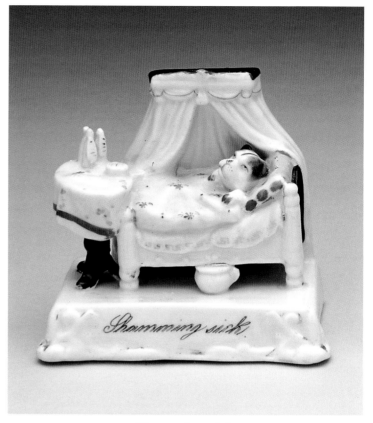

Shamming sick
Group D

Shoemaker in love, The
Group X

Sir! Where's your gloves?
If you think to go out with me?
Group X

PICTURE DUPLICATED
Six mois après la noce
Group B - large size
See: Twelve months after marriage

Slack
Group D

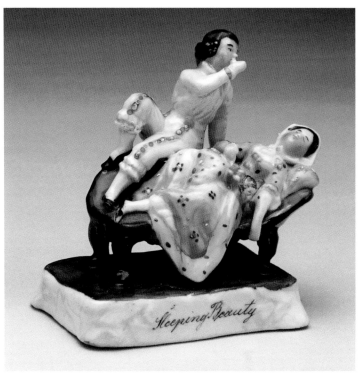

Sleeping Beauty
Group D

PICTURE DUPLICATED
Soft repose
Group D
See: How quietly they repose

Some contributors to Punch
Group F

Souter Johnnie – Tam O'Shanter
Group A single
Group B pair

Spicey Bit, A
Group B

Spoils of War, The
Group C standard size
Also captioned: Victoire, La

Spoils of War, The
Group C large size
Also captioned: Victoire, La

Stop your tickling, Jock
Group C

Stop your tickling, Jock
Group C

Sturm schwerer Cavallerie
Group F
(Heavy Storm Cavalry)

PICTURE DUPLICATED
Surprise, The
Group F
See: Wet reception, The

PICTURE DUPLICATED
Swansea to Bristol
Group B - pinbox
See: Great Nord of Scotland Railway

PICTURE DUPLICATED
Sweet song (love's old)
Group D
See: Love's old sweet song

Sweet violets, Sir?
Group C
Matchstriker

Swell, A
Group C

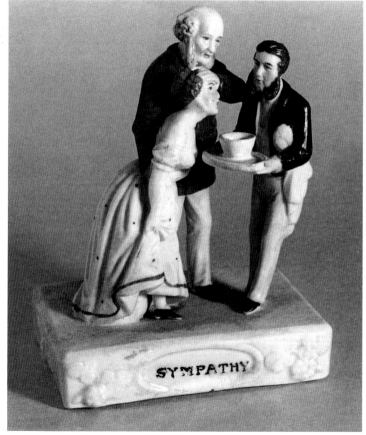

Sympathy
Group D
Caption doubtful

Taking a walk
Group B
Matchstriker

Taking the Cream
Group C

Taking the Cream
Group C

Taking dessert
Group X

PICTURE DUPLICATED
Tam O'Shanter
Group A
See: Souter Johnnie

Tea party
Group B

That's Funny! Very Funny! Very, Very Funny!
Group C

Three o'clock in the morning
Group A - standard size

Three o'clock in the morning
Group B - large size

To Epsom
Group X
Also captioned: To the Derby

Uncaptioned – possibly To Epsom
Group X

To Epsom
Group X

To Let
Group F

Tom Pounce
Group F

Top slice, The
Group C
Uncaptioned

Trespassing
Group E

Triple Alliance
Group B

Truly any form is not evil
Group F

Tug of War
Group C - standard size and large size
Also captioned: La bataille

Tug of War
Group C - large size
Also captioned: La bataille

Twelve months after marriage
Group A - standard size

Twelve months after marriage
Group B - large size

Twelve months after marriage
Group B - large size
Also captioned: Six mois après la noce

Reverse

Two different views
Group E

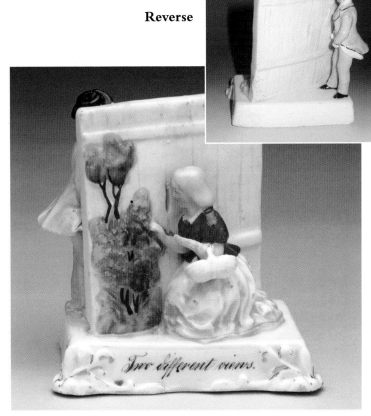

Two different views
Group X

PICTURE DUPLICATED
Une mauvaise rencontre
Group X
See: Girls of the period, The

Under petticoat government
Group D

Une heure monsieur
Group C
(One hour Sir)

Union for ever
Group X

United we stand, divided we fall
Group B

Unser Fritz
Group X
(Our Fred)
Watch holder

Unsere beiden, freundlichen nachbaren
Group X
(Our two friendly neighbours) – (Franco-Prussian map with court jester)

Velocipeding on a rainy day.

Velocipede for stout travellers
Group X

Velocipeding on a rainy day
Group X
Also with a different umbrella. (See page 34)

Very much frightened
Group B

Vet, The
Group A

PICTURE DUPLICATED
Victoire, La
Group C
See: Spoils of war, The

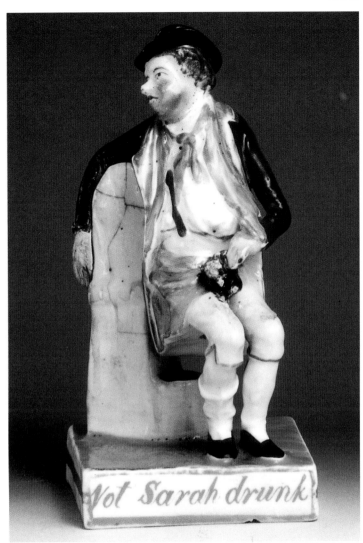

Vot Sarah drunk
Group X

Vy Sarah you're drunk!
Group X

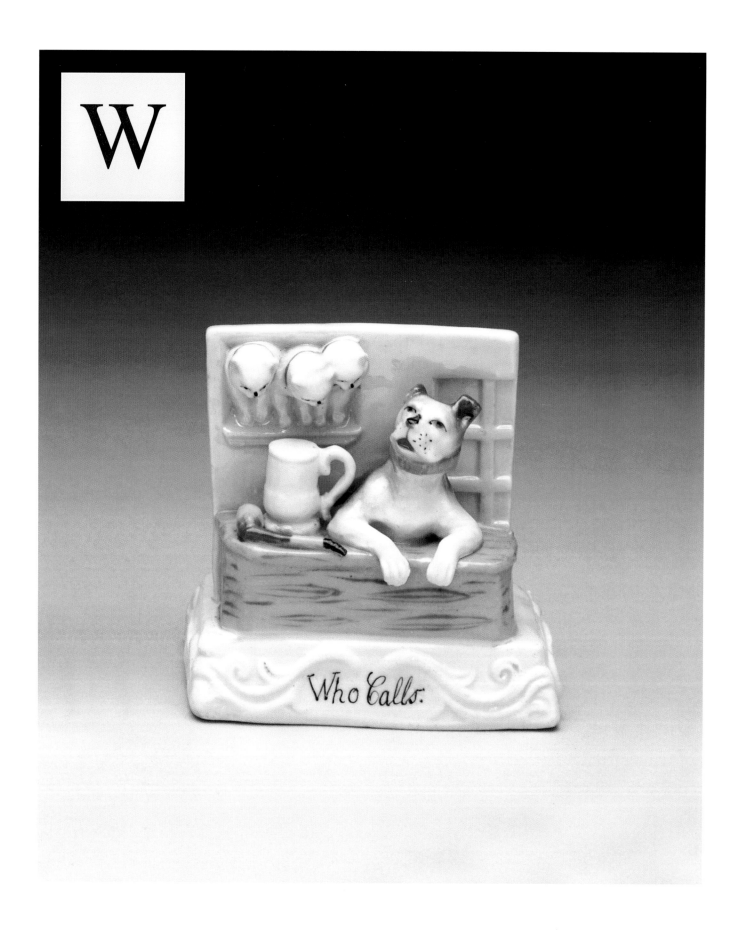

Who Calls.

Waiting for a bus
Group F - standard size
Group X - small size

Waiting for orders
Group B

Walk in
Group X

Walk in please
Group X

Was Blasen Die Trompeten Husaren Herans!
Group X
(What is the Hussar Trumpeter blowing)

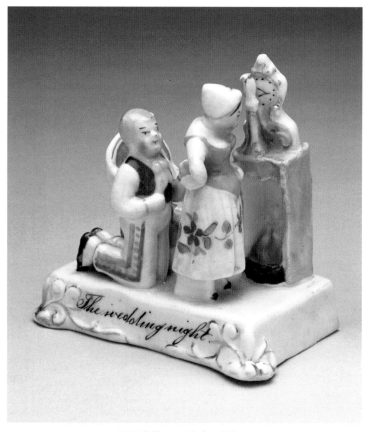

Wedding night, The
Group B

Wedding night, The
Group B

Well! What are you looking at?
Group X

Welsh costume
Group A

Welsh costume
Group A

Welsh Spinning party
Group A

Welsh Tea party, The
Group A
Numerous varieties

Welsh Tea party, The
Group A

Welsh Tea party, The
Group A

Welsh Tea party, The
Group D

Welsh Tea party, The
Group B

Wen das alter könte
Group X
(If old age could)

Wet reception, The
Group F
Also captioned: Surprise, The
Also captioned: Disagreeable surprise

We won't go home till morning
Group C

What have these met for?
Group X

What is home without a Mother-in-law?
Group B

What peace! When the old girl sleeps
Group B
Also in a pinbox

What is your fortune, my pretty maid?
Group C

When a man is married his troubles begin
Group A

When a man is married his troubles begin
Group B

When mother's at the wash
Group D

Where are you going to, my pretty maid?
Group C

Where are you going, my pretty maid?
Group C
Pinbox

Which is prettiest?
Group B
Also captioned: Quelle est la plus belle?

Who calls!
Group D
Matchstriker

Who is coming?
Group D

Who is the fastest of the three?
Group X

Who said Rats?
Group C
Also captioned: Où sont les rats?

Wide awake
Group F

Wine, wife and song
Group F

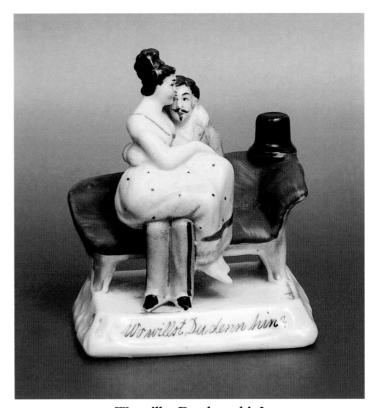

Wo willst Du denn hin?
Group X
(Where do you want to go to?)

You dirty boy!
Group B

You naughty Boy – You dirty Girl
Group B

Young Cups and Old Cups
Group B

You careless fool
Group B

The Royal Vienna Factory

There are five pieces in this series. Made in circa 1860, they are similar in size and theme to Fairings but the quality is much higher. These items were never made for the fairground market. They are all in Group X and are highly sought after by Fairing collectors. One is so rare that no picture is available. It depicts a man in a bath with a women entering the room.

Below are the four pieces which may have inspired *A mouse, a mouse!-1, The bedroom romp-2, The chaste Joseph-3, The landlord in love-4* and the missing piece appears to be *Did you ring sir?* They are all uncaptioned and bear the base mark of a shield with two line across it and the letter "R" in blue. They are exquisite in detail and design which puts them in a class of their own.

Vienna Series – 1
Group X

Vienna Series – 2
Group X

Vienna Series – 3
Group X

Vienna Series – 4
Group X

Alphabetical Index

OLYMPIC
TITANIC
BRITANNIC

THE ANATOMY AND EVOLUTION
OF THE
OLYMPIC CLASS

SIMON MILLS

ADLARD
COLES

LONDON · OXFORD · NEW YORK · NEW DELHI · SYDNEY

ADLARD COLES
Bloomsbury Publishing Plc
50 Bedford Square, London, WC1B 3DP, UK
29 Earlsfort Terrace, Dublin 2, Ireland

BLOOMSBURY, ADLARD COLES and the
Adlard Coles logo are trademarks of
Bloomsbury Publishing Plc

First published in Great Britain 2022

A catalogue record for this book is available
from the British Library

Library of Congress Cataloguing-in-Publication
data has been applied for

ISBN: HB: 978-1-4729-8865-2; ePub: 978-1-
4729-8864-5; ePDF: 978-1-4729-8863-8

2 4 6 8 10 9 7 5 3 1

Art Editor Louise Turpin - Typeset in Sukhumvit
Set by www.louiseturpindesign.co.uk
Printed and bound in China by Toppan Leefung

To find out more about our authors and
books visit www.bloomsbury.com and sign up
for our newsletters

CONTENTS

INTRODUCTION

'Day five. The Nicolakis *left harbour at 10.00 a.m. and within an hour all three teams were in the water. Evan and Richie K splashed at 10.44 and 10.46, Richie S and Barney at 10.47 and 10.49, with Barry and Stewie bringing up the tail-end at 10.54 and 10.56. After that there was nothing for me to do but sit around for the next four hours while the divers returned slowly to the surface. Yesterday's results are going to be hard to beat, with Evan and Richie K being the first humans in 105 years to enter the hull through the aft open shell door on E deck into Scotland Road, passing the remains of the ship's printing press en route to the casing doors at frame 52a and dropping down into the reciprocating engine room. Everything in there seems to be almost completely intact and today we're going to go for some closer detail. Evan and Richie will follow the same route they took yesterday, with Richie S and Barney entering through the skylight on the boat deck; the two teams will then link up inside the engine room to light up as large an area as possible for the cameras. Stewie and Barry are in the à la carte restaurant galley, on the eternal hunt for more crockery.*

Once the divers were all safely on the surface I found myself holding back as they came back aboard the Nicolakis, *probably because I don't think I could have got a word in edgeways if I had tried. All I needed to do was listen to the excited chatter of all six divers marvelling at what they had just seen, ranging from two intact reciprocating engines, an H&W builder's plate, the pristine engine telegraphs and associated machinery on the engineers' starting platform. These old campaigners have seen and done practically everything in their diving careers but today they seemed almost like kids in a sweet shop as I listened to their reactions at being inside an intact Olympic class engine room. I struggled to get my own thoughts into some sort of order as the* Nicolakis *headed slowly back to Vourkari, but the brief glimpses on the camera screens are only a taster of what's to come when I finally start to analyse the images on a larger screen in England. Back in port by 3.40 p.m., after which I strolled back to the Karthea hotel while the team sorted out their kit for tomorrow's dive.'*

The entry left, taken from my *Britannic* expedition journal for 25 September 2021, may seem like a curious way to begin a retrospective of the Olympic class liners, but as I was writing this particular entry it began to dawn on me just how much the *Olympic*, *Titanic* and *Britannic* have come to mean to so many diverse groups. To the technical divers, the wreck of the *Britannic* can almost be likened to a Holy Grail, with even the most hard-bitten techie unable to contain an almost child-like excitement as they swim over what is still the largest liner on the seabed, while in the case of the *Titanic*, arguments continue to rage over access for marine tourism and the rights or wrongs of commercial salvage. Meanwhile, legions of *Titanic* buffs eagerly follow every development on the two wrecks, as we continue to explore and reveal what lies inside.

For years, my focus has been largely on the history and exploration of the *Britannic*, but thinking back to 1993 I remember that I also wrote *RMS Olympic: The Old Reliable* (now probably long forgotten), the first serious book to focus exclusively on the career of the RMS *Olympic*. Three years later, this line of research effectively ground to a halt when I obtained the UK legal title to the wreck of the *Britannic*, which since 1996 is largely where my focus has been, but while I have often thought of picking up where I left off on the *Olympic*, somehow the opportunity to replant my flag on this particular mountain has never really presented itself. It was only during the autumn of 2020 that the Covid lockdown finally provided me with the incentive to revisit the work that I abandoned all those years ago.

So much has changed since 1993 that the notion of studying the *Olympic*, *Titanic* and *Britannic* as separate entities no longer seems appropriate. As we progress with our work inside the *Britannic*, it is becoming increasingly clear to me that to tell her story properly we need to see the ship in its full perspective, and the only way to do that is to study the Olympic class as a whole. This is probably just as well as it will be a while yet before we are ready to reveal fully what lies inside the wreck, but in the meantime this year's *Britannic* project has finally prodded me into picking up on my old research in order to put the story of all three ships into their full context.

This is that story.

TOP LEFT: *A composite sonar scan of the* Britannic *wreck,
taken in September 2003.*

BELOW: *The St Nikolo chapel and lighthouse, overlooking the
Kea Channel and the* Britannic's *final resting place.*

CHAPTER ONE

GENESIS

They were said to be the finest and most luxurious ships in the world.
Perhaps, but as ever it depends on your own individual perspective. Sitting
in first class and sipping champagne, you could be forgiven for thinking
that, whereas if you were a fireman toiling 80 feet below in the bowels
of the ship, then the view of the trimmers and firemen stoking the ship's
boilers would be more reminiscent of a scene from Dante's *Inferno*.

Looking back in time, it is easy to see why the Olympic class ships were supposed to symbolise everything that was good about the gilded age, in an era when, from the technological point of view, anything seemed possible. By the turn of the 20th century, shipbuilding technology meant that vessels had grown out of all proportion in a very short time. The first White Star liner, the *Oceanic* of 1871, had a gross tonnage of 3,707 tons, and although steam-powered she still required the use of sails to augment her speed and serve as backup in case of any mechanical failure. Forty years later, the SS *Olympic* would have no sails, three engines and a gross tonnage of over 45,000 tons – a twelvefold increase in carrying capacity.

By the end of the 19th century the White Star Line, in partnership with the Belfast shipbuilder Harland & Wolff, had secured their reputations in a period when

ABOVE: *Early advertising poster for the Olympic class, with many of the details still to be fine-tuned.*

British industrial power, for decades the envy of the world, was beginning to come under serious foreign competition. One by one, the other industrialised nations had caught up with British technology, although British shipbuilding and marine engineering continued to lead the world. Nonetheless, the gap was narrowing. Between 1892 and 1894, British shipyards had accounted for some 80 per cent of the gross tonnage of merchant vessels launched, yet by the early 20th century this figure had fallen to less than 60 per cent of the world share. To further rub salt into the wound, by the end of the century German vessels were also beginning to take the top honours with the speed records on the North Atlantic, with British pre-eminence in their traditional maritime stronghold suddenly coming under serious threat.

It was from this background that the Olympic class liners would evolve, although the catalyst that ultimately led to their conception came not from Europe but from the other side of the Atlantic. In 1901, the American railway baron, banker and financier John Pierpont Morgan arrived in the world of shipping. Already a formidable financial and industrial force on land, he had now set his eye on establishing American superiority on the oceans. His goal was simple – to buy out a select group of shipping companies, creating a common pool from which he would not only be able to eliminate an on-going rate war but at the same time would make the tonnage interchangeable. By 1902, Morgan's International Mercantile Marine Company (IMM) had gained control of the American, Atlantic Transport, Dominion,

ABOVE: *John Pierpont Morgan, the American financier who would ultimately make the Olympic class a reality.*

Inman, Leyland, Shaw, Savill & Albion and Red Star Lines. Now it was the turn of the White Star Line. His first approach came in February 1902, using his vast wealth to offer the White Star shareholders ten times the value of their individual investments. Had Thomas Ismay, the founder of the company, still been alive then it might have been a different story, but with three-quarters of the shareholders ready to accept the proposal there was little the Ismay family could do to stop the sale. In the end, a majority of the shareholders agreed to the sale of the company for the fabulous price of over £10,000,000, the first down payment of £3,000,000 payable on 31 December 1902.

It was at this point that the British government belatedly began to wake up to the threat posed by Morgan's expansion. Even if the growing foreign control of so many British shipping companies was acceptable to some, the potential loss of carrying capacity to the government in the event of a national emergency was not. This Damascene conversion came too late to prevent the sale of the White Star Line, but the national concerns were at least partially offset when IMM agreed that the ships would retain their British officers and crews, and would remain on the British register and at the disposal of the British government in any national emergency; in return, the British government would agree not to discriminate against the White Star Line as a foreign-controlled shipping line. If the government action had come too late to save White Star, at least a number of officials at Whitehall realised that any further attempt by Morgan to gain control of other British shipping companies had to be checked. The few shipping lines that were not controlled by the Morgan combine were not long in coming to terms with him, but only the French Compagnie Générale Transatlantique and the British Cunard Line remained truly independent. However, with the CGT enjoying financial assistance from the French government, the possibility of Cunard being able to hold out indefinitely was doubtful at best.

Cunard had already been operating a transatlantic mail service for more than 30 years before Thomas Henry Ismay's first White Star Line service between Liverpool and New York was instituted in March 1871, but if the company was to survive the financial

maelstrom, it could only do so with government support. Aware of the seriousness of the situation, in 1903 George Burns, 2nd Baron Inverclyde and chairman of Cunard, approached the British government with an offer they basically could not refuse. Inverclyde's proposal was for a subsidy to build two of the largest and fastest liners, able to compete with the Morgan combine on more equitable terms, in return for Cunard's guarantee to remain a British company for at least 20 years. Faced with the loss of even more mercantile tonnage and the even more serious prospect of having insufficient tonnage to transport troops to the furthest outposts of the empire, Parliament viewed the proposal sympathetically and agreed to a loan of £2,600,000, at 2¾ per cent interest, for the construction of two giant vessels, which would ultimately become the *Lusitania* and *Mauretania*. In addition, a 20-year annual subsidy of £150,000 would be payable to cover the additional Admiralty specifications that would be incorporated into the designs. The basic requirements, however, were simple enough. The ships needed to be capable of maintaining a minimum speed of 24.5 knots and were to be permanently available for government service as armed merchant cruisers in the event of war. In fact, both vessels would ultimately far exceed the contracted speed during their trials, with the *Lusitania* recording a speed of 26.45 knots while the *Mauretania* would even tip the scales at 27 knots during her trials off Flamborough Head.

The orders for the two Cunard sisters were awarded to two different shipyards, with Clydeside's John Brown & Company being given the contract to build the *Lusitania* and the Tyneside shipbuilder Swan, Hunter & Wigham Richardson awarded the contract to build the *Mauretania*, but while Cunard now had the financial backing to give IMM a run for its money on the North Atlantic, the practicalities of building the new generation of liners would be less easy to resolve. Months of testing ensued before Inverclyde, determined to live up to his end of the bargain, was ready to sign the contracts. Swan Hunter even carried out additional hull-form tests on a $^1/_{16}$th-scale model before construction began, while Cunard experimented with additional trials on the smaller liners *Caronia* and *Carmania*. *Caronia* had been designed with two quadruple expansion steam reciprocating engines, whereas the *Carmania* had been fitted with three propellers, each powered by a marine turbine. The initial results suggested that the turbine arrangement in the *Carmania* averaged over half a knot faster, although this may not have been wholly down to the use of turbines as the flow line for the triple propellers may have also played its part. Even so, it was all crucial data that would have an important impact on deciding the power plant and propeller combination that would be incorporated into the *Lusitania* and *Mauretania*.

The *Lusitania* was finally ready to be launched on 7 June 1906, with the *Mauretania* taking to the water three months later on 20 September, but it would be another year before the two vessels were ready to enter commercial service. In addition to the huge engineering undertaking, more mundane issues such as dredging the harbour alongside the Liverpool landing stage and building elevated platforms so that the gangways could reach the entrance on the upper decks needed to be addressed. Even *Skirmisher*, Cunard's tender at

Liverpool, would require an additional deck just to service the new vessels, but everything was in readiness in time for the *Lusitania*'s maiden voyage on 7 September 1907, from Liverpool to New York. Not surprisingly, she was an immediate sensation. At 31,550 GRT, the *Lusitania* was the largest vessel in the world, and by regaining the Blue Riband on only her second voyage from the North German Lloyd liner *Deutschland*, British pre-eminence on the North Atlantic was effectively reasserted at a stroke. With the marginally faster *Mauretania*

ABOVE: *An Autochrome Lumière plate of the 31,938 GRT* Mauretania, *taken during the latter stages of her career.*

joining the fleet on 16 November, the fact that Great Britain once again boasted the two largest and fastest vessels on the North Atlantic came as a welcome relief.

As the German shipping lines retired to lick their wounds and plan their own response, the directors of the White Star Line had also been closely watching events. White Star had long since withdrawn from the expensive race

PUBLIC BUILDINGS
PHILADELPHIA, 534 FEET HIGH

WASHINGTON MONUMENT
WASHINGTON, 555 FEET HIGH

METROPOLITAN TOWER
NEW YORK, 700 FEET HIGH

NEW WOOLWORTH
BUILDING,
NEW YORK,
750 FEET HIGH.

COLOGNE CATHEDRAL,
COLOGNE, 516 FEET HIGH

GRAND PYRAMID
GIZEH, AFRICA, 451 FEET HIGH

ST. PETER'S CHURCH
ROME, ITALY 448 FEET HIGH

R.M.S. OLYMPIC. 882 FEET LONG.

☆ **WHITE STAR LINE R.M.S "OLYMPIC"** ☆
COMPARED WITH VARIOUS FAMOUS BUILDINGS.

to make their ships the fastest in the world, their last record breaker, the *Teutonic*, having been built in 1889. The company's emphasis focused instead on larger and steadier vessels, although the disparity in speed could only be allowed to stretch so far. With the *Lusitania* and *Mauretania* both capable of exceeding 25 knots, whereas the *Adriatic* was barely able to maintain a service speed of a little over 16 knots, if the White Star Line was to maintain a credible express service then their next generation of vessels would need to be a lot faster. There would still be no question of returning to the field of competing for the Blue Riband, but their response would need to be no less sensational.

If the legend is to be believed then one evening during the spring of 1907 Joseph

ABOVE: *An early White Star postcard, emphasising the huge scale of the* Olympic *and* Titanic.

Bruce Ismay, chairman of the White Star Line and president of IMM, arrived for dinner at Downshire House, the Belgravia home of Lord William Pirrie. Pirrie was the chairman of Harland & Wolff, the birthplace of the entire White Star fleet, and during the course of the meal the two men speculated on their own plans for two super liners that would enable the White Star Line to regain the initiative on the North Atlantic. By the time the evening ended, Ismay and Pirrie had taken the first steps towards the construction of two ships, the like and scale of which the world had never seen.

US IMMIGRATION FIGURES 1841 TO 1910

US Fiscal Years	UK immigration to US	Irish immigration to US	Total
1841–1850	267,044	780,719	1,047,763
1851–1860	423,974	914,119	1,338,093
1861–1870	606,896	435,778	1,042,674
1871–1880	548,043	436,871	984,914
1881–1890	807,357	655,482	1,462,839
1891–1900	271,538	388,416	659,954
1901–1910	525,950	339,065	865,015

Suddenly, the concept of the *Olympic* and *Titanic* was no longer just speculation; but whatever Ismay and Pirrie had in mind, the new vessels were not built simply to be symbols of national pride, even if that was an undoubtedly useful bonus. If there were no clear commercial reasons for building such huge vessels then the Olympic class would have been an economic disaster, although in truth the economic reasons provided ample justification for their construction. In most respects, the *raison d'être* of the Olympic class vessels would be little different to any other White Star liner, namely the safe and effective transportation of passengers and cargo around the world. The North Atlantic, however, differed in one key manner when it came to the transportation of human beings. America was dependent on immigration and if the nation was to expand then it needed workers, be they low-skilled labour or higher-skilled intellectuals and engineers. An overpopulated Europe had proved an ideal source for the required immigrant labour throughout the

19th century, and even a cursory glance at the official immigration figures above illustrates the huge volume of emigrant traffic travelling from British ports alone.

Numerous shipping companies had willingly stepped forward to help transport huge volumes of emigrants from Europe to America, but despite the migrants' willingness to move thousands of miles from home, their pursuit of the American dream was not always easy. Not to put too fine a point on it, the quality and conditions aboard some of the earlier emigrant ships had been so bad that in March 1855 Congress introduced the Act to Regulate the Carriage of Passengers in Steamships and other Vessels. Setting out the requirements over 19 articles, the captains and owners of any emigrant vessels using American ports were required to allot minimum areas of deck space to passengers in certain parts of the ship, being subject to fines of $50 per passenger if they failed to maintain the required standards. Passengers also had to be allocated their own hospital space, minimum sized sleeping berths with dividers, deckhouses and adequate food of good quality.

In the event that any emigrant vessel failed to provide the required deckhouses or adequate ventilation, further fines for each failure to conform to the various provisions of the Act could be levied on the master and owners. On the face of it, the Americans did seem to have the best of intentions insofar as the transportation of emigrant traffic was concerned, and while the ship owners may not always have complied with the 1855 Act in the spirit in which it was intended, the gradual improvements in the size of emigrant vessels and shipbuilding technology enabled Congress to further tighten the regulations. The 1882 Act to Regulate the Carriage of Passengers at Sea contained even more specific regulations regarding adequate rules for occupancy, including light and air to passenger decks, ventilation, hatchways, companionways, water closets, food quality and meals per day, hospital compartments and even a surgeon.

The details of the legendary meeting between Ismay and Pirrie are shrouded in the mists of time, but it is probably fair to assume

ABOVE LEFT: *Joseph Bruce Ismay, chairman of the White Star Line since 1899 as well as president and managing director of IMM since 1904.*

ABOVE RIGHT: *Lord William Pirrie.*

OLYMPIC TITANIC BRITANNIC

that the minutiae of the luxurious fixtures and fittings would not have taken up much of their conversation. Both men would have been more than aware of the legal and economic requirements surrounding the concept, so there seems little doubt that the conversation would have been in relatively broad strokes, as they contemplated the size and speed of the two vessels that would ultimately take on the Cunard sisters. One thing we can be sure of, however, is that the White Star/Harland & Wolff partnership was ideally placed to make it happen.

Joseph Bruce Ismay, known to his family and friends as Bruce, was a very different individual to his father. Thomas Henry Ismay, a former director of the National Line, had founded the Oceanic Steam Navigation Company (more popularly known as the White Star Line) in 1869, and by the time of his death in November 1899 the company had risen to become one of the pre-eminent British shipping companies. Bruce was a far more introvert character than his father, his sensitivity and shyness sometimes mistaken for a brusque or even arrogant manner, but whatever he may have lacked in terms of his father's vision or ability to build up the firm, his organisational abilities and expertise in financial management made him an excellent administrator for the already established company. His business acumen did not help him to save White Star from being taken over by the Morgan combine in 1902, but Bruce's undoubted head for business was not lost on JP Morgan, who in February 1904 had persuaded him to accept the position of president of IMM, which despite its promising start was already in turbulent financial waters and in need of total reorganisation.

William Pirrie was an equally capable businessman, having joined Harland & Wolff as a gentleman apprentice in 1862 before becoming a partner in the firm 12 years later. Having assumed the chairmanship of the company on the death of Sir Edward Harland in 1895, Pirrie's domineering temperament seems to have been closer to that of Thomas Ismay. Some even considered him to be autocratic bordering on dictatorial, but the long-standing relationship between the two companies ensured that Harland & Wolff was contractually obliged to build all of White Star's vessels, and under Pirrie's stewardship Harland & Wolff had become one of the most powerful – perhaps even the most powerful – forces in the world of shipbuilding.

The practical problems facing Ismay and Pirrie in the construction of the two White Star behemoths were no less daunting than those faced by Lord Inverclyde four years earlier, although at least speed was not such an issue in this case. For the previous ten years, the competition for the fastest ship on the North Atlantic had been largely confined to Cunard and the German Hamburg America and North German Lloyd shipping lines, but while considerable prestige would always be associated with the company that operated the fastest ships, the fact remained that the faster ships were not always the most comfortable or cost-effective. Their fine lines not only made them less steady but also resulted in an additional loss of carrying capacity, while from the economic point of view they consumed huge quantities of coal and required a larger stokehold crew to feed the boilers in pursuit of that speed. The White Star business model was therefore aimed at larger, steadier and more economical ships. Ultimately, this proved to be a great success with the travelling public, but while Bruce had done nothing to change the company policy after assuming the White Star chairmanship in November 1899, the concept of increasingly large ships no doubt appealed to a shipbuilder like Pirrie.

The necessary expansion of the shipyard in order to make the project feasible would also result in a huge cost to Harland & Wolff and, coming at a time when Pirrie was already committed to establishing an additional ship repair facility at Southampton for the new White Star Southampton to New York express service, the timing was far from ideal. However, this was not the first time the Belfast shipyard had made alterations to accommodate the construction of White Star vessels. When Thomas Ismay ordered his first ships from the company, the slipways had to be specially constructed and then further strengthened when the *Britannic* and *Germanic* were ordered only three years later. Two completely new slips needed to be built before construction could begin on the *Teutonic* and *Majestic*, not to mention the construction of the Alexandra Graving Dock to accommodate the new generation of liners, but with a projected gross tonnage of 45,000 tons, the Olympic class would be nearly 50 per cent larger than even the *Lusitania*. Once again, the White Star Line was planning a generation of ships the like of which the world had never seen, and once again Harland & Wolff would

need to expand.

The first and greatest logistical issue was that they did not possess large enough facilities for the construction of one vessel of this size, let alone two. This meant that two completely new slipways would need to be built over a space that was already occupied by three, resulting not only in considerable capital expenditure but also the additional expenses of reduced shipbuilding capacity during their construction. Fortunately, the corporate muscle of IMM would provide a welcome loan to ease the financial burden as Harland & Wolff set about the two-year reconstruction of their north yard. By the time the work was completed, an area previously occupied by four slipways now had space for only three, while the supporting structures had been completely transformed. The gantry previously straddling what had been slips 2 and 3 had been dismantled and reassembled over slip 1, while the area that had occupied slips 2, 3 and 4 had been converted into a vast concrete apron for two berths, each capable of building a vessel of almost 1,000 feet in length.

If that wasn't impressive enough, the next stage of the reconstruction would provide Belfast with one of its major landmarks for the next 50 years. At 840 feet long, 270 feet wide and rising to a height of 228 feet, the Arrol Gantry came complete with four elevators, ten walking cranes and six travelling frames, while a huge cantilever revolving crane on the top of the structure ensured that there was ample lifting capacity to raise even the heaviest of objects. Not surprisingly, all this activity came at a considerable cost. The new gantry alone had cost £100,000, with an additional £30,000 being paid to the German Benrather company for a huge floating crane, which would be necessary to handle the fitting out of the two ships after launch. Combined with Harland & Wolff's £40,000 investment in the new ship repair facility at Southampton, Pirrie's commitment to the project was no idle boast.

As the work at Belfast continued apace, the White Star directors busied themselves with the issue of raising the necessary capital to finance the daunting construction costs. The company would go on to issue £2,500,000 of additional shares to cover the majority of the projected £3,000,000 cost, but on 29 July 1908 Ismay and the company's senior directors finally arrived in Belfast to peruse and approve the proposed general arrangement plan of what was then simply referred to as 'Design D'. In truth, the signature on this document was little more than a formality, with the order to proceed given as early as 30 May 1907, but on 31 July 1908 the contract was officially signed for the construction of Yard Nos 400 and 401 – the *Olympic* and *Titanic*.

RIGHT: *The expanded Harland & Wolff shipyard with the two enlarged slips in the northern yard.*

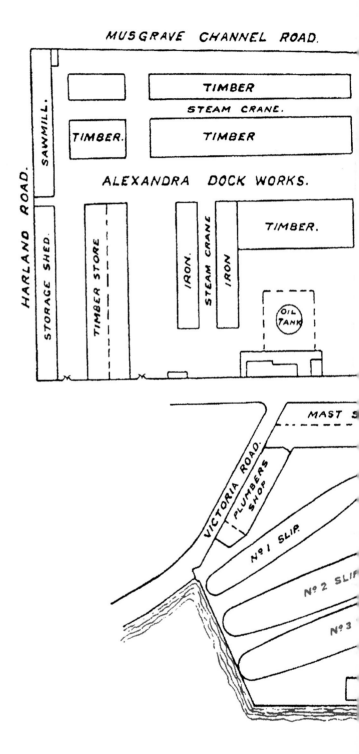

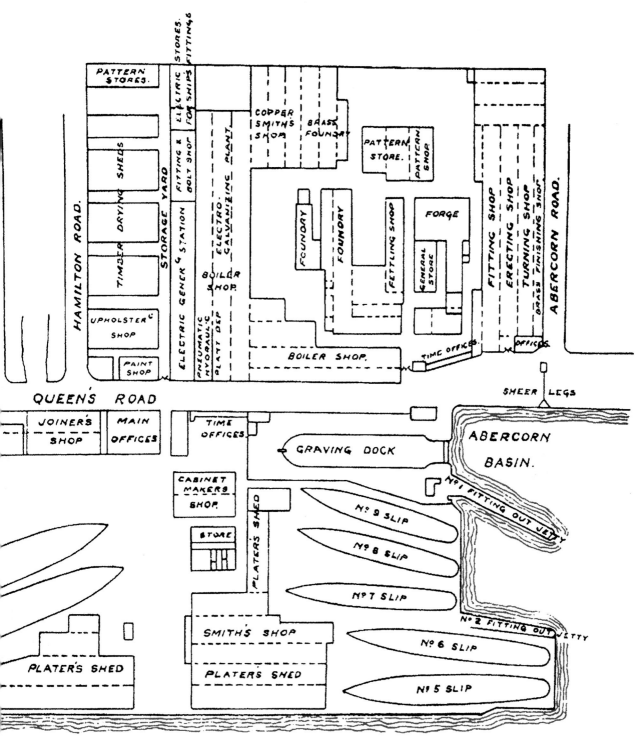

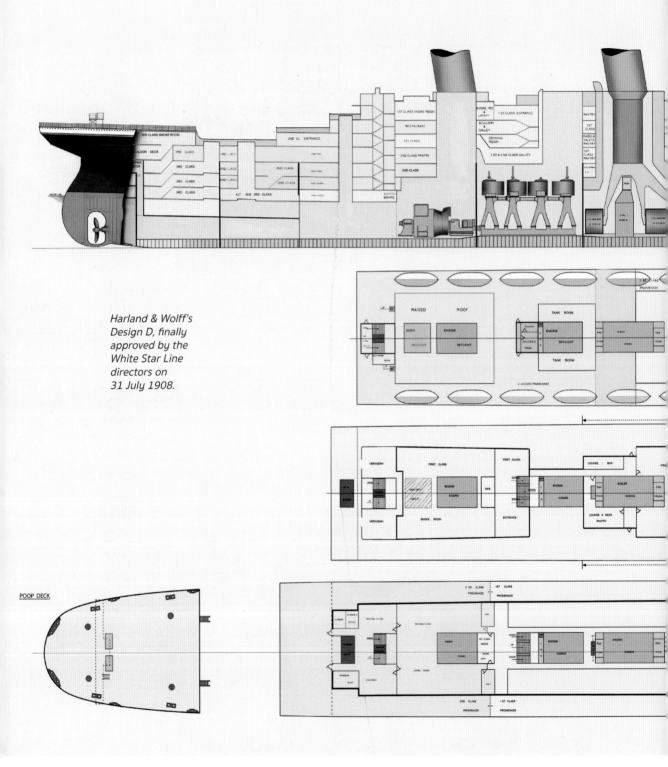

Harland & Wolff's Design D, finally approved by the White Star Line directors on 31 July 1908.

POOP DECK

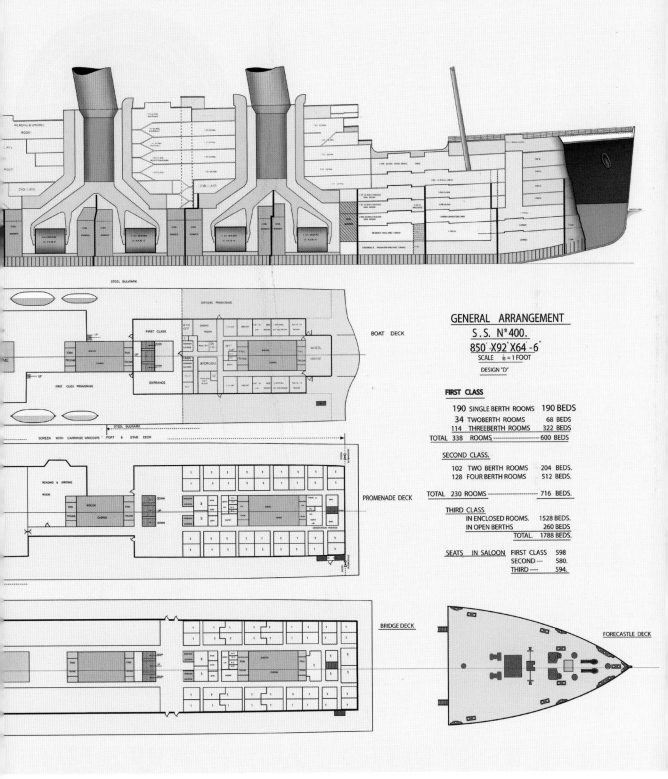

GENERAL ARRANGEMENT

S. S. Nº 400.

850ˈ X 92ˈ X 64ˈ -6ˈˈ

SCALE ⅛ = 1 FOOT

DESIGN "D"

FIRST CLASS

190	SINGLE BERTH ROOMS	190 BEDS
34	TWOBERTH ROOMS	68 BEDS
114	THREEBERTH ROOMS	322 BEDS
TOTAL 338	ROOMS	600 BEDS

SECOND CLASS.

102	TWO BERTH ROOMS	204 BEDS.
128	FOUR BERTH ROOMS	512 BEDS.
TOTAL 230 ROOMS		716 BEDS.

THIRD CLASS

IN ENCLOSED ROOMS.	1528 BEDS
IN OPEN BERTHS	260 BEDS
TOTAL.	1788 BEDS.

SEATS IN SALOON	FIRST CLASS	598
	SECOND ---	580.
	THIRD ----	594.

BOAT DECK

PROMENADE DECK

BRIDGE DECK

FORECASTLE DECK

CHAPTER TWO

THE DESIGN

Despite the threat posed by the *Lusitania* and *Mauretania*, the
design of White Star's latest generation of steamer was surprisingly
conventional. Thomas Ismay's policy of comfort rather than speed
remained the watchword and in that respect the Olympic class
would be little different to the company's four previous
vessels intended for the North Atlantic service.

The 20,904 GRT *Celtic*, the 21,035 GRT *Cedric*, the 23,884 GRT *Baltic* and the 24,541 GRT *Adriatic*, collectively known as the 'Big Four', had all entered service between 1901 and 1907, epitomising White Star's emphasis on comfort and luxury, but their service speed of 16 knots meant that they would need to be eclipsed in terms of both size and speed by the next generation of ships. Overseeing the Olympic class project, Lord Pirrie would be ably seconded by Alexander Montgomery Carlisle, the company's chief naval architect and, coincidentally, Pirrie's brother-in-law, and to complete the triumvirate Thomas Andrews, the head of the company's design department, as well as being Pirrie's nephew, ensured that the project remained resolutely in the family.

The objectives of the design team in this case were relatively straightforward. The two vessels would be designed with a beam broad enough to increase their displacement to the point where it did not exceed the available draught, so providing ample space for the carriage of both passengers and cargo. It has to be conceded that in the overall scheme of things the design of the Olympic class was anything but revolutionary, save for their huge size, which in terms of gross tonnage would make them 50 per cent larger than any previous liner, but even so the *Olympic* and *Titanic* would be the culmination of a tried and tested commercial design, which over the preceding decades had served the White Star Line well. The *Lusitania* and *Mauretania*, on the other hand, had been built to Admiralty requirements, including a modern balanced rudder, increased watertight compartmentalisation, turbine engines and high speed, but while this may have resulted in a fast and solid design, these accoutrements were of little practical use in the day-to-day operation of a commercial steamship.

THE HULL

While the design and construction of the Olympic class may have been more run-of-the-mill than state-of-the-art, the sheer length of the proposed structures would compel Harland & Wolff to upscale everything. Pirrie's original design called for a hull length of close to 900 feet, but while the *Olympic*'s overall length would be 882 feet 9 inches, the hull length between perpendiculars – ie from stem to sternpost – would be 850 feet. The hull would be built from mild steel based around a central keel, the keel itself formed by a single thickness of plating 1½ inches thick, with a keel bar 19½ inches wide and 3 inches thick. Either side of the keel was a double bottom, extending out to the extreme sides of the vessel. For the most part, this double bottom was designed to a depth of 5 feet 3 inches, although this was increased to 6 feet 3 inches beneath the reciprocating engine room, where additional strengthening was required to support the weight of the engines. The double bottom itself was subdivided into cellular tanks in order to assist with the trimming of the vessel, correcting any list brought about by the uneven emptying of the coal bunkers.

Above the double bottom, a vast network of over 300 frames extended from one end of the keel to the other. Generally, the frames were spaced 3 feet apart amidships, but towards either end of the keel they were closer together, reducing to 24 inches forward and 27 inches aft. The transverse strength of the hull would be maintained through a combination of 15 watertight bulkheads and the 11 non-watertight bulkheads forming the cross-bunker ends, with the beams of the bridge, shelter,

ABOVE: *Thomas Andrews.*

ABOVE: *Alexander Montgomery Carlisle.*

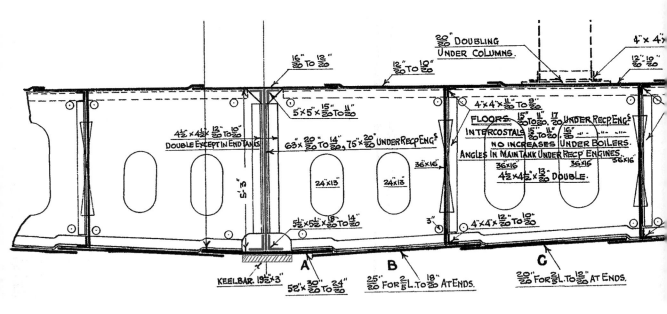

ABOVE: *Detail of the ships' keel and double bottom.*

upper and middle decks amidships reinforced by longitudinal girders. Below the middle deck, in the boiler rooms, the support pillars were spaced 9 feet apart, working in conjunction with strong beams at the lower deck level in way of each web frame. In the case of the inner rows, the beams were spaced so as not to interfere with the working passages, while in the engine rooms and hold the pillars below the middle deck were more widely spaced, with the number of pillars reducing forward and aft as the structure progressively narrowed. The ship's superstructure comprised the boat and promenade decks, which were also built to ensure a high degree of rigidity, supported at the sides by built-up frames in line with the hull frames. The deckhouses were stiffened by channel section steel fitted in the framework, reinforced by heavy brackets where the first-class public rooms pierced the boat deck above in order to increase the resistance to racking

forces when the ship was in heavy seas.

Due to the massive size of the vessels, it was also felt desirable that the individual hull plates should be as large as possible in order to reduce the number of overlapping plates, which would be linked using butts. Generally, the hull plates were 30 feet by 6 feet and weighed something in the region of 2½ to 3 tons, although some of the larger shell frames amidships measured 36 feet in length and weighed 4½ tons each. The entire skeleton and skin would be held together by no fewer than 3 million rivets in each ship, weighing something in the order of 1,200 tons. Of that number, half a million rivets, weighing 270 tons alone, would be used in the double bottom. Because of the immense size of the vessels, the decision was also taken to use

hydraulic steel riveting wherever possible, and as a result the majority of the hull, including the double bottom shell plating up to the turn of the bilge, the topside shell, stringer plates and doublings were all hydraulically riveted.

STEM AND STERN CASTINGS

Due to the triple screw arrangement, the stern frame itself incorporated an aperture for the centre turbine propeller shaft, while the two wing reciprocating engine propeller shafts would be supported by boss arm castings. The castings were manufactured by the Darlington Forge Company and for the most part were of the standard Siemens-Martin mild cast steel then in use. The rudder stock, however, was made from higher quality forged ingot steel, with the table at right indicating just how massive the stern structure alone would be.

STERN STRUCTURE WEIGHTS

Stern frame (2 pieces)	70 tons
After brackets (2 pieces)	73¾ tons
Forward brackets (2 pieces)	45 tons
Rudder (6 pieces)	101¼ tons (290 tons)
Stem bars	7¼ tons
Stem connection piece to keel	3½ tons (10¾ tons)

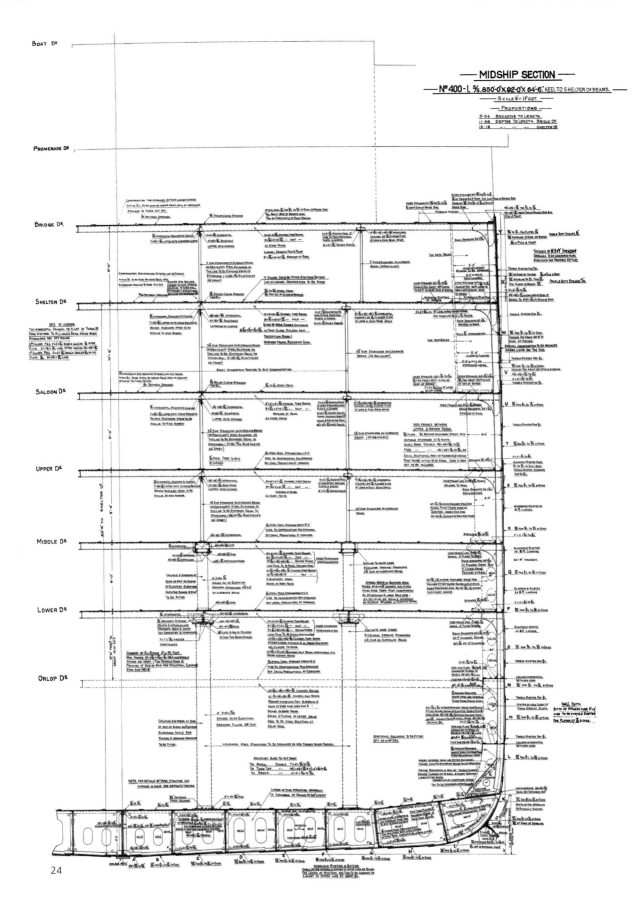

MIDSHIP SECTION

N⁰ 400 – L. S/S. 850'-0" x 92'-0" x 64'-6". KEEL TO SHELTER D⁰ BEAMS.

SCALE ⅛" = 1 FOOT.

PROPORTIONS

9·24 BREADTHS TO LENGTH.
11·26 DEPTHS TO LENGTH. BRIDGE D⁰
13·18   SHELTER D⁰

24

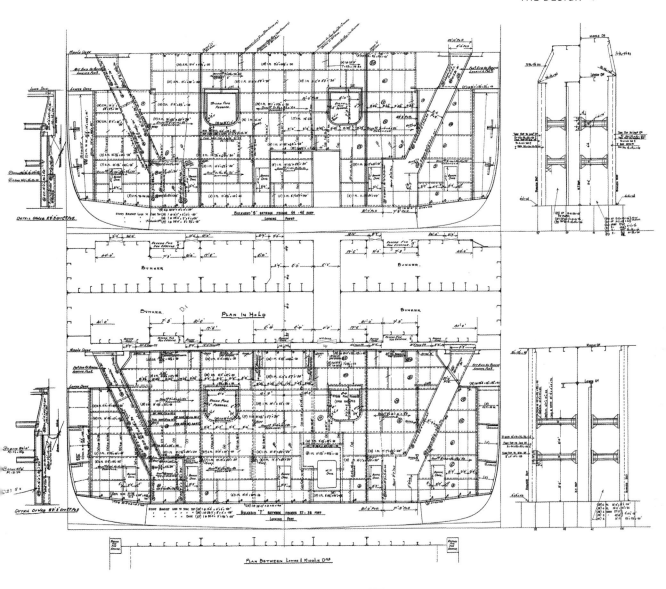

ABOVE: *Aside from adding to the transverse strength of the hull, the arrangement of the bunkers across the ship also ensured that the more than 600 tons of coal required on a daily basis to power the ship could be shovelled almost directly from the bunker into the boiler furnaces.*

LEFT: *Midship section of the final approved design. The seams of the bottom plating were double riveted and the topside treble and quadruple riveted. The butts of the bottom plating were overlapped and quadruple riveted, as were the butts in the side plating, except in way of the topside shell and doublings, where double straps were adopted.*

BOILER AND ENGINE ROOMS

The boiler rooms occupied six of the hull's watertight compartments, accounting for over 300 feet of the keel's length. To power the engines, the Olympic class vessels would require a total of 29 boilers, of which the 24 double-ended boilers, each 20 feet in length, accounted for 144 of the 159 Morrison-type furnaces, the remainder being located in the

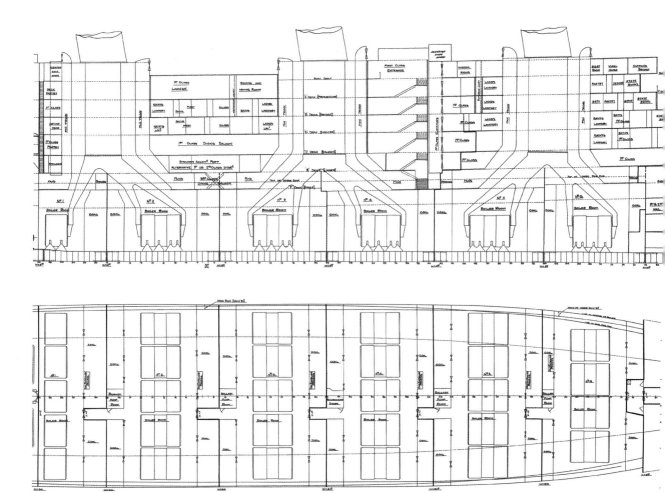

ABOVE: *With an overall length of 514 feet, the combined boiler and engine room spaces accounted for well over half the length of the hull. The above boiler room arrangement for the* Britannic *varied slightly from the two earlier vessels, but in all important respects the layout was practically identical.*

five single-ended boilers of boiler room 1. The forward boiler room was 54 feet long, while boiler rooms 3, 4 and 5 were marginally longer; with an overall length of 60 feet, boiler room 2 was the largest, while the five single-

ended boilers in boiler room 1 required only an additional 36 feet. The boilers themselves had a working pressure of 215 psi, and the generated steam was carried aft to the engines by two main steam pipes that passed through passages in the bulkheads, each pipe gradually increasing in diameter as they got closer to the forward bulkhead of the reciprocating engine room. A stop valve in the aft boiler room could close off the steam supply when necessary, while additional valves aft of the bulkhead directed the steam to the engines as required.

THE RECIPROCATING ENGINES

At 69 feet in length and covering the entire width of the tank top, the reciprocating engine room was easily the largest compartment in the ship. The *Olympic*'s two marine reciprocating engines, driving the wing propellers, were of the standard direct-acting inverted type, with the exhaust steam passing through four cylinders. The high-pressure cylinder measured 54 inches in diameter, the intermediate pressure cylinder was 84 inches, while the two low-pressure cylinders each had a diameter of 97 inches. By the time the steam had been expanded through all three stages, each engine was capable of generating some 15,000 horsepower when turning at 75 revolutions per minute.

After being expanded through the low-pressure cylinders, the steam, by now reduced to about 9 psi absolute, would then be channelled to the next compartment aft, where it could be directed either to the low-pressure turbine engine or into the main condenser. Experience with the *Laurentic*'s low-pressure turbine had proven the advantage of utilising a combination of reciprocating and turbine technology, both in terms of speed and economy, but because the Olympic class was designed to be less dependent on speed than the Cunard sisters, the turbine did not require so much power. The low-pressure turbine was therefore designed to use up the last of the remaining steam pressure, which would otherwise be directed straight to the condenser, before exhausting what little steam remained at about 1 lb absolute. Bearing in mind that the turbine could still develop some 16,000 SHP when running at 165 revolutions per minute, this represented a particularly economic use of the available steam pressure as it was exhausted from the reciprocating engines. The turbine itself was designed to operate only when the ship was moving forwards and in open water, so when manoeuvring in port or reversing the exhaust steam could be channelled directly into the condensers, immediately rendering the turbine non-operational.

All this engineering meant that with a total of 50,000 horsepower, the Olympic class could comfortably maintain a service speed of 21 knots. This came nowhere near the 25 knots developed by the turbines of the Cunard ships; nevertheless, the performance of the White Star triple-screw arrangement was still impressive. All this power, however, still had the potential to tear the hull apart if it was not properly harnessed. As the ship was pushed forwards by the screws, this in itself created huge stresses on the shaft, so in order for the engines not to be torn from their mountings, the impulse of the screws was transmitted into the hull by means of thrust blocks. At the extreme end of the three shafts, the *Olympic*'s propellers were also colossal in their scale. In practice, two-bladed propellers were the most efficient in terms of design, but they were also more prone to suffer from vibration so by the early 20th century practically all modern vessels were fitted with propellers of either three or four blades. In the *Olympic*'s case, the two triple-bladed wing propellers each weighed 38 tons and had a diameter of 23 feet 6 inches, the blades being cast from bronze and bolted

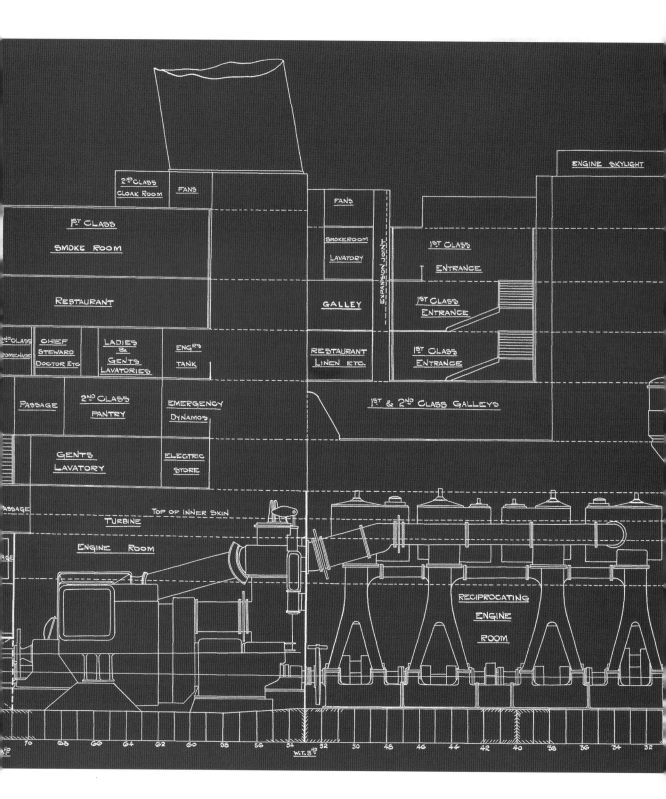

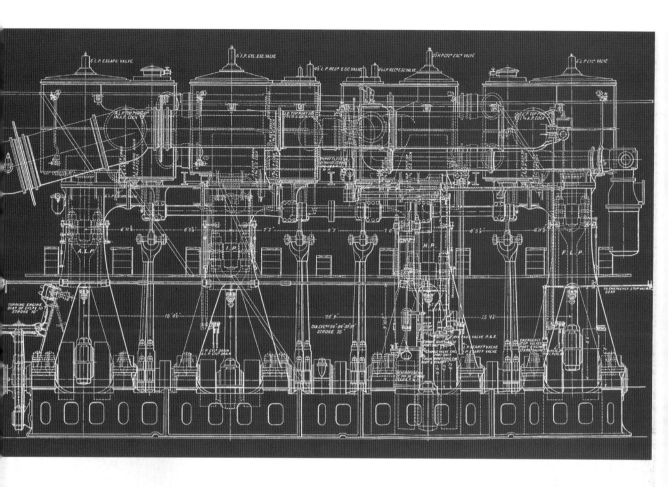

LEFT: *The arrangement of the Olympic class reciprocating and turbine engines. In the case of the* Britannic, *at 490 tons the marine turbine was the largest and more powerful of the three sisters', but still not the most powerful afloat.*

ABOVE: *The Yarrow, Schlick & Tweedy system meant that by using two low-pressure cylinders, as opposed to one, it was easier to balance the reciprocating engines, so that they would run more smoothly and with considerably less vibration.*

to a steel boss to more easily vary the propeller pitch. The central turbine propeller was smaller, with an overall diameter of 16 feet 6 inches, but having been cast in a single piece from 22 tons of manganese bronze, the pitch of the blades was fixed.

The final substantial piece of marine engineering in the hull was the steering gear, which bore little similarity to the *Lusitania*'s

balanced rudder design. The Olympic class rudder was actually little different to the standard rudder design of most mercantile vessels of the time, save perhaps for the scale. The rudder itself would be fabricated in six pieces with a combined weight of over 100 tons, so the steering gear required to operate it would need to be equally robust. The actual steering of the ship was controlled

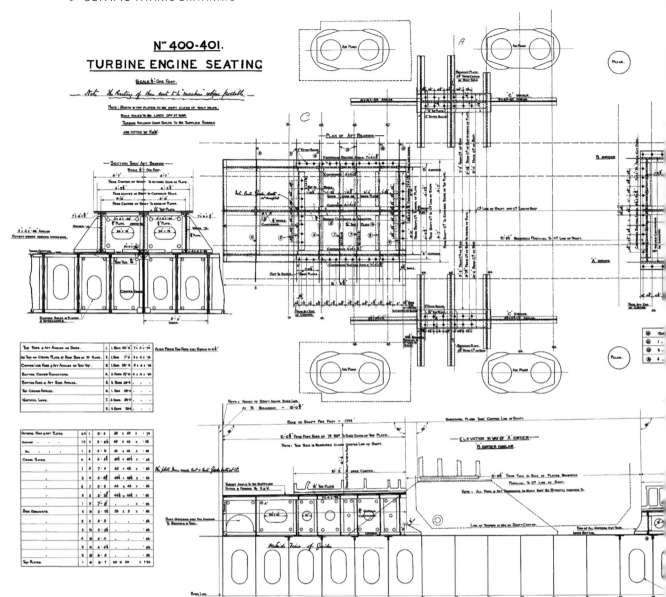

ABOVE: *Because Harland & Wolff did not possess turbine technology, the Olympic's 420-ton Parsons-type low-pressure turbine was subcontracted to John Brown & Co. However, the base for the engine was built into the ship prior to launch.*

by a telemotor in the wheelhouse, while the wheel on the aft docking bridge utilised a more direct mechanical link as it was much closer to the steering engines, so the steering gear could be effectively controlled from either of these two stations, with the exact position of the rudder always being visible on the electric helm indicator on the navigating bridge.

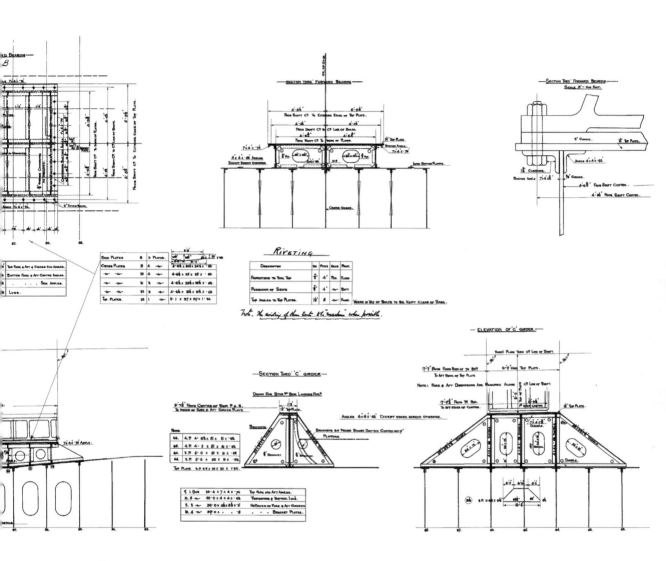

SAFETY AT SEA

In terms of watertight integrity, the *Shipbuilder* magazine described the *Olympic*'s subdivision as 'very complete'. The legal requirements called for a design whereby any two compartments could be completely flooded without threatening the ship's survival, and the designed 15 transverse watertight bulkheads

did just that, effectively dividing the ship into 16 watertight compartments. These bulkheads extended up from the tank top to the saloon deck at either end of the ship, although the forward collision bulkhead would extend one deck higher to the shelter deck. The bulkheads dividing the boiler rooms extended only as high as E deck, which was still well above the

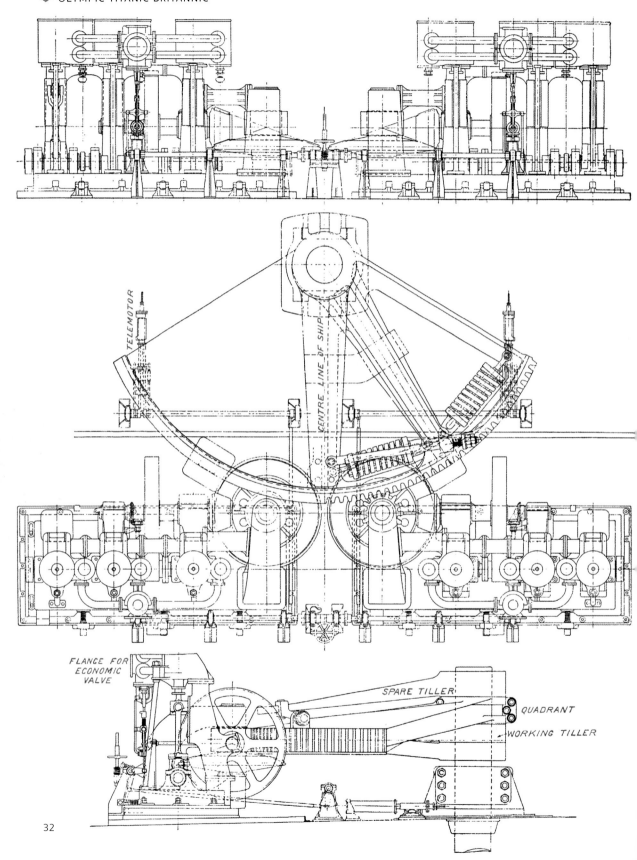

TELEMOTOR

CENTRE LINE OF SHIP

FLANGE FOR
ECONOMIC
VALVE

SPARE TILLER

QUADRANT

WORKING TILLER

waterline, while 12 watertight doors arranged on the Harland & Wolff drop system facilitated communication between the separate boiler and engine room spaces.

GENERAL ARRANGEMENT

The years leading up to the First World War were dominated by a class system that, if not exactly feudal, unquestionably resulted in a very clearly defined social structure. In this respect, the liners built in the early 20th century encapsulated in miniature the same social characteristics, and nowhere is this more apparent than in the Olympic class liners. White Star's reputation for luxury and comfort was well deserved, but ships of such a huge scale were not just built for millionaires. While first-class passengers may have sipped chilled champagne in the *Olympic's* ornate public rooms, life in steerage for the many thousands of emigrants en route to America was far more utilitarian. Even so, the vessels not only had to be constructed under survey by the Board of Trade in order to obtain the necessary passenger certificate, but in order to satisfy the White Star Line's legal requirements it was also necessary to meet the requirements of the UK Factory Acts and the Port Sanitary Authorities, as well as the requirements of the American immigration laws. Only then could the final certificates be issued. This was the main juggling act with which Pirrie and Carlisle had to contend, on the one hand providing the necessary comforts and facilities expected by the various classes on board ship, while at the

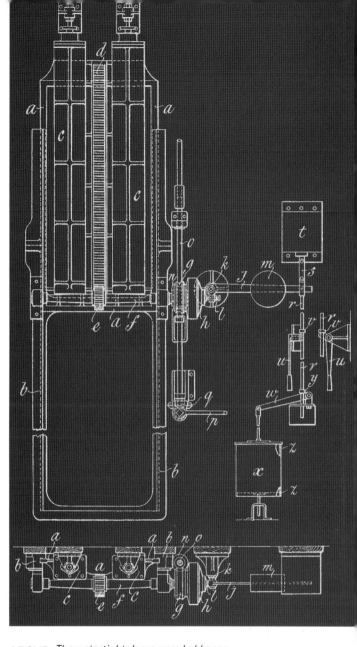

ABOVE: *The watertight doors were held open by a friction clutch, released by an electro-magnet controlled from the bridge or by a manual lever in the boiler room. If all else failed, floats beneath the floor level would also be lifted by the rising water, releasing the friction clutch, thereby closing the individual doors.*

LEFT: *The steering gear was situated in the poop on the aft shelter deck and consisted of a spring quadrant and tiller on a rudder head. It was worked through wheel-and-pinion and bevel gearing by either of the two sets of three-crank vertical steam engines.*

same time ensuring that the customary social barriers remained firmly in situ.

Perhaps the most palpable aspect of the ships' hierarchical structure was the fact that the upper decks were almost exclusively allocated to first class, but as we move further down into the ship the barriers between the various classes, although still undeniably there, seem to become increasingly blurred. Starting high up on the boat deck, this area was largely taken up with open promenades. Alongside the forward deck structure housing the navigating officers' cabins was the officers' promenade, while the first-class promenade extended from the forward main entrance back to a small engineers' promenade on either side of the reciprocating engine casing, just aft of the third funnel. The remainder of the promenade deck was allocated to second class. Both first- and second-class passengers had access to the boat deck via their own designated entrances, with the first-class passengers also enjoying their own gymnasium on the starboard side, just aft of their forward main entrance.

The promenade deck (A) below was more socially conscious, reserved exclusively for the first-class elite. Forward of the main entrance was allocated to staterooms, but moving aft a corridor on the starboard side led to the first-class lounge, panelled in the Louis Quinze style, while for the ladies there was the Georgian-style reading and writing room on the port side. From the lounge, another corridor on the port side led to the aft first-class entrance and staircase, leading in turn to the smoking room. The *Shipbuilder* magazine was moved to describe this room, finished in the early Georgian style

with mahogany panelling inlaid with mother-of-pearl, as '…without doubt the finest apartment of its kind on the ocean', while the deckhouses furthest aft were given over to two Palm Court veranda cafés, each with an ivy-covered trellis in the Louis Seize style. Only the veranda café on the port side could be accessed directly from the smoking room, via a revolving draughtproof door, but both had openings directly on to the aft promenade so that the two cafés would be less exposed to draughts during inclement weather.

The forward three-quarters of the bridge deck (B) was also given over to first-class staterooms, with an enclosed promenade on either side. Aft of the fourth funnel turbine engine casing, an additional first-class restaurant, a wholly new feature on White Star ships, would permit first-class passengers to dine à la carte any time they wished, as opposed to taking their meals at their designated sitting in the regular dining saloon. There was nothing to stop passengers from using the restaurant at any time during opening hours between 8am and 11pm, and any first-class passengers who had booked their voyage entirely without meals prior to departure would also benefit from a reduction on their standard fare. The remaining deckhouses astern of the restaurant were allocated to the second-class entrance and Louis Seize oak-panelled smoking room.

Once again, C deck accommodation was mostly given over to first-class cabins, extending from all the way forward to the enclosed second-class promenade aft of the turbine engine casing. There were no first-class public rooms on this deck, save for a barber's shop located on

ABOVE: *A contemporary artist's impression of the boat deck.*

BELOW: *The first-class main entrance.*

the port side of the aft staircase, but perhaps the most interesting inclusion was the maids' and valets' dining saloon on the starboard side of the aft staircase, indicating that servants were considered to be different from first-, second- and even third-class passengers. At the aft end of the first-class accommodation was an enclosed second-class promenade, which surrounded their own colonial Adams-style library, panelled in sycamore with a mahogany dado. It is only now, however, that we start to become aware of the spaces given over to the steerage passengers, with the aft well deck being allocated to the third-class open promenade, complete with cargo cranes and winches to access cargo holds 5 and 6. Aft of this open space, a third-class entrance in the poop led to a smoking room on the port side

and a general room to starboard, beyond which the compartment housing the ships' steering gear occupied the remaining space in the stern.

Although some first-class cabins were located forward, much of the allocated space on D deck was given over to the first-class reception room and dining saloon. At 114 feet in length and extending across the entire 92-foot width of the ship, the saloon, finished in the Jacobean English style and painted in white for a lighter and more airy feel, was large enough to accommodate 532 passengers at any one sitting. The reception room, some 54 feet in length and also extending the full width of the ship, was similarly finished, with the main

ABOVE: *The standard crew accommodation off the Scotland Road working passage along the upper deck.*

BELOW: *The steerage accommodation was utilitarian but comfortable.*

staircase contributing to an altogether more palatial effect, but unlike the tiled linoleum floor in the *Olympic*'s dining saloon, the floor of the reception room was covered by a dark and richly coloured Axminster carpet. Aft of the dining saloon were the first- and second-class galleys and pantries, leading to an oak-panelled second-class dining room, which could seat 394 passengers at long tables with revolving chairs. Aft of the dining saloon were more second-class cabins, with a small number of permanent third-class placed in the increasingly small area available in the ship's stern.

The upper deck (E) was the first deck to be allocated solely to accommodation, with first-class cabins extending along the entire length of the deck on the starboard side to a point located approximately amidships, after which second-class cabins extended back as far as the aft cargo holds. On the port side, however, was a working passage known to the crew as 'Scotland Road', after the similarly named street in Liverpool – a broad street near the north docks and on the old stage route to Scotland, with working-class housing laid out in the smaller streets on either side. A small number of third-class cabins occupied their allocated space at the forward end of this passage, but the vast majority of its length, running for some 500 feet, was taken up by accommodation for the ships' cooks, stewards, waiters and ancillary staff; even then, the crew accommodation extended along another two of the ship's compartments on the port side. In addition to being a working passage for the crew, Scotland Road served as a means for the steerage passengers to access the third-

class areas at either end of the ship, as well as providing access to the staircase down to their dining saloon amidships on F deck, effectively making Scotland Road one of the busiest parts of the ship at any stage of a voyage. F deck forward was almost entirely given over to steerage passengers, with some second-class cabins aft of the turbine engine casing, while on the aft lower deck (G) the remaining passenger accommodation was allocated to both second and third class.

Without exception, every White Star vessel was fitted out to the most exacting standards, but the construction of the *Olympic* and *Titanic* brought with it a number of logistical issues for Harland & Wolff. Because IMM intended to make the completion of the two White Star leviathans a priority, construction on other vessels ordered by the combine had to be held back. As a result, in the 1909/10 financial year, Harland & Wolff completed only six vessels, totalling 40,000 gross tons. The reduction of craftsmen engaged in finishing the ships also meant that the number of men working in the shipyard had decreased by about a third, so the London-based company Aldam Heaton & Co was taken over to ensure that the necessary skilled interior decorators would be available to complete the *Olympic* and *Titanic*. Prior to his death in 1897, John Aldam Heaton had often collaborated with the architect Richard Norman Shaw, who had designed and built Thomas Ismay's family home Dawpool at Thurstaston in Cheshire. Ismay must have been impressed as Shaw would subsequently be used as a consultant, advising White Star on the interior design of their vessels, so on the face of it the

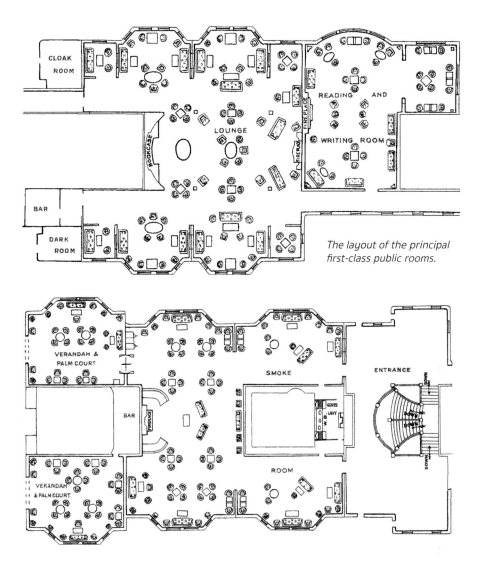

The layout of the principal first-class public rooms.

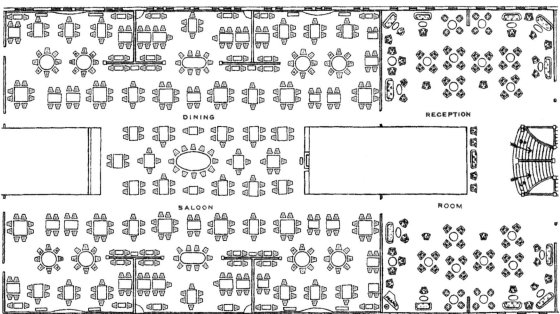

DECK F (MIDDLE DECK)

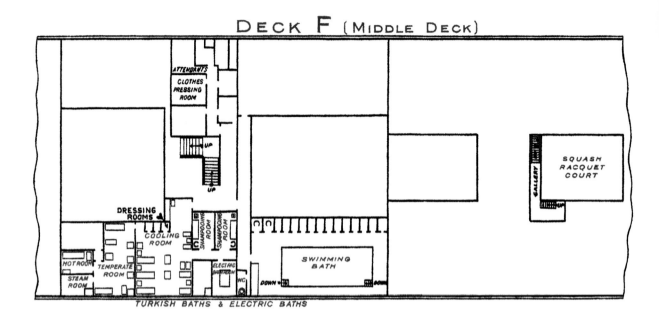

TURKISH BATHS & ELECTRIC BATHS

ABOVE: *The arrangement of the* Olympic's *Turkish bath and swimming pool. The layout of this area in the* Titanic *and* Britannic *would be substantially different.*

collaboration between White Star, Harland & Wolff and Aldam Heaton & Co seemed like an ideal partnership.

The lavish interiors would come as no great surprise to anyone familiar with White Star's proclivity for luxury, but it was not just in the fixtures and fittings that the *Olympic* would excel. For the first-class passengers, additional facilities, including a gymnasium, elevators, a swimming bath, a squash court, Turkish baths and even a Marconi apparatus, would help to ensure that the passengers would be able to keep themselves occupied, while at the same time keep in touch with the outside world.

In order to function effectively, the *Olympic* would require a combined crew of almost 900 in the deck, engineering and victualling

departments. These personnel also needed to be accommodated and, as a result, specific areas of the ship would be allocated to the various departments as best reflected the working layout. The navigating officers were housed in individual cabins in the forward boat deckhouses, just aft of the captain's bridge, while the captain's accommodation, located forward on the starboard side, incorporated a sitting room, bedroom and private bathroom. The ship's foc'sle, forward on the shelter deck, housed the crew's galley, along with the seamen's and firemen's dedicated mess areas, and it was from here that the seamen could access the forward windlass gear and the lookouts' observation cage, to which they could ascend via a ladder inside the foremast. The area directly below the foc'sle, spread over the saloon, upper, middle and lower decks, provided sleeping accommodation for the firemen and trimmers responsible for feeding the boilers,

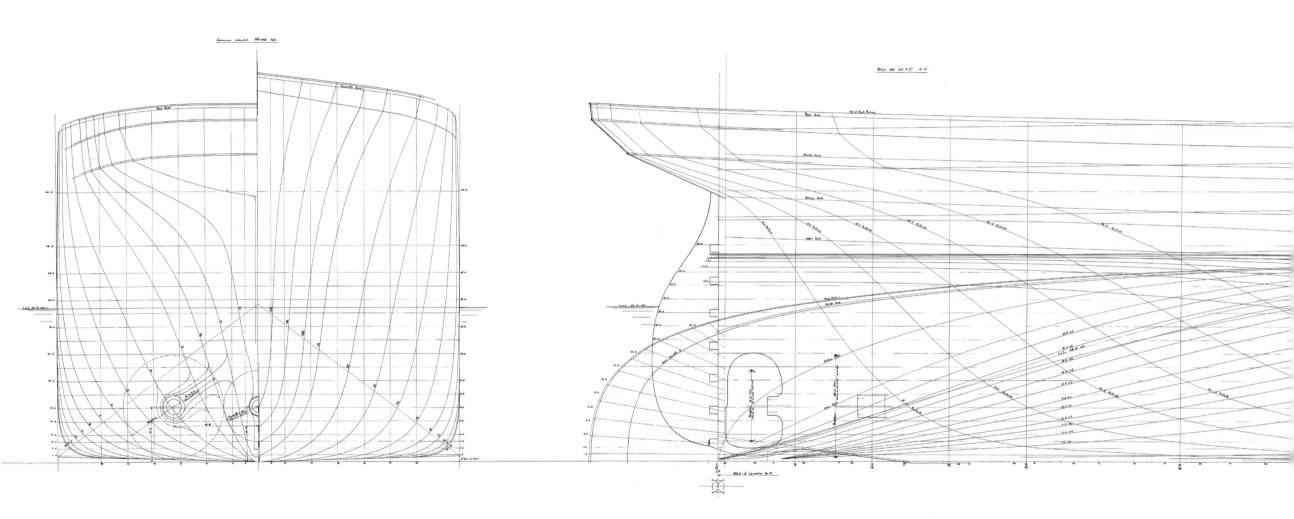

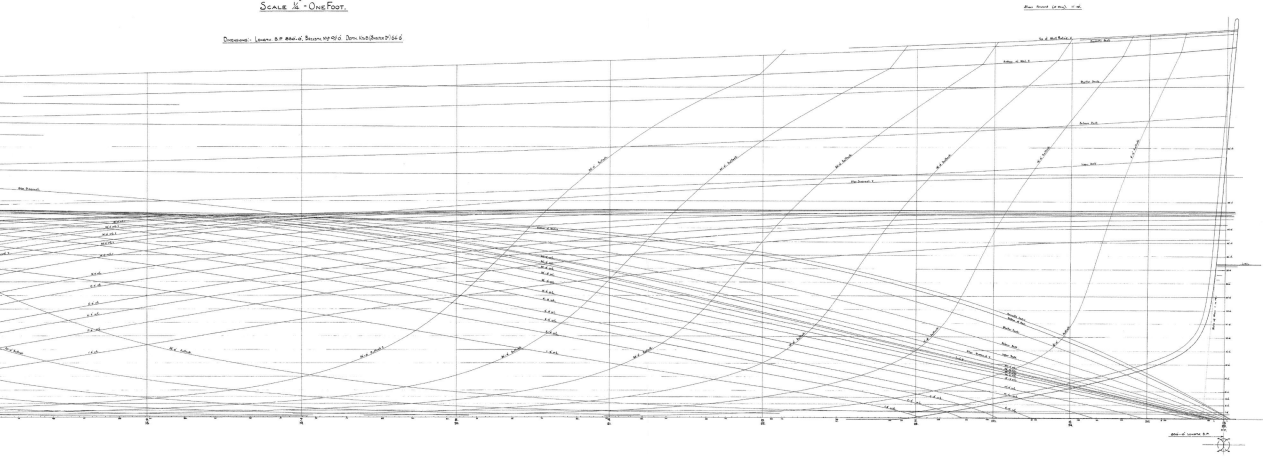

S.S. OLYMPIC.

— LINES. —

SCALE ¼" = ONE FOOT.

with two spiral staircases descending from the saloon deck directly to the tank top at the bottom of the ship, where a pipe tunnel led aft beneath holds 2 and 3 directly to the boiler rooms. The engineers' accommodation, on the other hand, was mostly located further aft on the middle deck, along either side of the reciprocating engine casing.

THE WORKING ARRANGEMENTS OF THE SHIPS

The task of navigating vessels of such a colossal size would fall to only the most experienced of commanders, although handling a ship with a displacement of over 52,000 tons would be a learning curve for even the most seasoned of skippers on the North Atlantic. Despite their huge size, however, at first glance the working arrangements in the Olympic class vessels seem to be broadly similar to those in the preceding ships. Perhaps the most noticeable equipment for handling the ship could be found on the foc'sle, where the ships' three anchors were located. The anchors for each ship would be manufactured by Noah Hingley & Sons at their works in Netherton, Staffordshire, but while Hingley's would also manufacture the stud link anchor chains for the *Olympic*, those for the *Titanic* would be contracted to the nearby British Machine Made Cable Company. The two anchors in the port and starboard hawsepipes each weighed 7¾ tons, while the largest anchor, resting in a well at the tip of the foc'sle, weighed in at 15½ tons and needed to be deployed over the side by an additional

crane, where it was then attached to a 9½-inch steel cable, specially manufactured by the Bullivant Company of Millwall, London, which fed through the additional hawsepipe built into the stem. Four capstans for working the warping cables were operated by the Napier Bros windlass gear, situated directly below on the shelter deck, while five additional capstans on the poop ensured that the vessels were always well secured at both ends when in port.

At sea, the all-important equipment for the safe handling of the ship was also state-of-the-art. Four compasses located on the navigating bridge, in the wheelhouse, on the aft docking bridge and amidships, on a non-ferrous platform above the raised roof of the first-class lounge, ensured the greatest navigational accuracy. The navigating bridge was situated in its customary location at the forward end of the boat deck, affording a clear view of any obstacles in the ship's path. The bridge itself housed the engine room, docking and steering telegraphs, ensuring easy communication with all key parts of the ship when at sea or manoeuvring in confined waters, while just aft of the bridge was an enclosed wheel house from where the ship was steered when in open water.

THE LIFEBOATS

At the time that the Olympic class was being designed, the British Board of Trade's lifeboat regulations had not been updated since March of 1894. Those regulations that did exist only covered vessels with a gross tonnage of up to 10,000 tons, but while that may have been perfectly adequate in 1894, with the *Olympic*

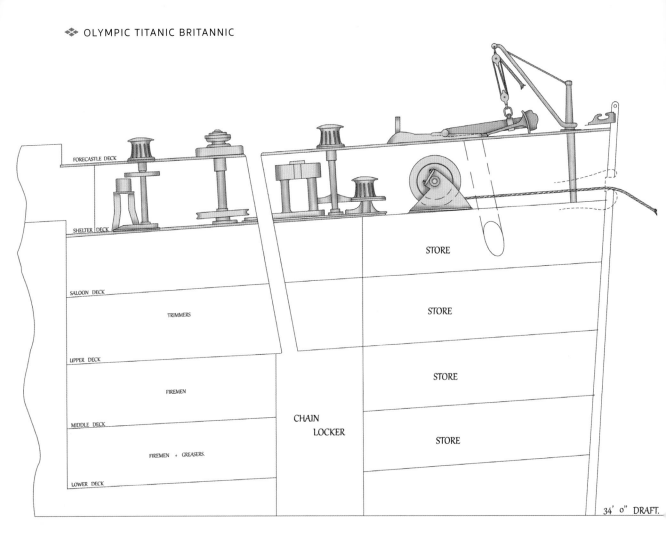

FORECASTLE DECK

SHELTER DECK

STORE

SALOON DECK

TRIMMERS

STORE

UPPER DECK

FIREMEN

STORE

MIDDLE DECK

CHAIN
LOCKER

STORE

FIREMEN + GREASERS.

LOWER DECK

34' 0" DRAFT.

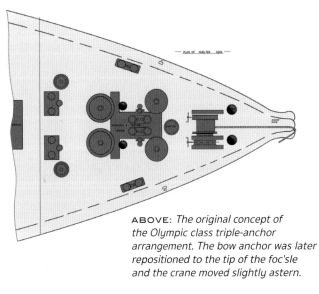

— PLAN OF SHELTER DECK —

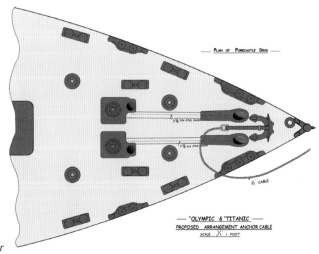

— PLAN OF FORECASTLE DECK —

"OLYMPIC & "TITANIC —
PROPOSED ARRANGEMENT ANCHOR CABLE

ABOVE: *The original concept of the Olympic class triple-anchor arrangement. The bow anchor was later repositioned to the tip of the foc'sle and the crane moved slightly astern.*

ABOVE: *The final configuration of the crane for the central bow anchor.*

having a projected gross tonnage of 45,000 tons those regulations were long overdue for revision. The existing regulations of the time required any vessels over 10,000 GRT to have 16 lifeboats with a combined cubic capacity of 5,500 cubic feet under davits, calculating the necessary space on the principle of 10 cubic feet per person. Filled to capacity, the

Olympic could carry over 3,000 souls, but with 14 rigid lifeboats, each able to take 65 people, two emergency cutters providing space for an additional 80 and four Engelhardt collapsible lifeboats each capable of taking another 47, this meant that the *Olympic* and *Titanic* actually had space in the lifeboats for only 1,178 people. Even that was over 200 more than was mandated by the rules of the day. While the regulations were long out of date, Alexander Carlisle was well aware that the

Board of Trade was in the process of discussing possible revisions to their lifeboat requirements. Even if the *Olympic* complied with the regulations in 1909, it was quite possible that modifications would soon be necessary to increase the existing lifeboat capacity, so with this in mind he approached the Welin Davit Company in London to discuss a system of davits that could, if called upon, each service up to four lifeboats.

Carlisle's primary consideration was for an improved system of davits similar to those fitted in the liner *Edinburgh Castle*, then completing at Belfast, so that with 16 sets of davits the *Olympic*, with four boats operated by each set of davits, could in theory have accommodated anything up to 64 lifeboats. Those figures may have been impressive, even if the additional capacity would have wreaked havoc with the open space on the boat deck, although even Carlisle saw a need for no more than 48. The reasoning behind the proposed system of double-banked lifeboats made perfect sense, and after meetings held with Pirrie and Ismay in London in October 1909 and January 1910, authorisation was given to proceed with the suggested designs, in order to be prepared for any potential changes in the regulations. At no time was the actual number of boats discussed, but it is clear that if the new regulations did call

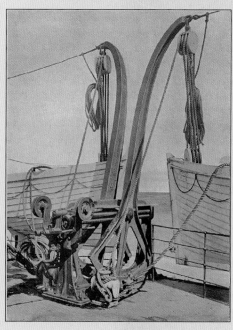

ABOVE: *An advertisement for the Welin Davit Company, highlighting the davit arrangement in the Olympic class.*

RIGHT: *The* Olympic *and* Titanic *were fitted with 16 sets of Welin double-acting quadrant davits, each of which could potentially handle up to four lifeboats. The outer boats would have been provided with shifting chocks, enabling them to be carried at the half-outboard position while at sea, so allowing ample gangway room between the two rows of boats. In the end the lifeboat regulations were not changed and only 16 rigid and 4 collapsible lifeboats were installed.*

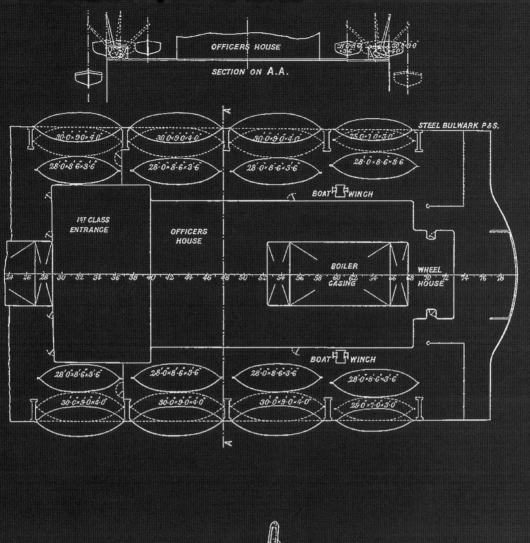

SECTION ON A.A.

OFFICERS HOUSE

STEEL BULWARK P&S.

30·0×9·0×4·0 30·0×9·0×4·0 30·0×9·0×4·0 25·0×7·0×3·0

28·0×8·6×3·6 28·0×8·6×3·6 28·0×8·6×3·6 28·0×8·6×3·6

BOAT ☐ WINCH

1ST CLASS ENTRANCE

OFFICERS HOUSE

BOILER CASING

WHEEL HOUSE

24 26 28 30 32 34 36 38 40 42 44 46 48 50 52 54 56 58 60 62 64 66 68 70 72 74 76 78

BOAT ☐ WINCH

28·0×8·6×3·6 28·0×8·6×3·6 28·0×8·6×3·6 28·0×8·6×3·6

30·0×9·0×4·0 30·0×9·0×4·0 30·0×9·0×4·0 25·0×7·0×3·0

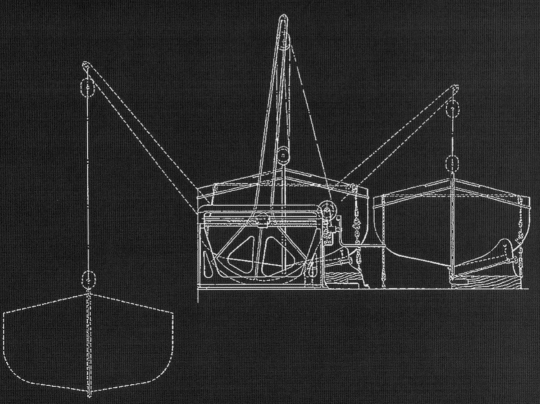

for additional lifeboat capacity then it could be achieved quickly and with minimal trouble or additional expense. In the end, the meeting of the Board's Life-Saving Appliances Sub-Committee in May 1911 chose not to extend the existing regulations; as a result, the original arrangement of one boat under each of the 16 davits remained in force.

BUILDING AND FITTING OUT

Even though the contract had been signed on 31 July 1908, it would still be several months before the modifications to the north yard were far enough advanced for the first of the keels to be laid. Construction began in earnest on 16 December when the *Olympic*'s first keel plates were finally ready to be laid on slip 2, but so as not to completely overwhelm the Belfast machine shops, work on the *Titanic*'s keel would only begin a little over three months later, on 31 March 1909. By building the two ships side by side, Harland & Wolff were undertaking an incredible feat of engineering, and yet construction on the *Olympic* still continued at a relatively brisk pace throughout 1909 as the huge vessel gradually took shape. Within three months the hull was framed to the height of the double bottom, by 20 November she was fully framed, and by 15 April 1910 the hull was fully plated. The timetable for the *Titanic* was slightly less impressive, having taken about one month longer than the *Olympic* to reach the stage where the hull was fully framed, but this delay was only because White Star was giving priority to getting the *Olympic* into service as quickly as possible. On the flip side, the delay meant that building experience with the *Olympic* allowed for any modifications to the *Titanic*'s design to be incorporated more easily.

Even though the *Olympic*'s shell was fully plated by the spring of 1910, considerable work still needed to be completed inside the hull on the deck plating, to say nothing of cutting the thousands of portholes and other openings that would be required in the finished vessel. However, by the autumn of 1910 work had finally progressed to the point where the first of the two ships was ready to be launched. The great day when the *Olympic* would take to the water came on Thursday 20 October 1910. Coincidentally, the plating on the *Titanic* had only been completed the previous day, providing an awe-inspiring view of the two hulls beneath the huge Arrol Gantry for those lucky enough to be invited to witness the event. With a guest list including the Lord Lieutenant of Ireland and the Lord Mayor of Belfast, Lord Pirrie would have been keen to ensure that everything went without a hitch. In line with established White Star tradition, there would be no official christening ceremony, even though the *Olympic* would ultimately be the largest ship in the world by a convincing margin; apart from the specially constructed stands, the only outward indications of a gala event were the signal flags spelling out the word 'Success' and the large White Star company burgee flying from the top of the gantry. At 11am, just as the water in the Victoria Channel was judged to be at its maximum height, the launch triggers were released; 62 seconds later, having reached a maximum speed of 12½ knots before the six

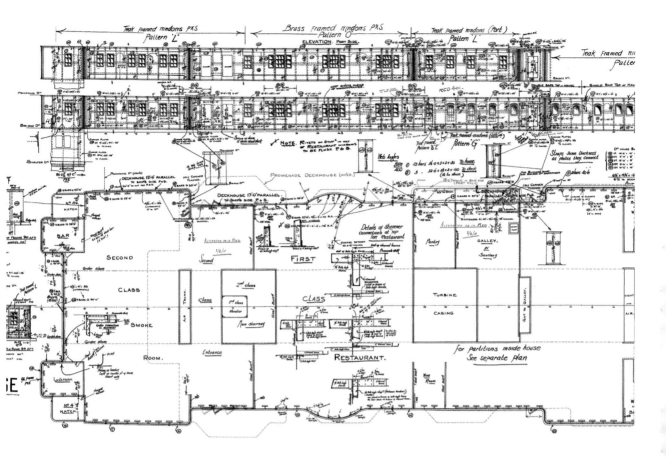

ABOVE: *Harland & Wolff did not need to produce a separate set of plans for each ship. Any modifications made to the* Titanic *were simply added to the same drawings as used for the* Olympic.

anchors and 80 tons of cable in the riverbed brought the 24,600-ton hull to a halt, the *Olympic* was safely afloat.

The launch had gone without a hitch, but there still remained many months of work to be done. At this stage the hull was still little more than an empty shell, but in the coming weeks the miraculous transformation into a floating palace would take place. It was here that the 200-ton Benrather crane would now demonstrate its worth, as the huge engine components and boilers were hoisted into the ship for assembly, before the superstructure was finally topped off with the four 60-foot funnels. Of course, it wasn't just the propelling

machinery that had to be shipped on board. Thousands of tons of piping, electrical cable and wood panelling were no less important, as the palatial accommodations were completed by armies of plumbers, electricians and carpenters. The work was still on-going on 1 April 1911, when the *Olympic* was placed in the brand-new graving dock in order to have her propellers fitted, and where the now dingy white-painted hull would be repainted in its White Star

steamed into Belfast Lough the following morning to adjust compasses and undergo two days of engine trials. Also being put through their paces over the two-day trial period were the two new passenger tenders *Nomadic* and *Traffic*, which had been specially constructed to service the *Olympic* and *Titanic* at Cherbourg. Little data on the sea trials was ever published, but we do know that the *Olympic* had taken on 3,000 tons of best Welsh coal and that speeds of up to 21¾ knots were recorded, comfortably exceeding the builder's expectations. However, the internal reports compiled by Thomas Andrews of the *Olympic*'s sea trials

colours: a black hull with a yellow band and white superstructure, and White Star's famous black-topped buff funnels. On 2 May, the ship's engines finally underwent their basin trials, the preliminary tests being described in *The Shipbuilder* as 'entirely satisfactory'.

With the transformation virtually complete, on 28 May the Liverpool tugs *Wallasey*, *Alexandra*, *Hornby* and *Herculaneum* swung the *Olympic* into position, before the vessel

were rather more forthcoming, noting that excessive vibration was particularly evident in the hull structure when the vessel was steaming at three-quarters of full speed, resulting in 'panting' of the shell in the forward upper decks, which increased exponentially with the speed. So too did the vibration, so much so that at one stage it was observed that even the coat pegs on the bridge were vibrating. The vibration in some of the accommodation areas was also

ABOVE: *9 January 1911: The giant Benrather crane towers over the* Olympic *alongside the deep-water berth.*

recorded as being at an unacceptable level and the issue would only be partially resolved with the fitting of additional stiffening, particularly in the transverse bulkheads and deckheads.

From a PR perspective, however, the timing of the *Olympic*'s completion could not have been handled better, when on the clear, sunny morning of 31 May 1911 the steamer *Duke of Argyll* arrived at Belfast from Fleetwood, having been specially chartered by the White Star Line to transport the guests and representatives of the press who would not only be present to see the *Olympic* handed over, but would also witness the launch that same day of the *Titanic*. For Lord Pirrie, the day took on an additional significance as it also happened to be his 65th birthday – not to mention his wife's 55th

birthday. In truth, the *Titanic*'s launch would be practically identical to that of her sister, except that while the *Olympic*'s hull had been painted a dazzling white, the *Titanic* had been finished for the occasion in the more traditional mercantile colours of a black hull and white superstructure; but the launch would be marred by tragedy when one workman, James Dobbin, was accidentally trapped beneath the hull when one of the supporting shores unexpectedly collapsed as it was being cut away. His fellow workers managed to drag him to safety before the hull began to move, but two days later

Dobbin would succumb to contusions and shock at the Royal Victoria Hospital. From the technical point of view, however, the launch had been a textbook success. Watched by an estimated 100,000 observers lining the riverbank, at 12.13pm the *Titanic* finally took to the water, the hull having travelled less than its entire length before the anchors secured to the riverbed brought her to a gentle halt.

As the crowds began to disperse, the invited guests and members of the press corps adjourned to the Grand Central Hotel for celebratory lunches to mark the occasion, and at 2.30pm Bruce Ismay, accompanied by Lord Pirrie, several directors of the White Star Line and even JP Morgan himself, went aboard the *Nomadic* to be taken out to the *Olympic*. At 4.30pm White Star's latest flagship, under the command of Captain Edward J Smith,

steamed into Belfast Lough accompanied by the *Nomadic* and *Traffic* as far as the mouth of the lough, at which point the *Olympic* headed across the Irish Sea to Liverpool, while the two little tenders headed south towards the French port of Cherbourg, where they would next rendezvous with the *Olympic* two weeks later.

In the meantime, Belfast's eyes were now finally fixed on the *Titanic*.

RIGHT: *Lord Pirrie with Captain Smith. One of the White Star Line's most experienced commanders, Edward Smith had been with the company since 1880, rising to command the* SS Republic *after only seven years. After serving as captain of the* Coptic *and* Majestic, *he was in 1904 given command of the 23,884 GRT* Baltic *before transferring three years later to the* Adriatic. *His seniority and experience with such large ships made him the obvious choice to take command of the* Olympic.

BELOW:
Starboard profile of RMS Olympic, *as completed in June 1911.*

CHAPTER THREE

NOMADIC AND *TRAFFIC*

Since the opening of the White Star Line's express service from Southampton to New York in 1907, the company's vessels had called at Cherbourg in order to benefit from any additional first class business on the continent and, equally important, to secure an additional chunk of the lucrative emigrant traffic from Europe to America.

The standard practice for any IMM vessels calling at the French port required the larger ships to anchor in the deeper Grande Rade, while shore-based tenders would bring out the passengers, baggage and mails.

Prior to the *Olympic*'s entry into service, White Star's tender at Cherbourg had been

BELOW: *Starboard profile of the SS* Nomadic.

the appropriately named paddler *Gallic*. Built by John Scott & Co in Fife, this vessel had originally been owned and operated by Birkenhead Ferries as the equally appropriately named *Birkenhead*, but while the paddler had done sterling service on that company's Rock Ferry to Liverpool crossing since 1894, by 1907 she was surplus to requirements and was gratefully taken over by the White Star Line

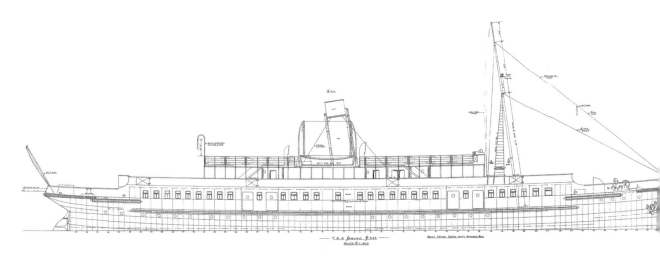

NOMADIC AND *TRAFFIC* SPECIFICATIONS

	NOMADIC	*TRAFFIC*
Harland & Wolff Yard Number	422	423
Slipway	1	1
Laying of keel to delivery	158 days	158 days
Length	233 feet 6 inches	176 feet 6 inches
Beam	37 feet 2 inches	35 feet
Number of engines	2	2
Length of service	57 years	30 years
Gross tonnage	1,273	675
Speed	10 knots	9 knots

for service as a tender at Cherbourg. However, while the 461-ton *Gallic* may well have sufficed for the smaller *Teutonic*, *Majestic*, *Oceanic* and *Adriatic*, the advent of the *Olympic* and *Titanic* meant that this arrangement could only have been seen as makeshift at best. When dealing with such magnificent vessels, each with a gross tonnage well in excess of 45,000 tons, something more special was needed, so a new class of purpose-built tender was conceived to service the Olympic class giants. The order for the *Nomadic* was officially confirmed on 5 June 1910, followed on 19 July with the order for the *Traffic*.

Although both designed as passenger tenders, the two vessels would serve very specific purposes. The larger *Nomadic* was designed to accommodate the first- and second-class passengers, while the smaller and more utilitarian *Traffic* was intended for third-class passengers and fitted with additional conveyer belts for the baggage and mail sacks. On 22 December 1910 the keels for Yard Nos 422 (*Nomadic*) and 423 (*Traffic*) were both laid side by side on slip 1, with the *Nomadic* taking to the water a little over four months later on 25 April 1911. She was followed two days later by the *Traffic*. From this point onward, work on the *Nomadic* generally preceded that on the *Traffic*, but only just, with the larger tender completing her trials on 16 May, followed by the *Traffic* on 18 May, so that both vessels were ready to be handed over to the White Star Line on 27 May – only 158 days after the laying of the keels.

The *Nomadic* and *Traffic* would also be different to every other White Star ship in one key respect. Each of the company's vessels was traditionally registered in the home port of Liverpool, but for administrative convenience the two tenders would instead be registered at Cherbourg, where they would be operated under the ownership of George Lanièce.

Despite all the expenditure and attention to detail, sadly the *Olympic*'s maiden arrival at Cherbourg was not the textbook success that Bruce Ismay had contemplated, noting that the working of the tenders at Cherbourg with passengers and baggage was '...extremely unsatisfactory, in spite of the fact that the

whole question had been very carefully gone into at a meeting held at Southampton on the 3rd May, when definite instructions were formulated for dealing with this important matter'. Captain Beresford, the White Star marine superintendent at Cherbourg, came in for additional criticism from the company chairman, who expressed his surprise that he felt himself to be 'justified in leaving the *Olympic* before all the baggage was on board the ship'. As far as Ismay was concerned, the marine superintendent was supposed to remain

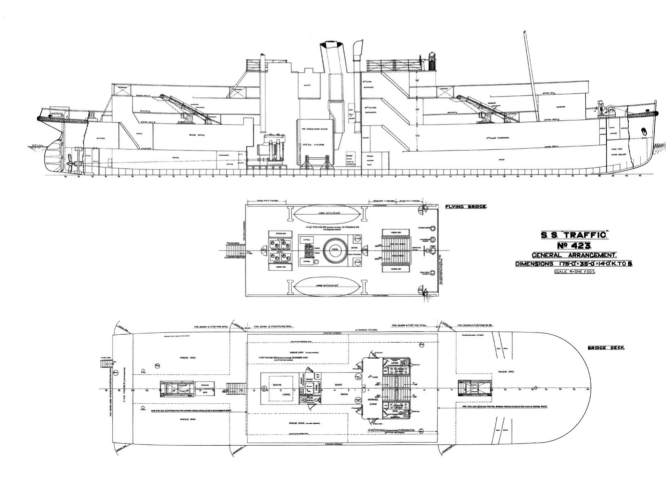

by the ship until the last of the baggage had been transferred and he wasted little time in forwarding a copy of the procedures drawn up by Thomas Andrews, which clearly laid down the manner in which the passengers and baggage should be embarked in future. Unfortunately, there is no known record of Captain Beresford's response, but it can be safely assumed that Andrews' procedures would in future be followed to the letter.

BELOW: *General arrangements of the SS* Traffic.

CHAPTER FOUR

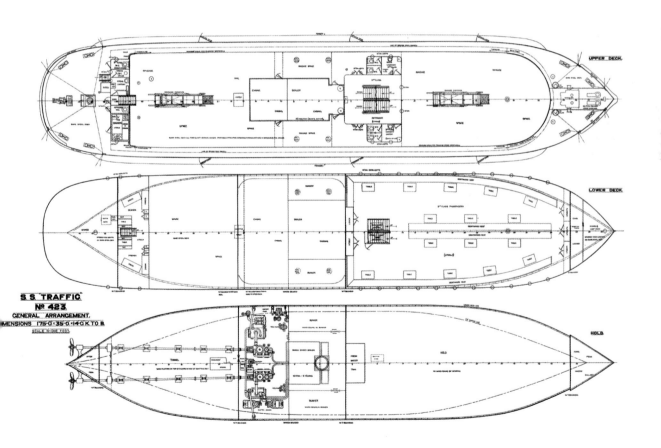

A MARVEL...

In the early hours of Thursday 1 June 1911, the brand-new RMS *Olympic* arrived for the first time at Liverpool, the home port of the White Star fleet. The reason for the visit had little to do with any operational requirements, except to provide the company with the welcome excuse to throw open the ship to public inspection for the day and to enjoy the adulation they knew would be coming their way in spades.

ABOVE: *The* Olympic's *officers for the maiden voyage. Left to right: First Officer William Murdoch, Chief Officer Joseph Evans, Fourth Officer David Alexander and Captain Edward J Smith.*

As the journalists marvelled at White Star's new wonder ship, shortly before midnight the *Olympic* once again weighed anchor for the passage south to Southampton, where she arrived in the early hours of 3 June. Once again, the significance of the arrival of the largest ship in the world could not go unnoticed and with the maiden voyage commencing not long before the coronation of King George V, the significance of the timing did not go unreported in the Southampton papers, as they bathed in the reflected glory of the *Olympic*'s maiden arrival at her home terminal.

After one final day of publicity and festivity, the more important task of preparing the ship for her maiden voyage had to take priority, not helped by the fact that the Southampton workforce responsible for coaling the ship happened to be on strike. At one stage the possibility of having to delay the *Olympic*'s maiden departure seemed very real, but by

bringing in their own workforce White Star were able to guarantee that the ship would at least have sufficient coal to reach New York, where she could then fill her bunkers. In the meantime, while the workers of the Harland & Wolff Southampton ship repair facility set about dealing with any last-minute issues, thousands of items, ranging from the company linen, cutlery and china to all necessary provisions, were embarked.

Sunrise came at 3.51am on Wednesday 14 June, bringing with it the glorious prospect of the *Olympic*'s maiden departure for New York from the huge dock that had been specially built to accommodate her. Exactly on schedule, at midday the White Star Line's latest flagship slowly reversed out of the White Star Dock, her ultimate destination being New York but with two scheduled stops, the first later that evening across the English Channel at Cherbourg, and a call the following afternoon at Queenstown, Ireland, where several hundred

TOP: *ABs swabbing the deck before the maiden voyage.*

ABOVE: *As the maiden voyage loomed, work continued on the* Olympic*'s paintwork right up to the last minute.*

additional steerage passengers would be taken on board. Also among the first-class passengers at Southampton were Mr and Mrs Joseph Bruce Ismay, the company chairman using the *Olympic*'s maiden voyage as the perfect opportunity to observe the vessel in action while en route to meetings in New York of the IMM board and finance committees.

Ismay was not the only person keeping a weather eye on things. Included in the passenger list was a correspondent from *The Times*, on board to record the maiden voyage of the world's largest liner for posterity and who was quick to note that as the *Olympic* left the White Star Dock he was able to see the Dutch ship *Kroonland* and the American Line's *New York* moored nearby, each ship over 10,000 tons but 'dwarfed into bewildering insignificance' from the passenger decks of the *Olympic*. The White Star chairman also found few things about which he could complain, noting that everything on board the ship worked most satisfactorily and that the passengers were very positive in their comments about the standard of the accommodation and the food. On top of that, the ship's engines performed flawlessly, without a hitch of any kind. All the same, there were areas where the chairman felt that things could still be improved. The first-class reception room, undoubtedly the most popular space on the ship, was always particularly crowded after lunch, at teatime and after dinner, meaning that all the spare cane chairs from the baggage room needed to be brought up to provide temporary seating. For a more permanent fix, an additional ten tables and 50 chairs were quickly ordered for

this room, while less noticeable issues, such as a potato peeler in the crew's galley, an additional water tube steam oven for the bakehouse and the lack of holders for cigars or cigarettes in the WCs, also found their way into the chairman's list. The only issue of any consequence seemed to arise from the springs of the beds being too 'springy', which in conjunction with the spring mattresses heightened the vibrations in the ship to such an extent that it seriously interfered with passengers' sleep, but as ever the chairman offered an immediate solution to the problem, requesting that lath bottoms (wooden slats) be fitted before the next voyage to take care of the problem.

Ismay's finely honed business eye was also quick to identify other revenue-increasing opportunities. The little-used after companionway between the lounge and smoking room on A deck provided an ideal space for installing additional staterooms, as did the excessive deck space of the B deck enclosed promenade. In time, Ismay's proposals for carrying out the rooms on B deck to the side of the ship would result in the main difference in the internal layout of the *Titanic*.

Other company men were also keeping a close eye on things. Chief Engineer Joseph Bell's report found few issues about which he could grumble, the only real items of consequence being additional sound insulation for the engine room telephones and additional insulation in some of the passenger areas. His most interesting suggestion was for the inclusion of a 'tell-tale' indicator on the bridge, noting which of the watertight doors were open or closed. Likewise, Thomas Andrews

found little to complain of, his notes including references to propeller noticeboards being permanently fitted to the outside of the ship's side rails in way of aft docking bridge, the first-class cloakroom on C deck not being sufficiently used to warrant the loss of earning space, the need for additional tables in the first-class restaurant, a carpet to be fitted in the captain's sitting room, additional sponge holders in the private bathrooms on B and C decks and back plates for the electric reading lamps fitted over the beds in the B and C deck suite staterooms. Perhaps his most intriguing note referred to the removal of the mirrors in the wardrobe doors adjoining the entrance doors to the inside staterooms on C deck, as anyone in the passage could see the occupant of the room dressing or undressing if the doors were left open.

The minutiae aside, after departing Queenstown the *Olympic* recorded daily runs of 428, 534, 542, 525 and 548 miles, which

ABOVE: *The* Olympic*'s enclosed B deck first-class promenade, regarded by Joseph Bruce Ismay as being excessively large. His memorandum of 22 June 1911 would result in additional first-class cabins being carried out to the side of the* Titanic.

all told would amount to a crossing of 5 days, 16 hours and 42 minutes, at an average speed of 21.7 knots. The fact that the passage had also been delayed for 1½ hours by fog, along with the five single-ended boilers having not been used at all in order to conserve fuel, would have further pleased Ismay, who noted that coal consumption had been extremely low, averaging about 620 tons a day instead of the anticipated 720 tons.

The *Olympic* duly docked at Pier 59, White Star's New York terminal located at the end of West 18th Street, at 10am on Wednesday 21 June, but her arrival would be marred by an unfortunate incident as the harbour tugs were turning the huge liner into her allotted

berth. Up on the bridge, Captain Smith briefly ordered the engines to slow ahead in order to increase the liner's momentum as she nosed her way into the berth, but positioned near the stern the 200-ton tug *O L Hallenbeck* was caught up in the suction from the 50,000-ton liner's propellers. Save for a few scrapes to her paintwork the *Olympic* showed little in the way of any notable damage, but the damage to *O L Hallenbeck*'s rudder and stern frame was more serious. Although few would have realised it at the time, it was a worrying sign of things to come, but none of that would dampen the celebrations on this day of days, and Ismay wasted little time in cabling his evident delight in White Star's latest flagship to Lord Pirrie in Belfast:

'Olympic *is a marvel, and has given unbounded satisfaction. Once again accept my warmest and most sincere congratulations.'*

ABOVE: *Stewardess Violet Jessop,
who would go on to serve on all
three Olympic class vessels.*

With the *Olympic* safely docked at her western terminal, it was also time to show off the latest addition to the White Star fleet in America, starting with on-board meetings of the IMM board and finance committee that same day. With masterly understatement, Ismay would describe them as being 'very much pleased with the ship', but Violet Jessop remembered a much more fraught time once they had departed:

*'Then pandemonium took possession
for two whole days. Panting visitors
rubber-necked everywhere. It was futile
trying to keep them within certain limits
and to cut short their innumerable
and sometimes ridiculous questions,
to which we were quite at a loss
for answers.'*

On the second night in port, a lavish dinner was given for 600 White Star agents. Well into the night they were conducted on tours around the ship, but by 3am things finally seemed to have settled down, even though throughout the night some of the guests could be found wandering about aimlessly, seemingly lost and desperate for some kind soul to rescue them, or passed out in baths and half under beds. However, by the time everyone had been rescued and escorted safely off the ship, everyone agreed that the *Olympic* and its crew were 'swell'.

The public reaction to the *Olympic* was vital as by now the IMM directors had more pressing matters on their mind. They already knew that the competition had been keeping a jealous eye on the *Olympic*'s progress, so much so that Cunard had even begun construction of the *Aquitania* six months earlier. This meant that, along with the *Lusitania* and *Mauretania*, Cunard would soon have a three-ship express service, while Albert Ballin's Hamburg America Line also had plans for an even larger trio of their own – the *Imperator*, *Vaterland* and *Bismarck*. Having come so far, the White Star Line simply could not afford to stop now and with discussions already well advanced for a third vessel it could only be a matter of time before a decision would need to be taken. The reality, though, was that the decision had already been made. The public reaction to the *Olympic* may only have provided the necessary reassurance when committing to such large expenditure, because on 20 June 1911, before the ship had even reached New York, Harland & Wolff had been authorised to proceed with a third vessel.

CHAPTER FIVE

GROWING PAINS

After the excitement of the launch day, the morning of Thursday 1 June 1911 at Harland & Wolff must have seemed like an anticlimax. The festivities were over, the *Olympic* had departed and the *Titanic*'s huge but empty hull was safely secured alongside the deep-water wharf, ready to follow in the steps of her elder sibling.

The *Olympic* had been received as an unqualified success with even Bruce Ismay, a man not exactly known for his exuberance, describing her as a 'marvel', and with the standard now set by the *Olympic*, Harland & Wolff had yet another mountain to climb if they were to surpass themselves with the second ship. The question they were probably asking themselves was how?

While the *Titanic* was finally getting all the attention at Belfast, in June 1911 the *Olympic* continued to catch the headlines as Captain Smith and his crew gradually came to terms with handling what was easily the largest ship in the world. After a week's stay in New York, at midday on 28 June the *Olympic* pulled away from Pier 59 for the voyage back to England. This time there would be no accidental mishap with the tugs as the ship backed out into the Hudson, save for one of the passengers conveniently discovering that he had misplaced his spectacles. In a suspiciously masterful display of American customer service, within an hour Wanamaker's department store had not only made a replacement set but had also dispatched them in the hands of the British aviator Tommy Sopwith. So the story goes, Sopwith flew over the *Olympic* while the ship was passing through the Narrows before dropping the package containing the spectacles on to the deck of the huge liner below. However, this is where the publicity stunt came to an unfortunate end, with Sopwith missing his target and the package bouncing harmlessly off the side of the ship to the bottom of the Ambrose Channel. For the remainder of the voyage, however, everything went according to plan; with the engines now settling in nicely, not to mention a strong following current, by the time the *Olympic* returned to Southampton she had averaged a speed of nearly 22.5 knots, well in excess of her designed service speed.

With the first round trip safely completed, Captain Smith and his crew settled into the daily routine of life on the North Atlantic mail run. Certainly, the *Olympic* continued to catch the public's imagination, even if the following voyage was largely uneventful, but on 13 August 1911, four days after leaving Southampton for the third time, Jeremiah Sweeney and Joseph Hipler had the dubious distinction of becoming the first stowaways to be recorded in the ship's log. One week later, second-class passenger William H Williams had the even greater misfortune to die on the return leg from a combination of heart disease and cirrhosis of the liver. Stowaways and deaths at sea were part and parcel of day-to-day life on the North Atlantic mail run, but the established procedures were straightforward enough: Sweeney and Hipler would be handed over to the authorities at Southampton, while Williams would be buried at sea.

It did not take long for the initial excitement of the *Olympic*'s entry into service to settle down, but on 20 September White Star's flagship would once again be in the headlines,

only not in a way that Roland Shelley, the company's publicity manager, would have wished. Certainly, the voyage began without any undue sign of trouble, when at 11.25am the *Olympic*, carrying 1,313 passengers, steamed out of the White Star Dock at the start of what was intended to be her fifth voyage to New York. After four uneventful trips, Captain Smith was by now reasonably adept at handling his new command, although in the enclosed coastal waters the vessel was nominally under the control of Captain George Bowyer, the Trinity House river pilot who would guide the *Olympic* as far as the Nab lightship, east of the Isle of Wight. About an hour after departing, the *Olympic* was abreast of the Black Jack buoy, marking the lower extent of Southampton Water and the point where vessels would begin the established reverse-S manoeuvre, taking them around the western extent of the Bramble Bank and into the Solent. Passing the Calshot Spit, North Thorn and Thorn Knoll buoys in quick succession, at 12.43pm the liner was alongside

LEFT: *The collision with HMS* Hawke *on 20 September 1911.*

the West Bramble buoy when two blasts on the whistle signalled that the *Olympic* was about to make a port turn; as soon as the manoeuvre was completed, Smith ordered course S 59° E as the ship's speed slowly began to increase.

So far everything was going according to plan, but coming up fast on the starboard quarter was the armoured cruiser HMS *Hawke*. By the time the *Olympic* was beginning her turn, the *Hawke* was already off Egypt Point on the Isle of Wight, and it was obvious to her captain, Commander William Frederick Blunt RN, that both vessels were now headed for the same channel. Accordingly, he altered course by five degrees to starboard, in order to give the *Olympic* more room as she entered into Spithead. Minutes later, the two vessels were almost beam to beam. Up until this point the *Hawke*, moving at an estimated 16 knots, had been the overtaking vessel, but at some crucial juncture during the manoeuvre the accelerating *Olympic* gradually began to overhaul the cruiser. It is at this point that the details begin to conflict; to Captain Smith it seemed as if the *Hawke*'s bow had come as far forward as the space between the *Olympic*'s second and third funnels, while Bowyer estimated that the cruiser's bow had progressed as far forward as the *Olympic*'s bridge. Chief Officer Henry Wilde estimated the *Hawke*'s progress to be somewhere between the two, but it was at this crucial juncture that the *Olympic*'s increasing speed meant that the cruiser now started to fall back. From here on, the actions of neither captain would have any influence on the laws of hydrodynamics. As the *Hawke* fell astern, Commander Blunt suddenly realised

that his 7,350-ton vessel was being pulled to port, directly into the 52,000-ton *Olympic*'s starboard quarter. Unable to believe what he was seeing, Blunt called the helmsman below, 'What are you doing? Port! Hard a port!' before ordering the port engine to be stopped and full astern on the starboard engine. Even at this stage Blunt may have hoped that he might be able to avoid the inevitable convergence of the two ships, until seconds later his helmsman shouted up that the helm had jammed. As a last resort, Blunt yanked the levers of the two engine telegraphs to full astern, but it was too late; with the *Hawke*'s helm jammed at 15 degrees to port, the cruiser was powerless to resist the invisible forces dragging her into the liner's stern.

High up on the *Olympic*'s bridge, Captains Smith and Bowyer were equally aghast at what they were seeing. At first, Smith could only assume that the *Hawke* was attempting to pass beneath his stern, yet knowing instinctively that the cruiser was too close to complete the manoeuvre safely. Bowyer was already in the process of ordering the helm hard over to port in a last-minute attempt to avoid a collision, but it was too late. Seconds later the *Hawke*'s bow slammed into the *Olympic*'s starboard quarter as the larger ship continued to move ahead, causing the cruiser to lurch violently to starboard. In Commander Blunt's words, 'She spun round like a top', and only narrowly avoided capsizing before the *Olympic*'s forward momentum caused the cruiser to shear away.

With her watertight doors closed the *Hawke* did not seem to be in any imminent danger of sinking, while collision mats rigged over the

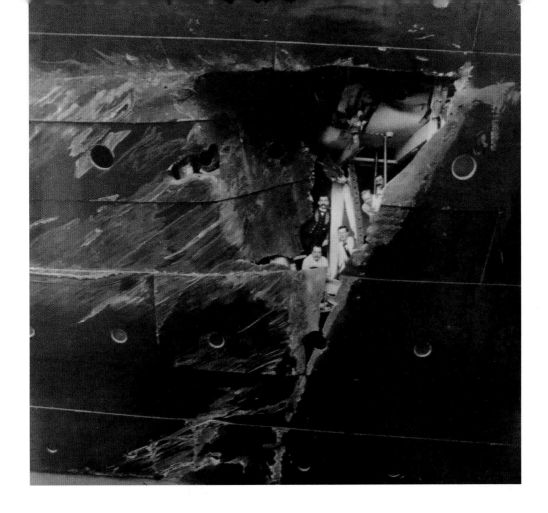

side did their best to slow the rate of water flooding into her crushed bow. The *Olympic*'s damage control systems may not have been as finely honed as those of the warship, but fortunately the damage only extended through one compartment, so the ship was never in any real danger of foundering. It could have been worse but fortunately a stoker positioned by the open door in O bulkhead, the aftermost section of the tunnel, saw the *Hawke*'s ram enter through the ship's side and used the lever to release the watertight door. During the time it took to close, sufficient water had come through the door to result in about three or four hundred tons of water in the forward section of the tunnel, but his quick action in closing the door had contained the flooding. Even so, there could be no doubting the scale of the damage. It was bad enough that a 12-foot triangular hole extended for some 14 feet from just above the waterline up to D deck, but the fact that the shell plating had been driven 8 feet into the *Olympic*'s flank indicated just how violent the full force of the impact had been. In many ways the timing of the collision could not have been more fortuitous, as the occupants of the second-class cabins in the damaged area were just sitting down to lunch and well away from the critical

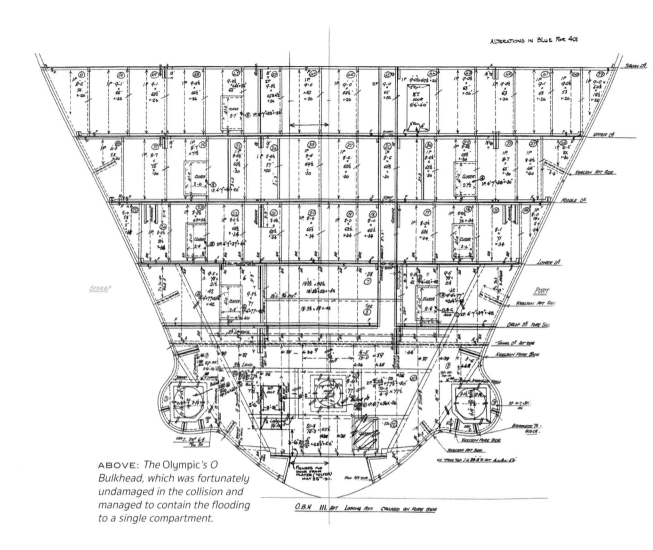

ABOVE: *The* Olympic's O *Bulkhead, which was fortunately undamaged in the collision and managed to contain the flooding to a single compartment.*

area. Amazingly, no one had been even slightly injured.

Beneath the waterline, the situation was even more serious. The *Hawke*'s old-fashioned ram bow may well have been obsolete, but it had performed the task for which it had originally been designed with clinical efficiency. Another pear-shaped hole, approximately 7 feet wide, had not only torn into the *Olympic*'s side but had damaged much of the bossing around the starboard propeller shaft, while all three of the starboard propeller's blades had been seriously

chipped by the cruiser's hull as the *Olympic* continued to move forwards.

One thing that was absolutely certain, the *Olympic*'s voyage was over. All Captain Smith could do was guide his stricken command into Osborne Bay off the Isle of Wight so that the passengers could be disembarked. The staff at White Star's Southampton Canute Road offices would find themselves having to deal unexpectedly with over a thousand passengers who now urgently needed to make alternative travel arrangements, and it is interesting to note

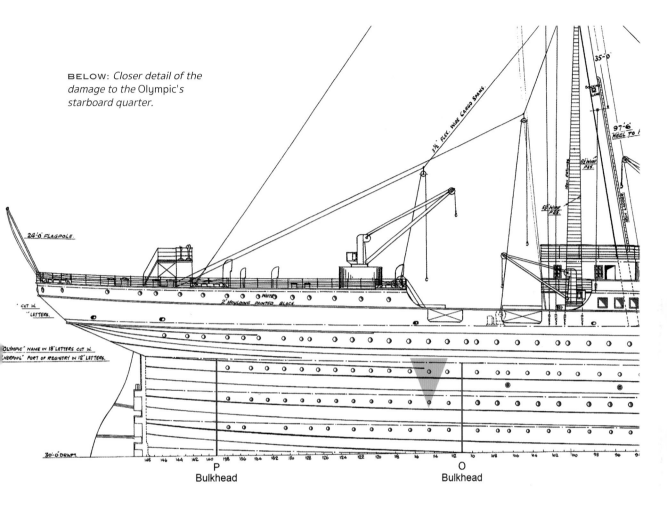

BELOW: *Closer detail of the damage to the* Olympic's *starboard quarter.*

P Bulkhead

O Bulkhead

that at least nine of the *Olympic*'s passengers were able to make it to Liverpool in time for the *Adriatic*'s scheduled departure the following day to New York.

By 4pm, HMS *Hawke* was safely secured alongside a boat house jetty in Portsmouth harbour. The following day she was moved to dock 12, while the *Olympic* returned to the Harland & Wolff repair facility at Southampton for temporary repairs. By 3 October the patching was complete and, travelling at a reduced speed of 10 knots, the *Olympic* departed from

Southampton for Belfast, arriving there safely three days later.

Sorting out the ensuing mess would keep White Star's legal representatives preoccupied for weeks to come, but in actual fact it was not just a case of deciding who was legally accountable for what had happened. The first legal case was a relatively simple matter of industrial relations. After the voyage had been abandoned, the *Olympic*'s crew had been paid off on 22 September. In accordance with the established practice at the time, the White

HMS HAWKE after COLLISION with OLYMPIC - 20 Sept 1911

Star Line was only obliged to pay them for the three days that they had been on board, rather than the full amount to which they would have been entitled had the voyage been completed. Feeling understandably aggrieved by what they saw as the unjustified withholding of their pay, several of the stokehold crew would later take the company to court, claiming that the White Star Line was obliged to pay the crew for the entire period for which the *Olympic* would have been away. Countering this argument at the petty sessions of the Southampton County Court, White Star's lawyers argued that under Section 158 of the 1894 Merchant Shipping Act, after the collision the *Olympic* was legally classified as a wreck because she had sustained a structural injury to her hull that made her incapable of continuing the voyage for which the crew had been contracted. There must have been persuasive arguments on either side as the magistrates were unable to reach a verdict and on 11 October the case was referred to an Admiralty court, but the final judgement, delivered on 1 April 1912, sided with the White Star Line, ruling that after the collision the *Olympic* was incapable of completing her voyage and that therefore she could legally be regarded as a wreck.

The issue of liability for the accident, however, would be a more hard-fought battle. Two days after the collision, an Admiralty board of inquiry held on board the HMS *Hawke* had exonerated Commander Blunt of all blame; satisfied with their decision, the Admiralty then set about putting together a case that would enable them to recover the cost of the repairs from White Star's insurers. The Admiralty based their argument on Commander Blunt's evidence that the *Olympic* had come too far south, had crowded the *Hawke* out of the channel, and that in overtaking the cruiser at such high speed the smaller vessel had been irresistibly pulled towards the liner by the force of the displaced water. Captain John Pritchard of the *Mauretania* would testify on White Star's behalf that he had never experienced suction of any description, but the Admiralty had marshalled its forces well. Among the witnesses was a US government official with specialist knowledge of interacting forces in water, but the crucial testimony would come from much closer to home. Professor John Biles conducted a number of experiments at the Teddington National Physical Laboratory, confirming that when a ship moves through water there is an area between the bow and amid-ships where water is pushed away from the ship, whereas further aft there was considerably more 'pull in'. However, it was not just the laws of physics that would resolve the case, with Biles's observations on the pre-collision manoeuvres probably dealing the killer blow to White Star's case:

'*Assuming the vessels to be parallel,
I do not think the* Hawke *could come through
the danger zone and get bridge-to-bridge
at a lateral distance of one hundred yards.
She would turn in.*'

Therein lay the crux of the matter. As far as the court was concerned, the fact that HMS *Hawke* had not been pulled in when coming up from astern supported Commander Blunt's assertion that the two vessels had been on converging rather than parallel courses, with the result that the *Olympic* had nearly crowded the *Hawke* out of the channel. It was this key point that prompted the court president to rule in the Admiralty's favour, citing the *Olympic* as being responsible for the collision by negligent navigation in coming too far south in the channel.

Round one to the Admiralty, but inevitably White Star sought grounds to contest the verdict and in January 1913 the appeal went ahead. To reinforce their case, White Star had even swept the channel to recover part of the *Hawke*'s broken underwater ram, hoping that by pinpointing the exact location of the collision they would be able to refute the judgement of crowding *Hawke* out of the channel. Unfortunately, however, Commander Blunt's testimony that the ram had detached sometime after the collision rendered the new evidence as worthless, and as the White Star lawyers had also failed to prove that the *Hawke* was the overtaking vessel at the time of the collision – largely due to the fact that just prior to the collision the *Olympic* had accelerated to a speed whereby she was going faster than the *Hawke* – the appeal was ultimately dismissed. Even then the legal arguments would continue up until November 1914, with a final appeal to the House of Lords, then the highest court in the land, but after three attempts at clearing their name the White Star Line was finally obliged to concede defeat. Even so, the company would always maintain that morally they were in the right.

From the White Star Line's point of view, the quick return of their flagship to service was an absolute priority, even though it would unquestionably mean delaying work on the *Titanic*. This meant not only that workers would be transferred from the second ship but also that, in order to further expedite the process, parts intended for *Titanic*, in particular the starboard propeller and even sections of the actual shaft, were cannibalised in order to speed the repairs as much as possible. It would take six weeks for Harland & Wolff to complete the work but by the afternoon of Saturday 18 November 1911 the *Olympic* was lying alongside the deep-water wharf, the post-collision repairs all but complete and scheduled to leave Belfast for Southampton two days later.

On the surface everything seemed to have gone well, but like any company Harland & Wolff was vulnerable to the occasional conflict between their workers. Industrial relations are one thing, but what came next at Belfast was by any standards unique. Shortly before 4pm that afternoon, James Stewart, a foreman labourer at the shipyard, was walking along Queen's Road, about a quarter of a mile from where the *Olympic* was lying. It was here that he bumped into a boilermaker named Edward Wilson, who was headed in the opposite direction. When Wilson asked Stewart if a leading hand boilermaker named Joseph Sharpe was still on board, Stewart confirmed that he was, only to be amazed when Wilson suddenly pulled out a revolver and said, 'I am going to blow Sharpe's

brains out!' As Wilson went on his way, all Stewart could do was call after him, 'Don't be making a fool of yourself', but he was still concerned enough to head back to find Sharpe and warn him of the danger before anything serious happened.

Wilson continued towards the *Olympic*, boarding the vessel by the gangway along the wharf and heading straight down to the boiler rooms. At 4.10pm he walked into the reciprocating engine room, where he immediately noticed Sharpe speaking with two holders-up named Thomas McKittrick and Joseph Turner; boilermaker William Walmesley was also present, and these three men would later graphically describe the events as they unfolded. At first there was nothing particularly remarkable about the conversation. As Wilson entered from the boiler room, he said, 'Sharpe, will you come into the boiler room as I want to say a few words to you.'

'Whatever you have got to say, say it here.'

'If you don't come into the stokehold, you'll be sorry for it.'

As Wilson attempted to pull his hand out of his pocket, Sharpe, seeing something he later described as 'bright and shiny', leapt forwards, catching Wilson by both wrists and pushing him back against the bulkhead. As the two men struggled the gun went off, the bullet lodging in Sharpe's left thigh as they fell to the floor. Walmesley later recalled that Sharpe fell on top of Wilson, who held the revolver in his right hand, and that as Wilson rolled over to his right two more shots rang out, striking Sharpe in his right leg below the knee and grazing the skin of his right leg. Within seconds, Sharpe's workmates

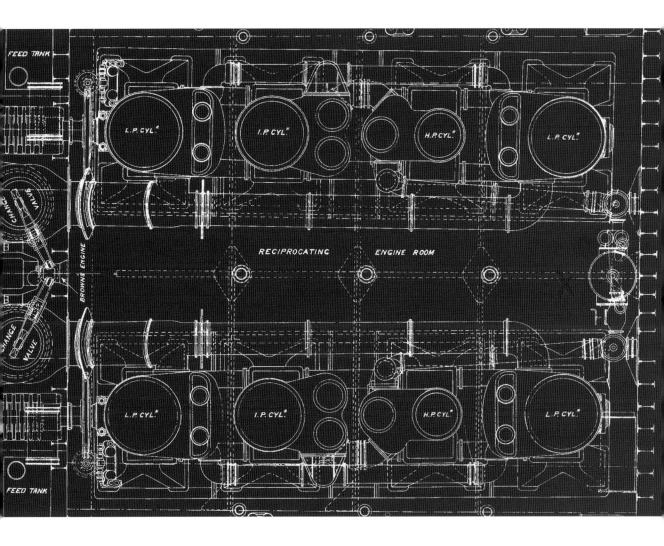

ABOVE: *The location of the armed struggle between Edward Wilson and Joseph Sharpe.*

were rushing to his aid, eventually succeeding in wrestling the revolver from Wilson's grasp and pinning him down on the tank top by his feet, but it was only when boilermaker William Plackett joined the struggle that Wilson was finally overpowered, just as James Stewart belatedly ran into the engine room.

Fortunately, Sharpe's wounds were not as severe as initially thought, and he was quickly carried topside and taken to the Royal Victoria Hospital. As dusk settled, harbour constable

Alexander Shannon arrived alongside the *Olympic* at 5.15pm, where John Dickinson, the manager of Harland & Wolff's ships' finishing department, immediately placed Wilson in his custody. Cautioned on a charge of shooting at Joseph Sharpe with intent to kill, all that the now distraught Wilson could be heard to say was: 'I am very sorry for what I have done. Is the injured man dead? Constable, blow my brains out with that revolver.'

It did not take long to work out what had happened. It quickly transpired that Wilson, who had known Sharpe for over ten years, had been drinking after the two men had argued over some overtime. After both he and his son had been laid off that Saturday, the previously teetotal Wilson, who already had problems at home with a seriously ill wife and child, proceeded to get drunk before somehow obtaining the revolver and returning to Queen's Island to settle the score with the man who, so he believed, was responsible for him being laid off. But for the intervention of McKittrick and Walmesley, he might have done just that. Meanwhile, he was taken before the court on 27 November, where he would be remanded in custody until the case was ready to go to trial.

It would not be until 18 March 1912 that the case of The King v. Edward John Wilson was finally ready to be placed before the Right Honourable Lord Justice Richard Cherry at the petty sessions of the Belfast assizes. Interestingly, there already seemed to have been an important alteration in the charge against Wilson, with the original charge of 'intent to kill and murder' having been watered down to 'intent to disable', but while there was no doubt as to Wilson's guilt, his legal counsel, Richard Best KC and Henry Hanna KC, probably pursued the only realistic option open to them by emphasising the mitigating circumstances. Certainly the 1907 Probation of Offenders Act provided the court with a degree of flexibility when considering Wilson's extenuating circumstances, character and mental condition

at the time of the shooting, and on that day it would seem that Wilson's prayers had been answered. Judge Cherry may have been an acknowledged authority on the Irish Land Acts, but his effectiveness as a judge was not universally respected. Maurice Healy, the Irish nationalist lawyer, writer and politician once observed that Judge Cherry 'erred towards charity', and Richard Best was just the man to exploit this characteristic, as he painted a heart-rending case for leniency on behalf of his client. The witnesses also helped Wilson's case no end, each prepared to testify to his previous good character, each in turn describing Wilson as 'a peaceable and law-abiding man', 'a quiet, decent hard-working man', 'a popular man amongst his fellow workers' and someone 'not inclined to quarrel with his fellow workmen'. Perhaps the most telling testimony came from Joseph Sharpe himself, who in his own deposition said, 'I have known the prisoner for a number of years, and we were very friendly, and although this has happened I have no ill feeling against him. I was aware previous to the Saturday that his wife and youngest child were seriously ill, he had told me that they were on the point of death.'

Considering the sympathetic legal testimony and Judge Cherry's charitable nature, it comes as no surprise that in his summing up the judge was satisfied that Wilson had committed the act while in a sudden fit of passion and under very trying circumstances. Cherry was convinced that he was justified in pardoning the prisoner under the Probation of Offenders Act, and after his four-month ordeal Edward John Wilson was duly discharged and walked free.

CHAPTER SIX

THE CALM BEFORE THE STORM

After launching, it had taken Harland & Wolff a little over seven months before the *Olympic* was ready to be handed over, but this had only been possible because the White Star Line had given priority to getting their new flagship into service. As far as the *Titanic* was concerned, there was less pressure, with tentative dates for the ship's maiden voyage being set for March 1912, ten months after the ship had been launched and, coincidentally, the beginning of the intermediate season on the North Atlantic.

Just as the *Olympic* had been an empty shell when she was launched, the same went for the *Titanic*. Even after the giant Benrather crane had lowered the engine machinery and boilers into the hull, little progress could be made on the accommodations until the task of sealing the engine room openings was complete; only then could the work of installing the electrical circuitry, plumbing and wood panelling really start in earnest. However, while the *Olympic* and *Titanic* had originally been cut from the same cloth, Harland & Wolff now had the added benefit of having observed the *Olympic* in service for several months, during which time literally thousands of design modifications had been incorporated into the *Titanic*.

Ismay had originally suggested, in a letter dated 22 June 1911, that additional first-class cabins on B deck should be carried out to the sides of the ship, but by the time Harland & Wolff had drawn up the revised layout the *Titanic* was already beginning to look like a

very different ship – at least on the inside. Ismay's additional cabins were all there, but in addition to the cabins having communicating doors, thereby forming mini-suites, the most noticeable change in the arrangements was the two parlour suites on each side of the ship, just aft of the forward main entrance. As in the *Olympic*, each of the suites came complete with a sitting room, two bedrooms and a private bath and toilet, but the *Titanic*'s suites also had their own private promenades, along with two inboard cabins slightly further aft (B101 and B102) to accommodate any servants travelling with their employers. In high season, each of these parlour suites could generate an additional $4,350 per crossing. Further aft, another discernible difference between the two ships was also there for all to see. Not only had the à la carte restaurant been significantly enlarged in the *Titanic*, having been extended across the open promenade to the port side of the ship, but an entirely new

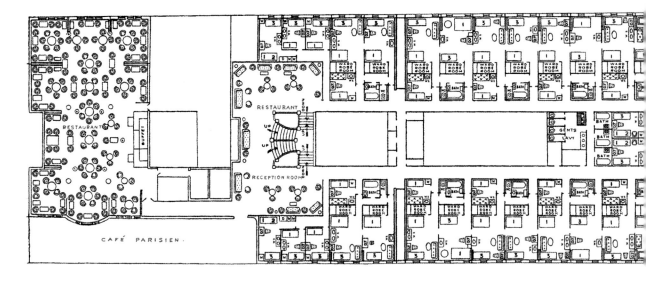

BELOW: *The layout of the* Titanic*'s Turkish bath marked another important internal modification to the* Olympic*'s original design.*

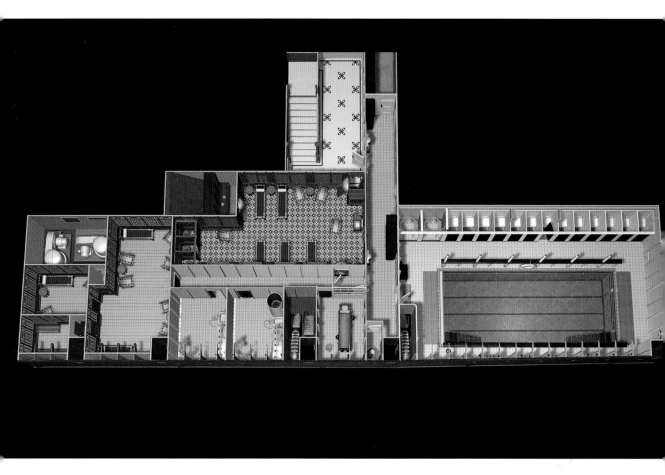

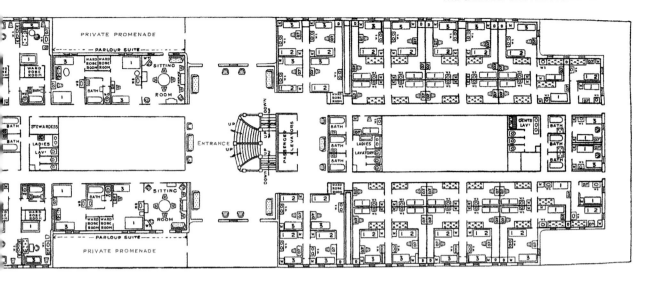

feature, the Café Parisien, now occupied what had previously been an open promenade in the *Olympic*, further enhancing White Star's first-class passengers' experience.

The *Titanic*'s modifications were not just limited to the ship's revenue-generating arrangements, however. On 24 February 1912, while on an eastbound crossing, the *Olympic*'s

ABOVE: *The* Titanic's *modified first-class B deck arrangement.*

BELOW: *Additional modifications were made to the ships' propellers in early 1912 in order to experiment with both the efficiency and economy of the engines.*

port propeller suddenly and unexpectedly lost one of its blades. Save for an initial shudder, neither the ship nor its passengers were ever

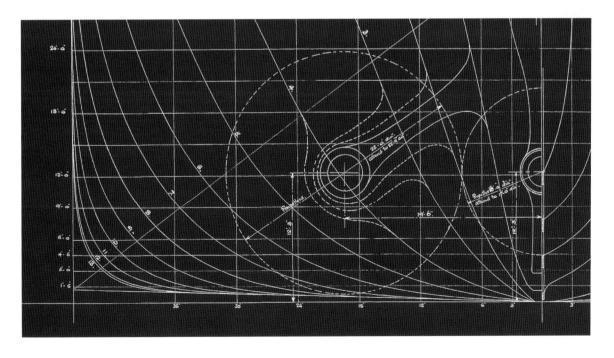

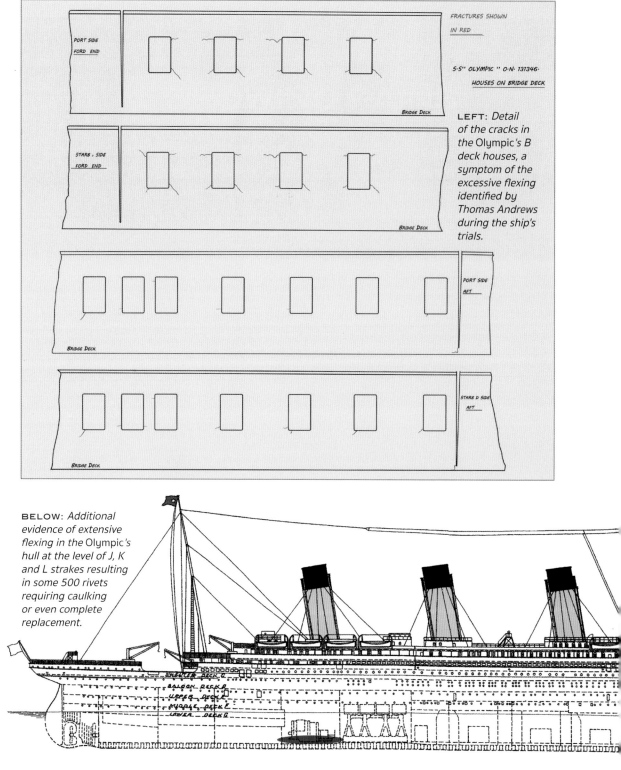

FRACTURES SHOWN
IN RED

S·S'' OLYMPIC '' O·N· 131346·
HOUSES ON BRIDGE DECK

PORT SIDE
FORD END

BRIDGE DECK

STARB · SIDE
FORD END

BRIDGE DECK

PORT SIDE
AFT

BRIDGE DECK

STARB D SIDE
AFT

BRIDGE DECK

LEFT: *Detail of the cracks in the Olympic's B deck houses, a symptom of the excessive flexing identified by Thomas Andrews during the ship's trials.*

BELOW: *Additional evidence of extensive flexing in the Olympic's hull at the level of J, K and L strakes resulting in some 500 rivets requiring caulking or even complete replacement.*

SHELTER DECK C
SALOON DECK D
UPPER DECK E
MIDDLE DECK F
LOWER DECK G

in any real danger, but there was no way that the ship would be able to remain in service until the missing blade had been replaced. After unloading her passengers at Southampton, the *Olympic* duly arrived back at Belfast on 1 March, where men and materiel once again had to be diverted from the *Titanic* to her sister ship. The loss of the propeller blade would be attributed to a chemical reaction between the bronze propeller blades and the securing bolts with the steel boss to which the blades were fitted, the close proximity of these two metals in sea water resulting in some form of electrolytic corrosion, but while science could explain the loss of the propeller blade, elsewhere a number of other problems were beginning to highlight a more troubling scenario. While on her first westbound crossing of 1912, the *Olympic* had run headlong into an Atlantic storm of such ferocity that even Captain Smith would later describe it as being one of the roughest he had ever experienced. It was certainly strong enough for the hatch cover of hold 1 to be torn

from its mountings, but the rough conditions had also exacerbated an earlier area of concern. While the *Olympic* was back at Belfast, Francis Carruthers, the Board of Trade's ship surveyor, took the opportunity to make an inspection of the hull, and while he found no signs of any undue stress in the sides of the vessel from the waterline upwards, he did observe a number of fractures in the side plating of the deckhouses on the bridge deck. There was no evident sign of stress in the promenade and bridge deck side plating, but he did note that the cracking was occurring at the portion of the deckhouses between and near to the two expansion joint openings.

Beneath the waterline, his observations were more detailed. On the starboard side forward, in way of boiler room 6, over 200 rivets had become slack and needed to be drilled out and renewed, while another 90 rivets on the port side showed enough slack to require caulking. Further aft on both sides of the ship in way of the turbine engine room, another 100 rivets also needed to be replaced. Carruthers himself carefully inspected the areas where the defective rivets had been observed, but while he could observe no further signs of stress, the issue of the cracking and riveting defects, combined with the vibration noted by Andrews during the ship's trials, indicated there was evidence to suggest that in some areas the *Olympic*'s hull was suffering from excessive panting. It was not yet a major structural issue, but additional strengthening would need to be carried out in the affected areas when the ship next returned to the shipyard for her annual overhaul.

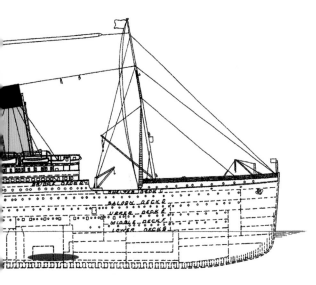

After a stay of only seven days, the *Olympic* was soon on her way back to Southampton, resuming commercial service on 13 March, but in terms of the ensuing structural modifications to the *Titanic*, this Belfast trip had been highly significant. The problems with the hull had highlighted a potentially serious issue, but in the case of the *Titanic* Harland & Wolff still had time to carry out more significant modifications by drilling out the double hand-riveted seams altogether and replacing them with quadruple-riveted one-inch steel straps. As far as the *Titanic* was concerned, the work would also be more extensive, extending between frames 63 and 81 forward at the level of the J and K strakes, and between frames 50 and 73 aft at the landing of K and L strakes.

It was at this point that perhaps the most distinctive feature would first appear in the *Titanic*'s external appearance, with the first reference dated 14 February 1912 to the permanent steel screen that would run along each side of the forward promenade deck. It is interesting that such a distinctive modification was only incorporated at such a late stage of the fitting out, but it would seem that the severe weather to which the *Olympic* had been subjected in early January, combined with the fact that extending the B deck cabins out to the side of the ship meant the *Titanic* no longer had an enclosed first-class promenade, may have obliged Harland & Wolff to reconsider this part of the design. As an added benefit, the enclosed promenade would incorporate a limited degree of additional stiffening in the area of the forward superstructure that had been an issue in the *Olympic*.

As the days ticked down to the maiden voyage, Harland & Wolff continued to tinker with the finishing touches that would make the *Titanic* worthy of her title as the new flagship of the White Star Line. In the meantime, Captain Smith would make one final round trip in the *Olympic* before returning to Southampton on 30 March. The voyage itself was largely uneventful, but as Smith left the *Olympic* for the last time, he would have had little notion of the momentous chain of events that were already being set in motion.

Shortly before 6am on the morning of Monday 1 April 1912, the sun rose over the Belfast skyline to find the *Titanic* still secured in the fitting-out basin. After ten months of work she was finally ready to depart on her trials that morning, but if anyone on board was overly superstitious at the thought of carrying out the engine trials on April Fool's Day, they would have breathed a sigh of relief when a strong north-westerly wind forced the decision to postpone the trials until the following day. Twenty-four hours later the winds had subsided and, guided by the tugs *Hercules*, *Herculaneum*, *Huskisson*, *Herald* and *Hornby*, the *Titanic* finally proceeded into Belfast Lough. Casting off the tugs at Carrickfergus, she then proceeded slowly to the mouth of the lough and the deeper waters of the Irish Sea, where for the next eight hours she would undergo a variety of speed and steering tests. Also on board would be representatives from the Southampton firm of C J Smith & Co, standing by to adjust the ship's four compasses for the voyage to Southampton, with the procedures being closely observed by Francis Carruthers on behalf of the Board

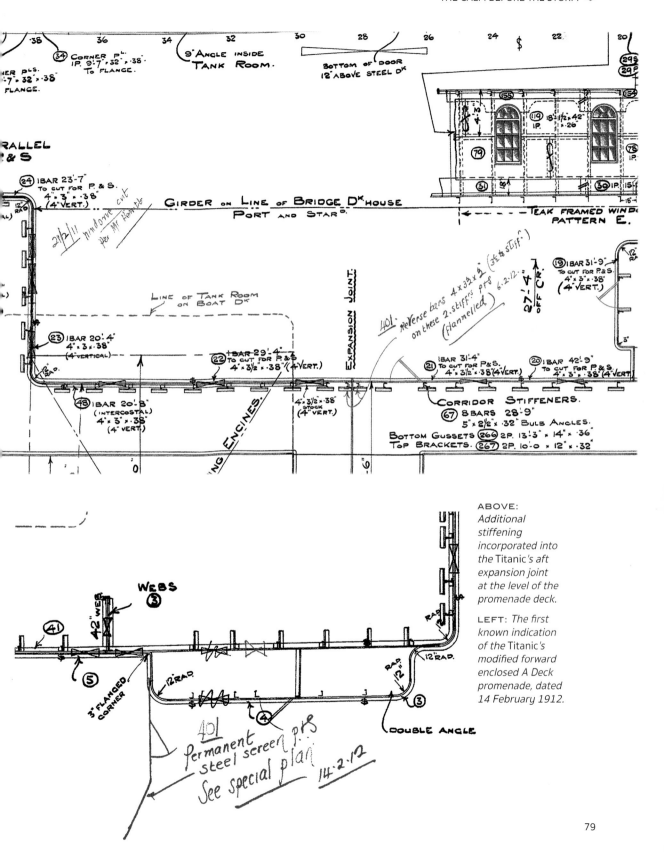

ABOVE: *Additional stiffening incorporated into the* Titanic's *aft expansion joint at the level of the promenade deck.*

LEFT: *The first known indication of the* Titanic's *modified forward enclosed A Deck promenade, dated 14 February 1912.*

of Trade. Little information would ever be published regarding the trials, but it is clear that throughout the day the ship lived up to her builder's expectations in every way. By 7pm the *Titanic* was back at Belfast and, with the final checks completed, Harold Sanderson finally took possession of the *Titanic* on behalf of the White Star Line, with Thomas Andrews signing off the paperwork for the shipyard. Shortly after 8pm, the *Titanic* was once again headed out to sea, scheduled to arrive at Southampton shortly before midnight on 3 April.

Taking advantage of the midnight flood tide at Southampton, the *Titanic* slipped quietly into Berth 44 of the White Star Dock, having already been turned by the five attending Red Funnel tugs so that she would be facing bow out on the day of her departure. By the time the sun rose on 4 April, White Star's newest flagship, safely secured in the berth occupied by the

Olympic only 12 hours earlier, would have presented an imposing sight to the inhabitants of Southampton, but unfortunately a distant look was just about all they were going to get; if the *Titanic* was to be ready to sail on 10 April then the already tight schedule, not helped by the delayed arrival from Belfast, left no time for any visitors or publicity-seeking journalists to inspect the ship. With barely one week to get her ready for sea, the workmen of the Harland & Wolff ship repair facility set about the tasks that had not been completed at Belfast, while the crew concentrated on the reams of bedding, linen, cutlery, glass and supplies that would be needed for what was now, at least in terms of gross tonnage, the largest ship in the world.

Charles Lightoller, then the *Titanic*'s first officer, recalled that just getting the ship ready was 24-hour day and night work, '...organising here, receiving stores there, arranging duties, trying and testing out the different contrivances, makers of the hundred and

ABOVE: *Second Officer Charles Herbert Lightoller.*

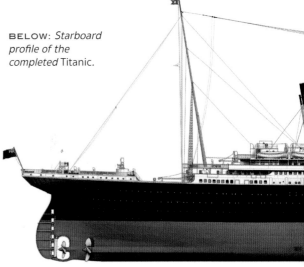

BELOW: *Starboard profile of the completed* Titanic.

one instruments with their chits to be signed certifying that this, that, and the other was in perfect working order'. However, to further complicate matters, there would also be a last-minute reshuffle among the senior officers. When the *Titanic* arrived at Southampton, William Murdoch held the position of chief officer, but when the *Olympic* had departed for New York on the morning of 3 April her chief officer, Henry Wilde, had not gone with the ship. Instead, he was to remain at Southampton where, 24 hours later, he would assume that same position on the *Titanic*. Murdoch would be bumped down to first officer and Lightoller would be made second; David Blair, Lightoller's friend and colleague from the *Oceanic*, would leave the ship altogether. As far as the junior officers were concerned, Third Officer Herbert Pitman, Fourth Officer Joseph Boxhall, Fifth Officer Harold Lowe and Sixth Officer James Moody would remain in their original positions. Needless to say, Lightoller wasn't overly thrilled

by the decision to restructure the ship's senior officers, later recalling that apart from the disappointment of having to step back in rank, for the next few days it also threw him and Murdoch completely out of their stride.

The White Star line also had other, more pressing issues. For weeks, an ongoing coal strike had wrought havoc with the shipping companies, resulting in numerous sailings having to be cancelled due to the lack of fuel. Even the speed of those vessels that did remain in service had to be limited in order to conserve supplies, but although the 37-day strike would be settled two days after the *Titanic* arrived at Southampton, it would still take days for coal supplies to return to normal. Fortunately, the ship already had some 2,000 tons on board when she arrived from Belfast, but it was only by emptying the bunkers of the remaining IMM ships berthed at Southampton that the White Star Line was able to ensure that the *Titanic* would have enough fuel on board to make it to New York.

Despite the apparent chaos, by the morning of Wednesday 10 April the *Titanic* was ready. Charles Lightoller certainly believed she was ready to go, recalling that 'It was clear to everybody on board that we had a ship that was going to create the greatest stir British shipping circles had ever known', but even as the Waterloo boat train arrived alongside and the passengers began to embark, there were still the customary last-minute formalities to be resolved. The Board of Trade's assistant emigration officer at Southampton was Captain Maurice Clarke, and it was his job to ensure that the lifeboats and all the life-saving equipment, not to mention the ship's distress rockets and signals, were properly tested, exercised and passed. If anything, Clarke was exercising even more scrupulous care than in an older and more

ABOVE: *10 April 1912: The* Olympic *arriving at New York on the same day* Titanic *departs from Southampton.*

settled ship, so he was not about to take any officer's word for it that everything was in order; he absolutely insisted on seeing everything for himself.

Shortly before noon, the last of the official paperwork was finally signed and as Captain Clarke returned ashore the order was given for the *Titanic* to slip her moorings. Guided by the expert hand of Captain Smith and Trinity House pilot George Bowyer, the ship slowly pulled away from Berth 44 and began her port turn into the River Test, where the first mishap of the journey threatened to bring the maiden voyage to a premature end before the ship had

ABOVE: *The tug* Vulcan *pulling the SS* New York *clear of the* Titanic's *stern, so avoiding a collision which could have ended the maiden voyage before it had even started.*

even cleared the dock. As the *Titanic* moved down the channel leading into the River Itchen and Southampton Water, she passed close to the liners *Oceanic* and *New York*, both tied up in front of the passenger sheds at Berth 38. It was here that the power of the *Olympic* class engines would once again be convincingly demonstrated. With the *New York* secured outboard of the *Oceanic*, as the *Titanic* began to accelerate through the partially obstructed channel the volume of displaced water caused the *New York* to range heavily on her moorings; it was at this point that the strain on the lines securing the American liner proved too

much as, one by one, they gave way with a loud cracking noise. Suddenly, the infamous inward pull of the Olympic class propellers was dragging the *New York*'s stern away from the side of the *Oceanic* and towards the *Titanic*'s port quarter. Perhaps it was because the *Titanic* was only moving at a relatively slow speed that a collision was averted, or maybe it was due to the timely intervention by Captain Gale on the tug *Vulcan*, who, on seeing what was about to happen, managed to get a line on to the *New York*'s stern just in time to avoid an accident. Even then, it was a near-run thing. On board the *Titanic*, Thomas Andrews would recall the situation as being 'decidedly unpleasant', with other witnesses confirming that the two ships came within 4 feet of each other, but the combination of the *Titanic*'s relatively slow speed, the *Vulcan*'s tow line and an order for the *Titanic*'s port engine to be put astern was just enough to avert disaster.

There were many who would regard this near miss as another example of the suction caused by the *Titanic*'s huge propellers, but in truth the hydrodynamic principles should already have been well understood. The most telling example had come nine months earlier, while the *Titanic* was secured at Belfast alongside the fitting-out basin. Shortly after midday on 20 July 1911, one of the cross-channel steamers had passed the vessel at speed, causing the much larger *Titanic* to range heavily on her moorings until one of the 5-inch fore and aft springs parted, causing a wire hawser to fall on to one of the barges alongside. Harland & Wolff's official letter of complaint to the Belfast harbourmaster even went so far as to say that several men working below narrowly avoided being killed or knocked into the water and, bearing in mind

that the midday channel steamers seemed to be making a habit of passing the *Titanic* at excessive speed, wasted no time in requesting that steps be taken to ensure that in future they passed more slowly. Considering that a vessel the size of the *Titanic* could be affected by the much smaller cross-channel steamers, the fact that the *New York* was similarly affected in the unusually crowded channel opposite Berth 38 should not be so surprising.

And so the *Titanic* resumed her course into Southampton Water, safely navigating the reverse-S manoeuvre around the Brambles Bank and into the Solent before pausing briefly at the Nab light vessel where Pilot Bowyer would disembark. The call at Cherbourg was reasonably routine, save for a slightly late arrival due to the delay caused by the near miss at Southampton, and it was here that a total of 142 first-class, 30 second-class and 102 steerage passengers would come

BELOW: *Details of the* Traffic*'s two designed positions alongside the* Olympic *and* Titanic *for transferring steerage passengers, mail and baggage.*

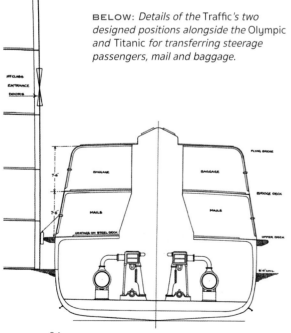

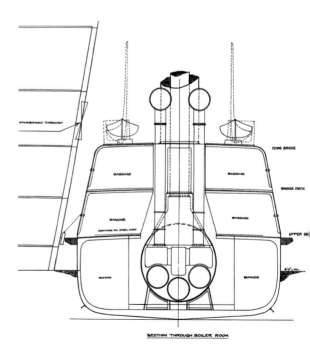

aboard. Included among the glitterati were the American millionaire John Jacob Astor and his young wife, Madeleine; Margaret 'Molly' Brown; mining tycoon Benjamin Guggenheim; John Thayer, vice-president of the Pennsylvania Railroad; George Widener, owner of the Ritz Carlton Hotel, with his wife, Eleanor, and son Harry; and American actress Dorothy Gibson. Also included in the list were British aristocrats Sir Cosmo and Lady Duff Gordon, travelling under the name of Morgan. During the transfer, Ismay would no doubt have been keeping an equally watchful eye on Captain Beresford's procedures aboard the *Nomadic* and *Traffic*, making sure that he now fully complied with the procedures detailed in Thomas Andrews' memorandum, while Andrews himself was watching the activities from above. After ten months in service, the procedures at Cherbourg now seemed to be working well, Andrews later writing in a letter to his wife, Helen, 'The two little tenders looked well, you will remember we built them about a year ago'. In a little under 90 minutes, 274 passengers, along with their baggage and mails for America, were taken aboard, while 22 passengers had gone ashore. Shortly after 8pm the *Titanic* once again headed into the English Channel, this time assuming a north-westerly course towards her second and final port of call on the southern coast of Ireland.

According to his last letter home, Thomas Andrews had expected the *Titanic* to arrive at Queenstown at about 10.30 on the morning of Thursday 11 April, but it was actually closer to midday before the ship finally dropped anchor off Roche's Point, some 2 miles from the entrance to the harbour. The two paddlers, *America* and *Ireland*, would then ferry out the final passengers who would be embarked in the ship, along with another 1,385 sacks of mail. This time, however, the White Star clientele would be very different to the millionaires who had boarded at Cherbourg. Queenstown was largely an emigrant port, from which tens of thousands of Irish nationals would leave the country every year. This time the *Titanic* took on a further 113 steerage passengers, along with seven second-class. Only seven second-class passengers were supposed to disembark at Queenstown, but unbeknown to Eber Sharpe, the port's Board of Trade emigration officer, his final calculations would be slightly off. The final certificate of clearance confirmed that the *Titanic* had on board 606 cabin-class passengers, 710 third-class and 892 crew: a total of 2,208 souls. However, 23-year-old fireman and Queenstown resident John Coffey had decided to take the opportunity to desert the ship, secreting himself beneath the piles of mailbags on one of the tenders. One of those mailbags contained a final letter from Thomas Andrews to his wife, writing of the kindness of everyone on board and that everything was going splendidly.

Within a couple of hours, the process was complete. Sharpe signed off the last of the paperwork before the passenger tenders returned to shore to the tones of the uilleann pipes of Eugene Daly, standing on the *Titanic*'s poop for a last glimpse of Ireland as the great liner took him from his old life to the new world. New York was now less than six days away.

CHAPTER SEVEN

TITANIC

As the *Titanic* sped westwards, Charles Lightoller recalled that 'everybody's admiration of the ship increased; for the way she behaved, for the total absence of vibration, for her steadiness even with the ever-increasing speed, as she warmed up to her work'. Certainly, Chief Engineer Joseph Bell was working the engines up gradually, recording consecutive daily runs of 484, 519 and 546 nautical miles.

All the same, it had not all been a case of plain sailing. Throughout the voyage, in boiler room 5 a team of firemen had been working to extinguish a coal fire burning in the forward starboard bunker. Fireman Charles Hendrickson later spoke of the fire possibly having been burning since the ship had left Belfast, but evidently no one thought it serious enough to report the matter to Captain Maurice Clarke before the ship sailed. It was only after the *Titanic* had departed from Southampton on the Wednesday afternoon that work to empty the bunker finally started, but by noon on Saturday 13 April the last of the coal had been removed from the bunker and the fire had finally been extinguished. Other niggles, inevitable on any maiden voyage, continued to crop up. For the most part, Thomas Andrews' notes apparently concerned relatively trivial issues, be they problems with the hot press in the restaurant galley, the pebble-dashing in the private promenade being too dark, or just too many screws on the stateroom coat hooks. More concerning perhaps were the problems with the Marconi transmitter, which kept wireless operators Jack Phillips and Harold Bride working well into the Saturday night to complete the repairs. The problem was eventually traced to a burned-out secondary winding in the transformer, but by early Sunday morning power had been restored, enabling Phillips to finally set about dealing with the large backlog that had built up from the previous day.

The repairs could not have been completed a moment too soon, as one by one a series of ice warnings began to arrive, warning of the potential hazards that lay ahead. The *Caronia*'s message was the first to arrive at 9am, containing the two-day-old coordinates of a

RIGHT: *Once in the open sea, the* Titanic *heads for New York via Cherbourg and Queenstown.*

number of icebergs, growlers and field ice, while at 1.42pm another message arrived, this time from the *Baltic*, advising that the Greek steamer *Athenai* had also reported icebergs and field ice in the area. Captain Smith duly acknowledged receipt of both messages. This second ice warning would later become a matter of some controversy as it would be pocketed by Joseph Bruce Ismay when Captain Smith showed it to him just as he was going into lunch; it would remain in his pocket until 7.15pm, when Smith requested its return so that he could post it in the chart room. During lunch, a third message was intercepted from the HAPAG liner *Amerika* to the US Hydrographic Office in Washington, reporting the presence of icebergs ahead, while a fourth message from the *Californian* to the *Antillian* was also intercepted and delivered to the bridge. While Phillips and Bride would not have been navigators, had they but known it the cumulative result of these messages was a

large barrier of ice lying directly in the *Titanic's* path. Despite the information in his possession, Captain Smith elected not to reduce speed, although it was enough for him to slightly delay the customary course change in position 42N, 47W, commonly known as the 'Corner', by about half an hour, possibly to take the ship slightly further south than the ice position reported by Captain Barr of the *Caronia*. The diversion, however, was minimal and at 5.50pm he ordered course N 71° W, as the *Titanic* assumed her final westbound heading for New York.

As Captain Smith retired for dinner in the à la carte restaurant with the Widener family, other indicators began to urge caution. Throughout his watch, Lightoller noted the temperature dropping four degrees to 43° (Fahrenheit)

BELOW: *The two bunkers in boiler rooms 5 and 6 compromised by the fire.*

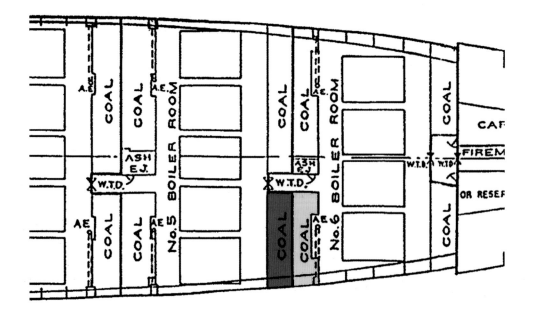

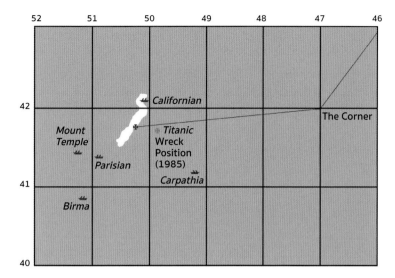

LEFT: *The* Titanic's *intended course from "The Corner" towards New York and the ice barrier.*

BELOW: *The* Titanic's *final position, over 1,200 miles east of her intended destination in New York.*

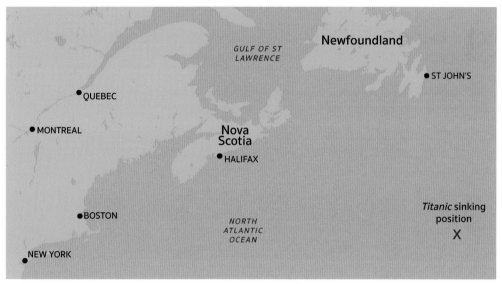

between 6.30 and 7.30pm and by 9pm the water temperature had plunged to 33°, barely one degree above freezing point and certainly cold enough to send word to the carpenter to drain off the freshwater tanks to prevent the pipes from freezing. All told, the temperature had dropped by ten degrees Fahrenheit in two hours.

Shortly before 9pm Captain Smith returned to the bridge, where Lightoller later recounted

a curiously distant exchange. Smith remarked that it was cold, giving Lightoller the perfect opening to mention that it was only one degree above freezing and that he had sent word to the carpenter and the engine room to keep an eye on their fresh water. They then began to speak about the weather, noting that the lack of any wind had resulted in a flat calm, to which Smith pensively muttered, 'A flat calm...' Lightoller then commented that it was a pity there was no breeze while they were going through the ice region as it made it more difficult to see the water breaking on the base of any bergs, although both men agreed that there would be a certain amount of reflected light from any bergs; even if the blue side of a berg was towards them, the white outline would still give them sufficient warning of any danger ahead. If there was a last chance for Smith to take the decision to slow down then this surely was it, but as he left the bridge at 9.30 he said to Lightoller, 'If it becomes at all doubtful then let me know at once. I will be just inside.' Lightoller knew this remark undoubtedly referred to ice, and no sooner had Smith left the bridge than the message was being sent to lookouts Archie Jewell and George Symons, reminding them to keep a sharp watch for small ice and growlers until daybreak.

ABOVE: *Frederick Fleet, the lookout who sighted the iceberg just too late to save the* Titanic.

At 10pm, eight bells sounded. First Officer Murdoch arrived on the bridge to take over just as lookouts Reginald Lee and Fred Fleet were relieving Jewell and Symons up in the crow's nest. Lightoller passed on the usual 'items of interest' regarding course, speed, weather conditions and ice reports, before setting off on his rounds once Murdoch's eyes had adjusted to the darkened conditions on the bridge. For the next four hours the *Titanic* would be his responsibility, yet crucial events that may have saved the ship even at this late stage were still unfolding in the wireless room, barely 100 feet from the bridge. While Bride was sleeping in his bunk, Phillips was preoccupied with clearing the backlog of wireless traffic to Cape Race. During this time, two crucial ice warnings would be received, the first from the *Mesaba* at 9.40pm – about the time Lightoller was already in the process of warning the lookouts to keep a sharp watch for ice. For reasons unknown, this message would never reach the bridge, nor would a final message sent at 11pm from the Leyland liner *Californian* by wireless operator Cyril Furmston-Evans, who had been instructed by Captain Stanley Lord to warn all nearby shipping that they were stopped and surrounded by ice. Unfortunately, the *Californian*'s message was never completed as Phillips, almost deafened by the noise due to the strength of the signal – a clear indication that the two ships were very close to each other – cut in, saying, 'Keep out. I am working Cape Race.' It was a common enough occurrence and Evans would later testify that he did not see the rebuff '...as an insult or anything like that'. Instead, he promptly closed down for the night

and went to bed. The last opportunity to warn the *Titanic*'s bridge officers of the potential danger ahead had come and gone.

Seven bells sounded as Sixth Officer James Moody probably started to contemplate a nice warm bunk after going off duty at midnight, but whatever thoughts may have been going through his head would have been quickly shut off when, at 11.40pm, three loud clangs suddenly rang out from the lookouts' bell. Seconds later, the crow's nest phone rang as he moved to answer it.

ABOVE: *The foremast crow's nest provided the lookouts with an unimpeded view.*

'*What did you see?*'
'*Iceberg right ahead!*'
'*Thank you.*'

The subdued calm on the darkened bridge became one of frantic activity as Murdoch ordered, 'Hard-a-starboard'; seconds later, Quartermaster Robert Hichens was turning the ship's wheel to move the tiller to starboard as ordered, initiating a sharp turn to port. Meanwhile, Fourth Officer Joseph Boxhall, just approaching the bridge from the officers' quarters, also heard the ringing of the bridge engine telegraphs as the order 'full astern' was rung down to the engine room. No sooner were the orders given than Murdoch was pulling the lever to operate the 12 watertight doors, but already it was too late. Seconds later, the *Titanic*'s flank brushed against the huge immoveable iceberg as a rock-hard spur of ice sliced into the ship's starboard side. The *Titanic*'s fate was sealed in the next ten seconds.

Within moments of the collision, Captain Smith was on the bridge.

'Mr Murdoch, what was that?'
'An iceberg, sir. I hard-a-starboarded and reversed the engines and I was going to hard-a-port round it but she was too close.

I could not do any more. I have closed the watertight doors.'

After giving orders for the carpenter to sound the ship, the information, when it came, was not encouraging. The damage to the lower starboard side of the vessel, about 10 feet above the keel, extended along some 250 feet of the ship's forward six compartments, but while the forepeak was not flooded above the level of the peak tank itself, water was rising quickly in the next four compartments. Within ten minutes of the collision, it had risen to a level of about 14 feet above the keel, except in boiler room 5, where the pumps were, for the time being at least, sufficient to contain the flooding. Despite the damage, no one was contemplating any

BELOW: *The enclosed wheelhouse, immediately aft of the bridge. The door at right led to the navigating room and beyond that the captain's sitting room.*

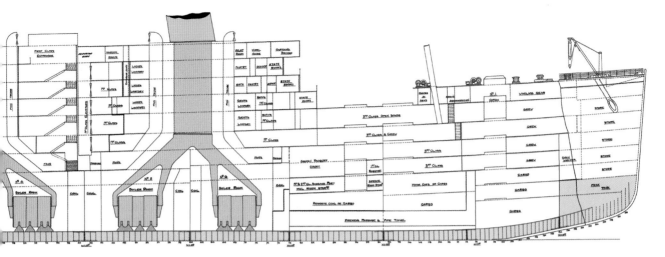

thoughts of abandoning ship at this time, but while the legend of the unsinkable ship may well have engendered a sense of false security among the *Titanic*'s officers, there was one man on board who had little doubt as to the true seriousness of the situation.

In 1912, the concept of any damage to a hull extending beyond two compartments seemed unthinkable, hence Pirrie's design provided for any two of the largest contiguous compartments to be flooded without endangering the ship. The *Titanic*'s watertight subdivision was so efficient that theoretically it was even possible for the ship to remain afloat with all four of the forward compartments flooded, but, critically, the damage extended aft of Bulkhead D and into boiler room 6. All of a sudden, Thomas Andrews' calculations were focused not so much on how low in the water the bow might sink, but rather on how long the ship would last.

For all the ongoing calculations that night, undoubtedly the worst was saved until last. In May 1911, Alexander Carlisle's recommendations for additional lifeboat capacity in the larger vessels had been rejected

ABOVE: *Edward Wilding's testimony at Lord Mersey's enquiry would accurately sum up the nature of the fatal damage to the* Titanic: *'I cannot believe that the wound was absolutely continuous the whole way. I believe that it was a series of steps; that before the ship finally cleared the iceberg, as the helm was put over, she would be tending to swing her side into the iceberg.'*

by the Board of Trade's Life-Saving Appliances Sub-Committee, and the consequence of this lack of foresight was something with which Captain Smith now had to contend. At his disposal was a total of 14 rigid and four Engelhardt collapsible lifeboats, along with the two emergency cutters, but while this number was more than enough to meet the regulations – and indeed exceed them – it was wholly insufficient for the 2,201 passengers and crew on board that night, never mind the 3,547 who might have been aboard had the ship been filled to capacity. If Andrews' calculations were to be believed then the *Titanic* had barely two hours to live when at five minutes after midnight, almost half an hour after the collision, Captain Smith gave the order to uncover the boats. Bad though the situation was, it could have been

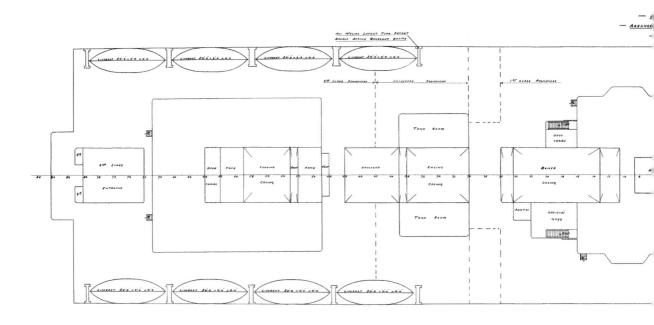

ABOVE: *The layout of the boat deck on the* Titanic *and the all-too-apparent lack of lifeboats resulting from the Board of Trade's failure to update the 1894 regulations.*

BELOW: *The* Titanic's *Marconi and silent rooms, where wireless operators Phillips and Bride worked into the early hours of Sunday morning to repair the faulty transformer.*

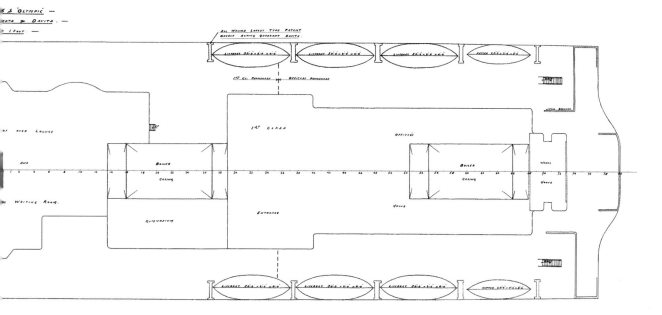

worse. But for the wireless repairs carried out the previous evening by Phillips and Bride, the ship may well have been incapable of calling for aid, but at 12.15am on Monday 15 April – 35 minutes after the collision – Phillips began to transmit the CQD distress signal in a desperate attempt to call for the help of any nearby vessels.

The unsinkability myth also seemed to be working against the crew in their attempt to lower the lifeboats. Although mortally wounded, the *Titanic*'s condition had, to all intents and purposes, seemed to stabilise. The initial scale of the flooding had initiated a noticeable dip in the ship's forward trim, but as the water level inside the hull continued to rise, the reduction in the head of water gave the understandable impression that the ship had not only stabilised, but that she was not in any immediate danger. Even in a sinking condition the *Titanic*, still with electric power and heating, seemed to be a safer option than a flimsy lifeboat, but the result of this overconfidence

meant that many of the early lifeboats would be sent away carrying only a fraction of their capacity. Even then the pace was slow. It was not until 12.40am that First Officer Murdoch finally lowered lifeboat 7 on the starboard side, the first to be sent away. The lifeboat itself had space for 65 people, yet it contained only 28, including American film actress Dorothy Gibson, Connecticut banker William Sloper, and Margaret Hays, who carried her Pomeranian dog with her. Thirteen minutes later Murdoch ordered Third Officer Pitman to take charge of lifeboat 5, once again with a capacity for 65 but holding only 36. Murdoch's third boat, number 3, contained only 32 occupants, by which time nearly 100 spaces had already been lost.

On the port side, it was little different. Murdoch had interpreted the captain's orders of women and children first to mean just that, but giving space to men if there were any women unwilling to go. Lightoller, on the other hand, interpreted the order more literally, allowing no men into the boats save for the required

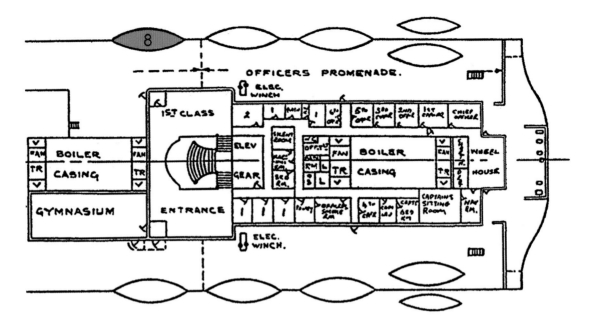

The following labels appear within the deck plan diagram:

8

OFFICERS PROMENADE.

ELEC. WINCH

1ST CLASS

BOILER   FAN   BOILER

FAN

CASING   TR   TR   CASING

GYMNASIUM   ENTRANCE

ELEV

GEAR

WHEEL HOUSE

CAPTAINS SITTING Room

ELEC. WINCH.

ABOVE: *Lifeboat no 8 was the first to be lowered on the port side. Among the passengers would be the Countess of Rothes, who Seaman Thomas Jones would later describe as '...more of a man than any we had on board.'*

number of seamen to man them safely. Some have described Lightoller's lack of imagination as a major contributory factor in dozens if not hundreds of unnecessary deaths, yet at the American inquiry seaman Thomas Jones recalled Captain Smith's more direct influence in the lowering of lifeboat 8, the first to be lowered on the port side at 1am:

'The captain asked me was the plug in the boat, and I answered, "Yes, sir." "All right," he said, "Any more ladies?" There was one lady came there and left her husband. She wanted her husband to go with her, but he backed away, and the captain shouted again – in fact, twice again – "Any more ladies?" There were no more there, and he lowered away.'

The man who Jones saw back away was almost certainly Isidor Straus, the 67-year-old owner of the American department store Macy's. After seeing his wife and her maid safely into the lifeboat, Isidor had refused to go before the other men, at which point his wife, Ida, also stepped back at the last minute to remain on board with her husband. Jones estimated that his boat had contained 35 ladies, with two sailors and two stewards to man them. This still left space for another 25 occupants, yet when asked by Senator Francis Newlands at the American inquiry into the disaster as to why they had not taken more on board, he replied, 'I don't know, sir. There were no more women to come in, they would not leave.'

At about the same time that lifeboat 8 was being lowered, the lowering of emergency boat 1 on the starboard side at 1.05am would provide one of the most controversial moments of the evening. In a boat capable of holding 40, only 12 occupants would be aboard, of which only two were women: Lucile, Lady Duff Gordon and her secretary, Laura Francatelli. Murdoch's flexibility in allowing men into the lifeboats when there were no women also enabled Sir Cosmo Duff Gordon to join his wife, along with two more passengers and an additional five firemen, before the boat was lowered over the side. Then again, although many of the boats had originally been lowered half empty, the intention had still been for them to take on additional passengers from the open gangway doors in the hull, the only problem with this plan being that once the lifeboats were in the water, fearing the suction they had instead moved away from the ship.

As the deck officers struggled to instil a sense of urgency in the passengers, in the radio room Jack Phillips was initially having little success. Just over the horizon, Cyril Furmston-Evans had gone off duty on the *Californian*, while the *Frankfurt*'s operator seemed not to understand the call for assistance. The *Mount Temple* was at least able to receive the *Titanic*'s CQD but could get no further response, and it was only by the greatest of good fortune that Harold Cottam, the wireless operator on the Cunard liner *Carpathia*, cut in to ask Phillips if he was aware of a growing number of messages coming through from Cape Cod for the *Titanic*. Seconds later, he received his response: 'Struck a berg; come at once!' The *Carpathia*'s skipper, Captain Arthur Rostron, later recalled Cottam being in his cabin at the time, simply listening as he was undressing at the end of a long day, when the *Titanic*'s CQD came in, but either way Cottam's intervention would turn out to be a game changer. Immediately rousing his sleeping captain, within minutes the *Carpathia*

was headed north-west, squeezing every ounce of pressure out of the ship's engines as she rushed towards Fourth Officer Boxhall's CQD position. Rostron called out an additional watch of firemen to maintain and even exceed the *Carpathia*'s usual service speed of 14 knots, but with 58 miles to cover there was little chance of the Cunarder being able to reach the *Titanic*'s position in time.

Other ships were also nearby, including a mystery vessel sighted directly ahead at about the same time as Murdoch was lowering his first lifeboat. At the American inquiry, Boxhall would give the approximate distance of this vessel, seemingly steaming towards the *Titanic*, as being about 5 miles, but despite the fact that he claimed to be able to see the vessel's masthead and port running lights, she seemed to get no closer. Using the ship's electric Morse lamp, Boxhall had even attempted to signal her while firing off intermittent rockets, but although she seemed at one stage to be getting closer, when he observed what he took to be the illusive steamer's stern light he instinctively knew it could mean only one thing – she had turned away from the sinking *Titanic*.

Throughout the evacuation, Bruce Ismay had also been assisting where he could to help passengers into the lifeboats, although his over-enthusiastic input was not always appreciated. About an hour after the collision, just as Fifth Officer Harold Lowe was in the process of lowering lifeboat 5, Ismay was shouting frantically 'Lower away, lower away...' while gesturing with his arm in broad circles, seemingly in an attempt to speed up the evacuation. It was too much for Lowe, who

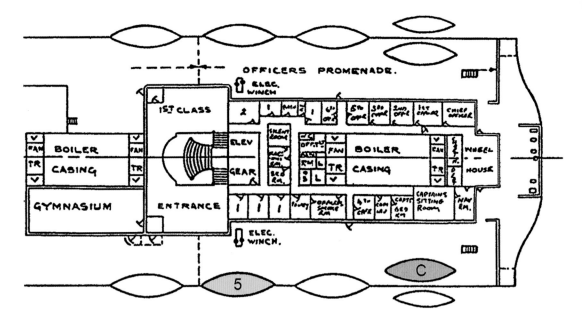

ABOVE: *Lifeboat no 5, where Fifth Officer Lowe would confront Ismay. A little over an hour later the White Star chairman would escape in collapsible C, the last boat to be lowered on the starboard side.*

quickly told him to get the hell out of the way. Clearly, Lowe wasn't about to be intimidated by Ismay, even if he was the chairman of the line: 'Do you want me to lower away quickly? You'll have me drown the whole lot of them!' Without saying another word, the subdued chairman stepped back, returning to assist the passengers of lifeboat 3 as best he could while Lowe continued with the lowering of lifeboat 5.

Throughout the hour or so that Boxhall continued to fire his rockets, the *Titanic* appeared to have steadied herself, so much so that by the time the water in the forward holds and boiler room 6 had reached the level of E deck, the rate of flooding had decreased considerably due to the decreasing differential head across the openings in the side of the ship. As a result of this near equalisation, the speed of the decreasing draught and increasing angle of trim had slowed to an almost imperceptible speed. It would not be until 90 minutes after the collision, with the combination of water flowing over the top of the bulkhead between boiler rooms 6 and 5 and the upward flooding of E deck, that the process would once again start to accelerate, but fortunately there was by that time an increasing sense of urgency on the boat deck. After the relative slowness in getting the first few boats away, by 1am not only was the pace quickening but the number of passengers now willing to take up the number of available spaces was also increasing. Stewardess Violet Jessop, standing by on the aft port-side boat deck, suddenly found herself being shepherded into lifeboat 16 by Sixth Officer James Moody; moments later, he handed a tightly wrapped bundle to Jessop with the cheery words 'Look after this, will you?' Closer inspection revealed a seemingly forgotten baby, saved at the last minute by Moody's actions when, at about 1.30am, lifeboat 16 was lowered into the water.

By 1.50am the last of the rigid boats had been launched, leaving only the four Engelhardt collapsible lifeboats for the more than 1,500 souls still remaining on board. Minutes earlier, boiler room 6 had finally flooded to the point where bulkhead E was no longer high enough to keep the water from flowing over the top and into boiler room 5; from this point onward the *Titanic*'s life could only be counted in minutes rather than hours, as moments later the ship's foredeck slipped beneath the surface.

Ten minutes later the ship's propellers had risen clear of the water, when, as the crew struggled to launch the two collapsible lifeboats from beneath the forward set of davits, one of the great controversies of the night would be played out. The *Titanic*'s boat deck was still as congested as ever, as First Officer Murdoch endeavoured to fill collapsible C, the last remaining lifeboat on the starboard side, calling for any more women passengers. First-class passenger William Carter would later recall that he, Ismay and several officers were also calling for any more women, but with none coming forward one of the officers – most likely Murdoch – said that they could take the place of seamen and get into the boat. Augustus Weikman, the ship's chief barber, later endorsed Carter's version of events, saying that Ismay and Carter were both ordered in as the boat was being lowered and that there were no women in the vicinity. Ismay himself would never refer to any specific order for him to get into the boat, simply saying that there was space and that he got in. His departure, barely 20 minutes before

the *Titanic* sank, may not have been the craven action depicted in the movies or American press, but it would cast a huge shadow over his reputation for the rest of his life, as the chairman who deserted his sinking ship while leaving over 1,500 people to drown.

The last boat to be lowered on the port side, at 2.05am, was collapsible D, after which all that could be done was to release the two Engelhardt collapsible boats (A and B) on the roof above the officers' deckhouse. By this time, however, the forward promenade deck was already submerged, and with the water now flooding up the stairwell to the boat deck, neither Lightoller nor Murdoch had time to hook them up to the davits. It was at this time – about 2.12am – that the *Titanic*'s hull could no longer withstand the stresses building up in the now largely unsupported stern. Lightoller would not recall being aware of the ship actually breaking in two, but a clue to his feeling the start of the process may come in his testimony at the British inquiry into the sinking, when in response to question 14052 he replied, 'Well, she seemed to take a bit of a dive, and I just walked into the water.'

As the water surged along the boat deck, the two remaining Engelhardts were washed clear of the ship. Neither had their canvas sides raised and, to further complicate the situation, collapsible B had also landed on the boat deck upside down, yet they would still provide limited sanctuary for a handful of survivors. Among them would be Lightoller himself, who, after being trapped against the fidley just in front of the forward funnel by the force of the water as it flowed into the air vents,

was blown clear by a rush of air and found himself alongside the upturned collapsible B. Lightoller's situation left him perfectly placed to observe the *Titanic*'s forward deck as the base of funnel 1 crumpled and collapsed on to the forward starboard wing of the bridge, but he would always remain adamant that the *Titanic* did not – could not – break in half. The ship's hull, however, had undeniably given way as the slow build-up of stresses overwhelmed the side plating. For a moment the darkened stern settled back, almost as if it had righted itself and would remain afloat, before slowly sliding

ABOVE: *With the* Titanic *only minutes from sinking, the location of Engelhardt collapsibles A and B on the roof above the officers' deckhouse proved totally unsuitable, with no practical way for the crew to lower them down to the boat deck.*

forward and gradually upending as it began the final plunge, following the now detached forward section of the hull. At 2.20am, 2 hours and 40 minutes after the collision, the *Titanic*'s stern finally disappeared beneath the surface, the White Star's latest and greatest flagship having been in service for only four and a half days.

CHAPTER EIGHT

AFTERMATH

The early hours of the morning of Monday 15 April 1912 found the *Titanic*'s
dazed survivors anxiously scanning the horizon for any signs of rescue. The
only lifeboat to even make an attempt to return and rescue survivors from the
water was number 14, commanded by Fifth Officer Harold Lowe, although
he would succeed in picking up only four survivors, of which one, first-class
passenger William Hoyt, would die from exposure within the hour.

ABOVE: *Captain Arthur Rostron and the officers of the SS* Carpathia, *who raced
fifty miles through the night to rescue over seven hundred* Titanic *survivors.*

ABOVE: *Monday 6 May 1912: Lord Mersey's inquiry adjourns to Southampton to visit the* Olympic.

Ninety minutes after the *Titanic* had gone down, the first of the *Carpathia*'s rockets could be seen to the south-east, and shortly after 4am Captain Rostron ordered the engines stopped as the first of the *Titanic*'s lifeboats – number 2, commanded by Fourth Officer Boxhall – moved alongside and began to offload its passengers. The rescue would take over four hours but by 8.30am lifeboat 12, in the charge of a half-frozen Charles Lightoller, who had spent much of the night knee-deep in near freezing water on the upturned hull of collapsible B, was the final lifeboat to arrive alongside. As soon as the last of the 705 survivors had been taken on board, Rostron made one last search of the area, in the forlorn hope of finding any more survivors, before handing over the task to Captain Stanley Lord of the *Californian*, who had finally arrived at the scene at 8.30am. At 8.50am the *Carpathia* set course for New York, leaving in her wake the 1,502 passengers and crew – over two-thirds of

Titanic's original complement – who had either drowned or died from exposure.

This time, the cruel sea had not distinguished between man and woman, rich or poor. Third class bore the brunt of the losses with only 178 out of 706 being rescued, yet among the 122 first-class passengers who also failed to make it were American millionaires John Jacob Astor, Benjamin Guggenheim, Isidor Straus and George Widener. All the money in the world could not save them that night. Gone too were Captain Smith, Thomas Andrews, William Murdoch, Joseph Bell and, incredibly, his entire complement of engineers, who had stayed below to keep the lights burning right up to the last minute.

With all the key personnel lost with the ship and Pirrie's ongoing recovery from a prostate operation, it fell to Alexander Carlisle, although long retired from Harland & Wolff, and Edward Wilding, Thomas Andrews' successor as chief designer, not only to answer the questions of Lord Mersey's *Titanic* inquiry to the best of their ability but also to salvage the company's reputation, to say nothing of the reputation of British naval architecture as a whole. Certainly, the evidence seems to suggest that they were successful in their aim, Wilding's evidence even acknowledged by Lord Mersey himself as being of great assistance to the inquiry. Perhaps the

BELOW: *Harold Sanderson accompanies Joseph and Julia Bruce Ismay to Lord Mersey's wreck inquiry. Sanderson would later succeed Ismay as president of IMM and chairman of the White Star Line, following his prearranged retirement in June 1913.*

only positive thing that can be said to have come from the *Titanic* disaster is that, in the end, both the British and American inquiries would recommend the most far-reaching reforms in mercantile shipping. By the time they were done, all foreign-going passenger ships would be subject to universally tighter regulations regarding watertight subdivision and lifeboats for all, while more practical arrangements to prevent such an accident from ever happening again, including round-the-clock radio watches, the formation of the International Ice Patrol and the signing of the first Safety of Life at Sea convention in January 1914, would all be directly attributable to the tragic sequence of events that had overtaken the *Titanic*.

But all that lay in the future. Of more immediate concern to the White Star Line was the fact that the Achilles heel of the Olympic class design had been laid bare by the loss of the *Titanic*; if the *Olympic* and *Britannic* were to have any future then Harland & Wolff would quite literally need to go back to the drawing board. It would begin on Thursday 10 October 1912, when the *Olympic* duly arrived back at Belfast to undergo a major reconstruction of her interior that would take the better part of six months to complete. Bearing in mind that the ship had been in service for barely 16 months, such an extensive reconstruction was far from routine, but in truth the preceding six months had, especially in the *Olympic*'s case, been extraordinary to say the least. To be fair, it was not just the White Star Line who had a problem. The sinking of the *Titanic* had been an unmistakeable wake-up call for the entire shipping industry to the fact that the safety regulations had failed utterly to keep pace with the huge leaps in technology that had culminated in the creation of the latest generation of vessels.

The fate of the *Titanic* had well and truly shattered the era of Edwardian self-confidence, and although the *Olympic* had safely completed a further six voyages following the loss of her sister ship, it would only be a matter of time before those deficiencies needed to be put right. Indeed, the loss of the *Titanic* had so unnerved the travelling public that demand for cabins on board the *Olympic* had suddenly plummeted, so even before Senator Smith and Lord Mersey had highlighted the need for universal lifeboat capacity, the White Star Line had already realised that the court of public opinion would also expect no less. Within days of the sinking, the shipping companies had set about increasing the deficient number of lifeboats on their vessels, but for the White Star Line the matter would become an even greater priority, not just because of what had happened to the *Titanic*, but also because the *Olympic* was soon to be back in the headlines herself, and for all the wrong reasons.

The first indications of a problem occurred on Wednesday 24 April. The *Olympic* had returned three days earlier to her Southampton terminal, where Captain Benjamin Steele, White Star's marine superintendent at Southampton, immediately set about embarking an additional 40 Berthon collapsible lifeboats to ensure that there was enough lifeboat capacity for everyone on board. The work was being closely monitored on behalf of the Board of Trade by Captain Maurice Clarke, the man who two weeks

earlier had cleared the *Titanic* to sail, when a message arrived from the White Star offices at Liverpool saying that only 24 additional boats would be necessary for the coming voyage. Work immediately began on landing the surplus boats, which were urgently needed for other vessels anyway, but even as the boats were being taken ashore, rumours were beginning to circulate that they were being landed because they had not been passed as fit for use. By the morning of departure, the required number of additional boats had been secured and covered, additional temporary wire falls had been installed and additional deckhands had also been signed on to ensure that there would be enough men to handle them in the event of another emergency.

Aware of his additional workload for the day, Captain Clarke had even boarded the *Olympic* at 7am for his final inspection of the new arrangements, as he continued to put the crew through their paces. By the time he was done, Clarke was quite satisfied with the new boat arrangements, estimating that it took an average of only 12½ minutes to lower each boat; at 11.50am, ten minutes before the ship's scheduled departure time, he was just handing the certificate of clearance to Captain Haddock when word reached the bridge that the stokehold crew were deserting the ship. The *Olympic*, it appeared, was going nowhere.

The reason for the mass desertion quickly became apparent. Quite simply, the stokehold crew lacked confidence in the additional boats, but even though Clarke assured them that they were completely safe, the men obstinately refused to return on board unless the company replaced the collapsibles with rigid lifeboats. With such an impossible demand, White Star could only postpone the ship's departure until a replacement stokehold crew could be mustered, so while Second Engineer Charles McKean remained ashore to muster a new crew, the *Olympic* – supposedly to vacate the berth, but more likely to make any further desertions impossible – moved to a safe anchorage off Spithead.

Dawn on 25 April found the *Olympic* still anchored in the Solent. To pass the time, Captain Clarke, who had remained on board in order to be able to give the ship clearance to sail as soon as the replacement crew was embarked, continued to exercise the deckhands at their lifeboat stations, although the efficiency of the previous day seemed to have deteriorated noticeably, Clarke noting that it took nearly two hours to uncover and lower only a few boats. But for the passengers beginning to come up on deck at around 8am the activity might have continued for longer, but Clarke decided to suspend the exercise so that no one would be alarmed. Later in the morning, a union delegation arrived on board to negotiate a settlement to the dispute, during which time six of the collapsible boats were lowered into the water. When examined after two hours, five were seen to be totally dry inside, while the sixth contained a small amount of water. Closer inspection revealed a tiny hole in the side, but even then the two hours' leakage was easily bailed out in less than three minutes, at which point the delegates retired to the captain's cabin, agreeing that if the faulty boat was replaced then they would advise their members that the lifeboats were safe.

It was not until 10pm that the tender arrived alongside, carrying a total of 168 replacement stokehold crew and a number of additional men in order for the ship to be run at a faster speed than normal to make up for some of the time that had been lost. However, just before midnight, as Captain Haddock was preparing to take his ship to sea again, another message arrived on the bridge advising him that his crew was once again deserting. This time the problem wasn't so much a lack of faith in the new boats but rather a lack of faith in the new stokehold crew. Fifty-three men of the deck department were suddenly refusing to sail with the ship, believing the replacement crew to be either 'the dregs of Portsmouth' or firemen who were not experienced in the running of a large ship. Despite their evident sympathy for Captain Haddock, the deserting seamen twice refused his orders to return on board. One seaman, named Lewis, even admitted that the actions of the firemen at Southampton had been 'a dirty low down trick', but as their replacements were not fit to be aboard it would be unsafe to put to sea. With no prospect of any resolution, Haddock signalled to the commander of the cruiser HMS *Cochrane*, lying half a mile away off Spithead: 'Crew deserting ship, request your assistance, Haddock, Master.'

Before long, Captain William Goodenough RN had boarded the *Olympic* to help mediate in the dispute, but he would have no more success than Haddock. Several of the men remained dissatisfied with the new boats, while the majority stood by their belief that the new stokehold crew not only lacked experience but were not even union members. Perhaps it was this last point that was the real crux of the matter, as Goodenough later reported that the deserting seamen seemed to be more afraid of their union than any possible repercussions from their actions. Even a potential charge of mutiny failed to influence the men, and as nobody had been hurt or threatened – in fact, the men had shown every respect for the two officers – any use of force could not be justified. And so the dispute continued into a third day. At 11am, the tender once again returned alongside, this time carrying another 30 additional deck crew, but as the hours continued to tick by it was looking increasingly unlikely that the ship would ever leave port. Sure enough, at 3pm the news arrived from the White Star head office

that the voyage had been cancelled altogether. The *Olympic* duly returned to disembark her passengers at Southampton, where she would remain until her next scheduled voyage on 15 May.

The mutiny was over, but for the White Star Line it could not be an end to the matter. One week later, on 30 April, the 53 seamen who had deserted the *Olympic* after she had sailed from Southampton found themselves at the Portsmouth Police Court, charged with '...wilful disobedience to the lawful commands

BELOW: *The* Olympic, *having returned to her berth at Southampton after the mutiny of April 1912.*

of Captain Haddock, the Master of the steamship *Olympic*, contrary to section 225 of the Merchant Shipping Act, 1894'. The union's defence hinged on Article 458 of the same Act, alleging that the White Star Line was legally bound to ensure the seaworthiness of their ships, and that by allowing the *Olympic* to sail with an incompetent crew it almost amounted to rendering her as unseaworthy as if she had a hole in her hull. To dispute this argument, Norman Raebarn, acting for the White Star Line, called upon Captain Benjamin Steele to testify that the lifesaving equipment on board was adequate, while Captain Clarke was called to confirm that he had passed the boats as seaworthy, with an adequate number of seamen to handle them. As for the competence of the replacement stokehold crew, Second Engineer Charles McKean acknowledged that while many of the replacements lacked experience, he did not particularly consider the job of fireman to be skilled labour, although he did admit, much to the amusement of the court, that it was hard work. On 5 May the judge delivered his verdict, not surprisingly in favour of the White Star Line, but in summing up he concluded that it would be inappropriate to fine or imprison the mutineers as they had probably been 'unnerved' by the *Titanic* disaster.

If nothing else, White Star had at least gone some way to restoring their reputation, albeit at the cost of a small legal case and an additional £16 payment to the Board of Trade for the three days that Captain Clarke had to spend on the ship, but even then the issue was not quite forgotten. On 14 May, George Terrell MP tabled a question in Parliament, enquiring what

ABOVE: *Captain Haddock leaves the Portsmouth Police Court, after giving evidence at the* Olympic *mutiny case.*

action was to be taken against the officials of the British Seafarers' Union who had prevented the departure of the *Olympic* and consequently delayed His Majesty's Mails. The Board of Trade, however, also felt it best to let sleeping dogs lie, conceding that as a result of the Portsmouth court case, no additional prosecutions would be worthwhile.

The next seven voyages were mercifully uneventful, save for the unfortunate death on 20 September of third-class passenger Isaac Guttenberg from overloading his already diseased stomach with food, but on 10 October 1912, with the summer season drawing to a

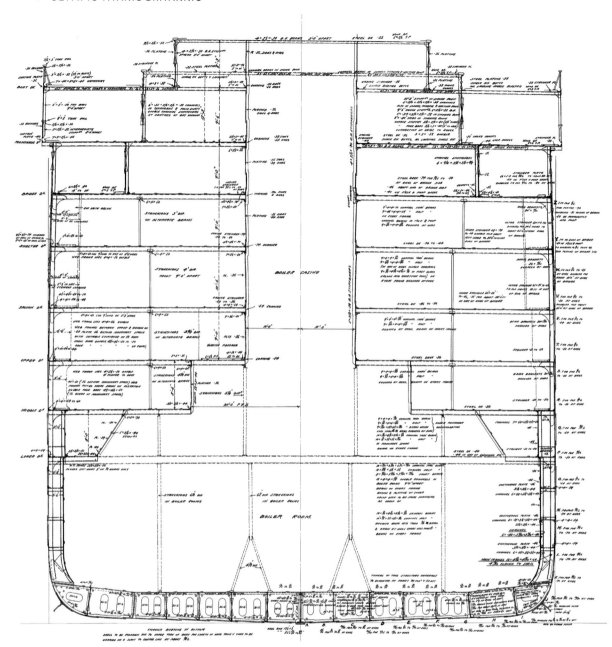

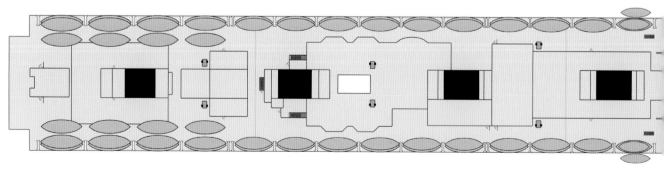

close, the *Olympic* arrived back at Belfast. The revised lifeboat arrangements had always been regarded as a temporary fix at best, but if public confidence in the ship was to be fully restored then a complete rebuild would be necessary. In actual fact, Harland & Wolff had been wrestling for weeks with a list of what needed to be done, which on closer examination extended well beyond the need for additional lifeboats and higher watertight bulkheads. By the time they had completed the work, not only would the rebuilt *Olympic* incorporate a new watertight inner skin, but considerable work had also been carried out to strengthen and stiffen the hull itself. Francis Carruthers would later record the structural modifications in considerable detail:

'An alteration has been made in the structure of this vessel by fitting an inner skin extending over the boiler and machinery spaces, from the forward end of the permanent bunker to the after end of the turbine engine room.

• No. 1 (collision) bulkhead has been carried up water-tight to the forecastle deck.

• No. 4, 6, 10 and 13, counting from forward, have been carried up W.T. to bridge deck and a new bulkhead has been fitted between No. 12 and 13 to level of upper deck, where it joins No. 13... On account of the increased height of the 5 bulkheads mentioned, the W.T. doors on these bulkheads have been removed and stronger W.T. doors fitted. The following additional stiffening has also been fitted to the bulkheads:–

• No. 1. Collision Bulkhead 134 forward. Hold 3½" x 3½" x ½" angles on existing channels.

• Orlop to Upper. 5" x 3" x .56" angle reverse bar making 8" girder.

• Upper to Saloon. 5" x 3½" x .44" reverse on existing stiffeners.

• Saloon to Shelter. 5½" x 3½" x .42" bulb angles.

• Shelter to Foc'sle Head. 4" x 2½" x .32" bulb angles.

• No. 4 bulkhead No. 78 forward. Mid to Upper 4" x 3" x .38" reverse bar on existing stiffeners.

• No. 10 bulkhead No. 30 aft. Below Lower Deck 9" x ⅝" plate riveted to face of webs from top to bottom.

• Mid to Upper. 4" x 3" x .38" reverse bar to existing stiffeners.

• Upper to Saloon. Continuous bar – casing 5" x 2½" x .38". Outside casing 4" x 3" x .38" reverse to existing stiffeners.

• No. 16. Aft Peak. No. 139 aft. Lower to Middle Deck. 3½" x 3" x .38" reverse bars to existing stiffeners.

• Middle to Upper. 4" x 3" x .38" reverse bars to existing stiffeners.

• Upper to Saloon. 5" x 3½" x .44" reverse bars to existing stiffeners.'

TOP LEFT: *Midship section of the* Olympic*'s modified hull after her 1912/13 refit.*

LEFT: *The* Olympic*'s modified lifeboat arrangements following the loss of the* Titanic *resulted in much of the original first-class promenade space being lost.*

— T.S.S. "OLYMPIC" —

PLAN SHEWING ARRANGEMENT OF BOAT STANDS.

SCALE ½ = 1 FOOT.

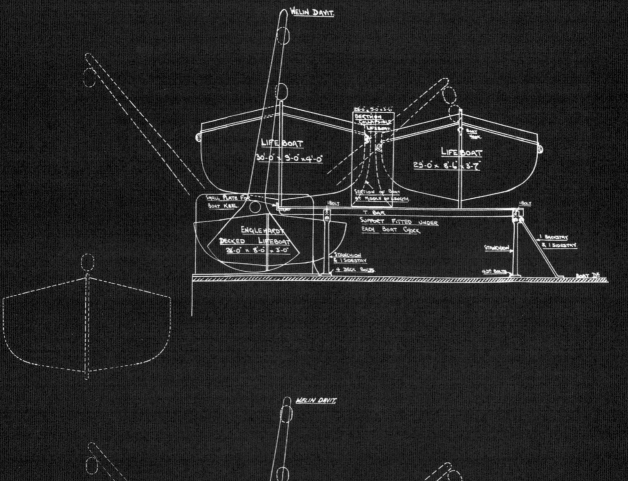

WELIN DAVIT.

LIFEBOAT
30·0" × 9·0" × 4·0"

25·0 × 5·0 × 3·6
BERTHON
COLLAPSIBLE
LIFEBOAT.

SECTION OF BOAT
AT MIDDLE OF LENGTH.

LIFEBOAT
29·0 × 8·6 × 3·7

BOAT HOOK

SMALL PLATE FOR
BOAT KEEL.

1 BOLT

1 BOLT

ENGLEHARDT
DECKED LIFEBOAT
25·0" × 8·0" × 3·0"

T BAR
SUPPORT FITTED UNDER
EACH BOAT CHOCK

1 BACKSTAY
& 1 SIDESTAY

STANCHION

STANCHION
& 1 SIDESTAY
4 DECK BOLTS

4 ⅛" BOLTS

BOAT DK

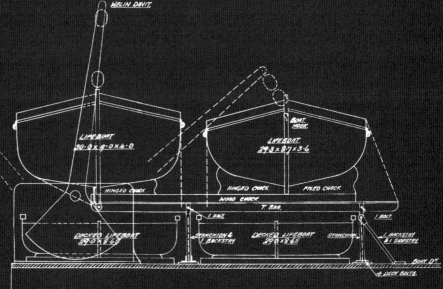

WELIN DAVIT.

LIFEBOAT
30·0 × 9·0 × 4·0

LIFEBOAT
29·3 × 8·7 × 3·6

BOAT
HOOK

HINGED CHOCK

HINGED CHOCK

FIXED CHOCK

WOOD CHOCK

T. BAR.

1 BOLT

1 BOLT

DECKED LIFEBOAT
25·0 × 8·6·5

STANCHION &
1 BACKSTAY

DECKED LIFEBOAT
29·0 × 8·6·5

STANCHION

1 BACKSTAY
& 1 SIDESTAY

BOAT DK

4 DECK BOLTS.

S.S. "OLYMPIC"

PLAN SHEWING ARRANGEMENT OF
BOAT STANDS.

SCALE:- ½" = ONE FT.

16.11.10.

DRG: 46.S.

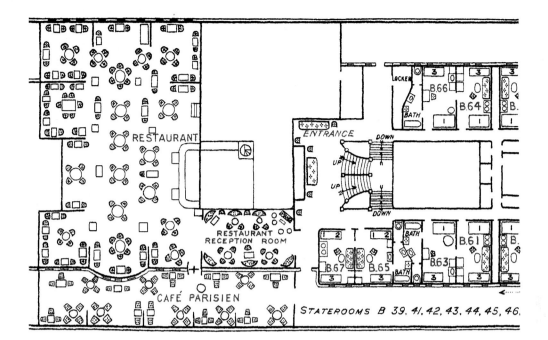

ABOVE: *The 1913* Olympic's *enlarged B deck à la carte restaurant and new Café Parisien, which had proved so popular on the* Titanic.

LEFT: *Detail of the* Olympic's *revised aft davit stands, designed to serve three or four lifeboats.*

Outwardly, the most noticeable modification was the 28 sets of davits – 14 along each side of the boat deck – which all told would be capable of serving 68 boats, with a capacity for 3,500 people. The lessons of the *Titanic* had been learned at a terrible cost, but at least Carlisle's foresight in installing the Welin double-acting davits would finally prove its worth. Even then, not all the modifications would relate to the safety of the ship, with Harland & Wolff also taking the opportunity to install additional first-class cabins on the boat deck, although no attempt was made to modify the arrangement of the *Olympic*'s B deck staterooms to bring them in line with the layout in the *Titanic*. Certainly, it would have been possible, but the additional

lifeboats on the boat deck had resulted in the loss of much of the previously open deck space, so that the *Olympic*'s previously superfluous B deck promenade now appeared that much more attractive. Even so, to increase the ship's earning capacity, the à la carte restaurant was extended out to the port side of the ship, with a new Café Parisien on the starboard side to match the layout in the *Titanic*.

The task of retrofitting the *Olympic* through the winter of 1912/13 would be enormous, but by 22 March 1913 the ship was once again ready to depart for Southampton, where for the last six months the White Star express service to New York had been maintained by the *Oceanic*, *Majestic* and *Adriatic*. The timing could not have been better when on 2 April – the start of the intermediate season and coincidentally exactly a year to the day since the *Titanic* was delivered – the new *Olympic* finally departed on what would be her 18th crossing to New York.

CHAPTER NINE

IMPROVING ON PERFECTION

The contract to proceed with the construction of the *Britannic* had been confirmed on 23 October 1911, but six days prior to that date a table of particulars prepared for Lord Pirrie indicated that Yard No 433 had already been planned with an increased beam of 93 feet 6 inches. At this stage there was still no talk of any watertight double skin, but structural issues with the *Olympic*'s excessive flexing may well have had an influence on the subsequent decision to increase the beam.

In an ideal world Harland & Wolff might even have gone further, but with the entrance to the graving dock being no wider than 96 feet, short of rebuilding the dock itself there was no possibility of increasing the beam any further. After the *Titanic* had sunk, the options for further strengthening the *Britannic*'s hull were largely achieved through a combination of an increased number of longitudinal beams supporting the double skin, stronger and higher transverse bulkheads, as well as thicker plating in the superstructure. The two ships

BELOW: *The huge 50,000 GRT* Britannic, *compared to the original 5,004 GRT* Britannic *of 1874.*

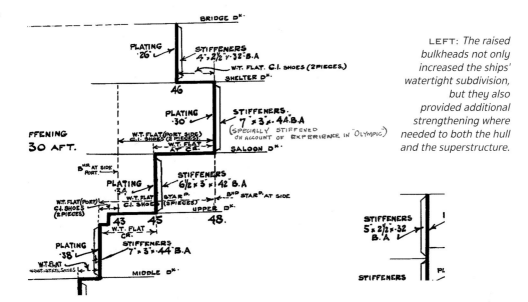

LEFT: *The raised bulkheads not only increased the ships' watertight subdivision, but they also provided additional strengthening where needed to both the hull and the superstructure.*

might still have looked similar, but in terms of structural design the *Titanic* and *Britannic* would be very different.

Legend has it that immediately after the *Titanic* sank, all work was suspended on the *Britannic* while the White Star Line considered whether or not to proceed with her construction at all. It's an interesting fable, but closer analysis of the construction data shows little evidence to support it. At the time the *Titanic* was leaving Belfast, the *Britannic* was already framed to the height of her double bottom, but if you bear in mind that it took 42 weeks from that stage for the *Titanic* to be fully framed, and only three weeks longer for the *Britannic* to reach the same stage, then considering the *Britannic*'s stronger and more elaborate hull it is evident that any delays in her construction were minimal. Even so, while it continued to be business as usual for the shipyard, the *Titanic*'s fate could not fail to have a dramatic impact on the hundreds of designs and technical drawings from which the *Britannic* would ultimately evolve.

In truth, the White Star Line's commercial options were few and far between. Five years on, the original concept of the *Olympic* and *Titanic* being built to compete with Cunard's *Lusitania* and *Mauretania* was already a distant memory. After casting a jealous eye at the new White Star steamers, Cunard had begun to explore the possibilities of constructing their own version, so much so that less than a week after the launch of the *Titanic* the first keel plates of the *Aquitania* had already been laid. To further complicate matters, Albert Ballin's Hamburg America Line was planning an even larger trio, with the *Imperator*, *Vaterland* and *Bismarck* each having a projected gross tonnage well in excess of 50,000 tons. Faced with this competition, White Star's option to cancel the third ship – if indeed it ever was an option – was limited to say the least.

Even so, from a commercial point of view the basic template of the Olympic class was undeniably sound, despite what had happened to the *Titanic*. As far as the public spaces were

No. 433, TRIPLE S.S. "BRITANNIC" — handwritten engineering record

ABOVE: *One of the Harland & Wolff engineering records, detailing the decision to increase the* Britannic's *beam almost three months prior to the loss of the* Titanic.

concerned, the *Britannic*'s layout would be near identical to those in the *Olympic* and *Titanic*; in fact, even the most cursory of glances at the general arrangements leaves no doubt that they were indeed sister ships. However, while the public rooms were largely similar, behind all the elaborate wood panelling there were marked differences in the structure. The February 1914 edition of *Engineering* magazine described the *Britannic*'s structure in considerable detail, although in this case all comparisons were with the *Olympic* only, any reference to the *Titanic* being discreetly omitted. At first the comparisons between the two ships seemed reasonably close, with the writer waxing lyrical about the double bottom being carried up above the turn of the bilge, the double bottom at the centreline being increased to 75 inches beneath the machinery space, the thickness of the keel, the web frames, the intercostal members... All of this techno-babble could have

been cut and pasted from previous technical specifications published when the *Olympic* entered service, but from the tank top upwards the *Britannic* provided the journalists with an altogether different emphasis.

It had taken six months to install the *Olympic*'s double skin, which, considering the limited available space, would probably have been a Herculean task for the Harland & Wolff workforce, whereas in the *Britannic*'s case the additional skin could be incorporated into the hull more easily during the actual construction. As a result, the *Britannic*'s framing and longitudinal reinforcement, although hidden from sight, would be considerably different to the original design. The inner frames comprised 6-inch channels placed at 3-foot intervals, with heavy brackets connecting them to the inner bottom; at intervals of 30 feet there were transverse watertight divisions, secured by 6-inch channel stays, while at certain frames bracket stays had also been fitted to further reinforce the strength of the structure. In conjunction with the transverse watertight bulkheads and a watertight division halfway up the double sides along the entire length of the eight engineering compartments, the cellular subdivision of the *Britannic*'s flanks was particularly complete. Concerns about the practicalities of inspecting and maintaining the internal spaces were dealt with by fitting manhole doors to the inner wall but, crucially, the writer also acknowledged that the double-

skin construction would not only keep water from entering the ship in the event of the outer hull being damaged, but that it would also add enormously to the strength of the structure due to the extent of the stiffening members between the double skin.

To further increase the *Britannic*'s watertight subdivision, as well as providing additional stiffening further aft, an additional bulkhead was installed dividing the electric engine room into two compartments. As a result, 16 transverse bulkheads would divide

BELOW: *The rebuilt sides of the 1913* Olympic, *already very different to the original 1908 design, were further strengthened in the* Britannic.

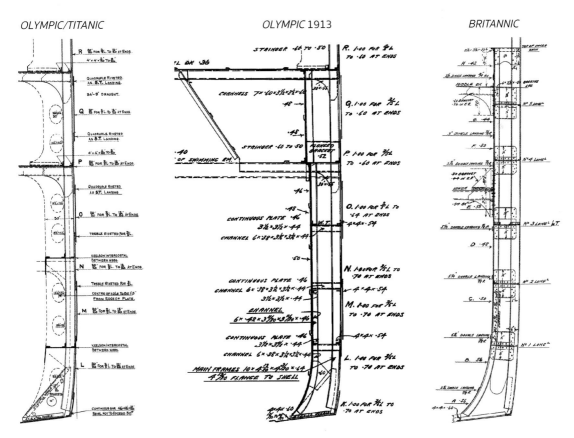

OLYMPIC/TITANIC   OLYMPIC 1913   BRITANNIC

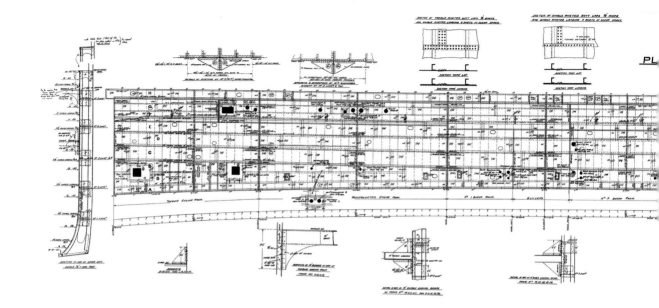

the *Britannic* into 17 watertight compartments, with five of these bulkheads extending to the level of the bridge deck, 76 feet above the keel and 40 feet above the load line. The remaining 11 bulkheads extended to at least the upper deck, which was still over 21 feet above the load line.

Inside the eight boiler and engine room compartments, the layout was equally familiar. The diameters of the main reciprocating engine cylinders were identical to those in the *Olympic*, although in the case of the *Britannic* they were all fitted with piston valves as opposed to the *Olympic*'s low-pressure cylinders, which had flat slide valves with relief rings at the back. This modification was incorporated because of the enhanced pressure in the low-pressure chest, as it was intended to develop a higher power and to exhaust into the ship's larger and more powerful turbine at a slightly increased pressure – about 10 lb absolute. As in the case of her sisters, the *Britannic*'s turbine was of

ABOVE: *The* Britannic*'s watertight inner skin extended 30 inches inside the outer shell, up the sides of the ship to a height of 6 feet 6 inches above the load line and, longitudinally, from the after end of the turbine engine room to the forward end of boiler room no 6.*

the Parsons' exhaust type, but the design was considerably different to the turbine in the two earlier ships, with the much larger bladed rotor weighing 150 tons. With an overall length of about 50 feet and when complete weighing in at 490 tons, although its 18,000 shaft horsepower meant that it was by no means the most powerful marine exhaust turbine afloat, it was undeniably the largest.

All this engineering was largely hidden from the prying eyes of the public, but the one essential safety feature that could not be missed was the innovative arrangement of the lifeboats. The lessons regarding the woeful lack of lifeboats on the *Titanic* had been acted upon long before the findings of the British

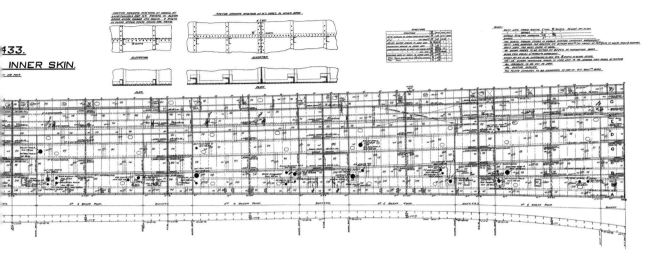

433.
INNER SKIN.

BELOW: *The Britannic's wing propellers each had a diameter of 23 feet 9 inches, and consisted of three manganese-bronze blades bolted to a cast-steel boss. The screws were designed to run at 77 revolutions per minute when the two engines were indicating collectively 32,000 horsepower. Interestingly this original elevation for the Britannic shows that by 1912/13 Harland & Wolff were already experimenting with the propeller configuration, with a triple-bladed central turbine screw hidden in plain sight.*

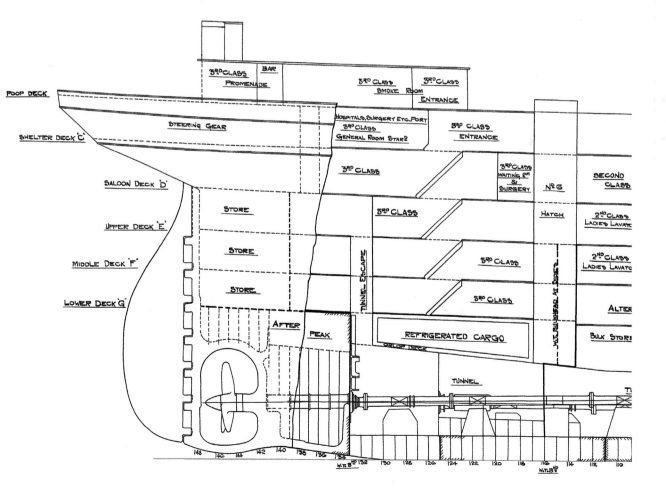

and American *Titanic* inquiries were published, and certainly no one looking at the *Britannic*'s modified profile could ever accuse the White Star Line of not taking the matter seriously. Several general arrangement drawings exist regarding the number of boats planned for the *Britannic*, but although the number was never finally settled upon, *Engineering* magazine confidently announced that 48 wooden boats would be carried on the *Britannic*. This may seem small compared to the 62 boats in the rebuilt *Olympic*, but at 34 feet long and 10 feet wide, the *Britannic*'s lifeboats would be the largest on any liner.

The mode of launching would also be unique; in fact, nothing like it had ever been seen before. The eight sets of electrically driven davits were of a huge lattice-girder construction, each pair mounted like shear-legs on horizontal pivots and designed to move simultaneously through a considerable angle on each side of the vertical line. Aside from it being possible to lower the boats at a greater distance from the ship – a particular advantage on the high side if the ship is heeling over at a considerable angle – the lifeboats were also stacked in strategically placed tiers across the boat deck, which even allowed for some of the boats that were not stacked abreast of the funnels to be transferred from one side of the ship to the other. The *Britannic*'s superstructure would need to undergo considerable strengthening just to support the additional weight of the six sets of girder davits positioned on the boat deck, but the modification, if perhaps unsightly, would at least result in the boat deck retaining much of its open space.

THE *BRITANNIC*'S SPECIFICATION BOOK

The intriguing thing about the *Britannic* specification book, when compared to the *Olympic* and *Titanic*, is that the alterations to the internal arrangement of the public spaces seem reasonably minimal. Clearly the basic template conceived in the *Olympic* and fine-tuned in the *Titanic* was working well, but if the *Britannic* was to compete with the *Aquitania* and the three HAPAG leviathans then the design would still need some refinement.

Inevitably, the majority of the effort and expenditure would be concentrated in the first-class areas. Starting with the forward main entrance, the first thing the White Star Line chose to do was to improve the lifts. In the *Olympic* and *Titanic* the three forward lift shafts extended from the promenade deck (A) to the bottom of the grand staircase on the upper deck (E), whereas in the *Britannic* all three lifts would be extended upwards to facilitate access to the boat deck; to make it easier for first-class passengers in cabins amidships, an additional lift was installed between the third and fourth funnel casings, running up

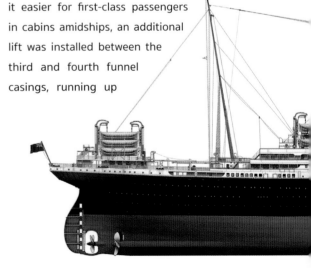

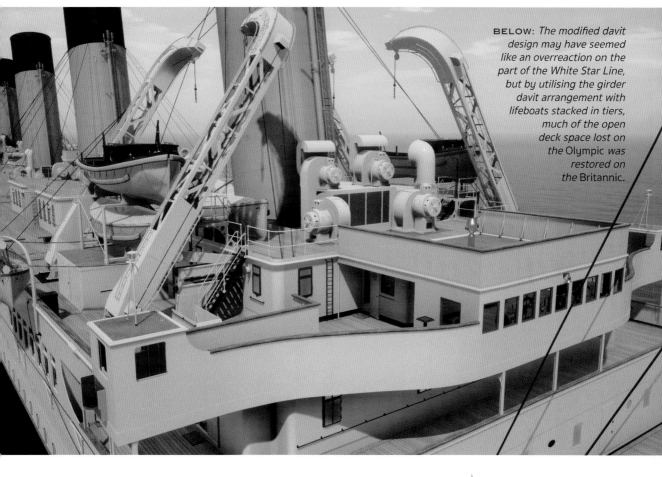

BELOW: *The modified davit design may have seemed like an overreaction on the part of the White Star Line, but by utilising the girder davit arrangement with lifeboats stacked in tiers, much of the open deck space lost on the* Olympic *was restored on the* Britannic.

BELOW: *Starboard profile of the RMS* Britannic, *in her intended White Star colour scheme for commercial service on the North Atlantic.*

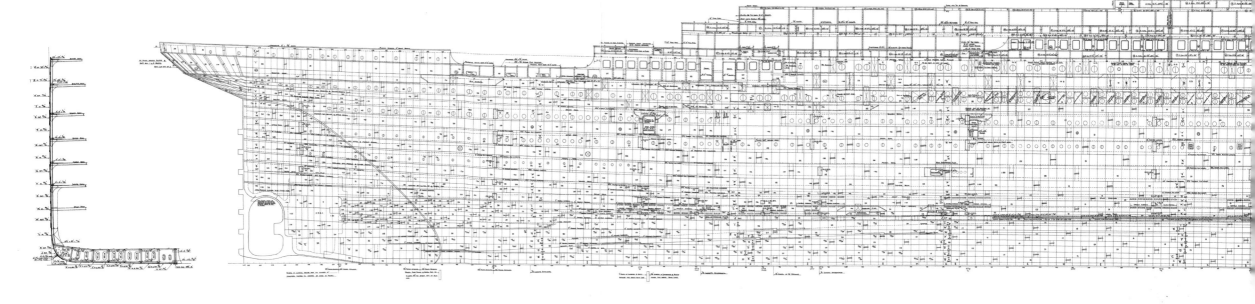

SS "OLYMPIC"
SHELL PLATING PLAN

Nº 433.

PLATING AND STIFFENING OF W.T. BULKHEADS.

SCALE ⅛" = ONE FOOT.

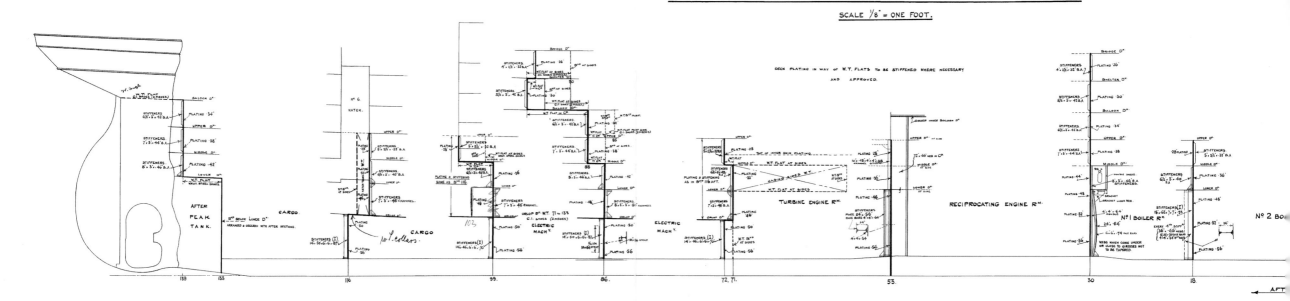

DECK PLATING IN WAY OF W.T. FLATS TO BE STIFFENED WHERE NECESSARY AND APPROVED.

AFTER PEAK TANK.

CARGO

Nº 6 HATCH.

TURBINE ENGINE Rᵐ.

RECIPROCATING ENGINE Rᵐ.

Nº I BOILER Rᵐ.

Nº 2 BOILER

ELECTRIC MACHᵞ.

ELECTRIC MACHᵞ.

◄ AFT

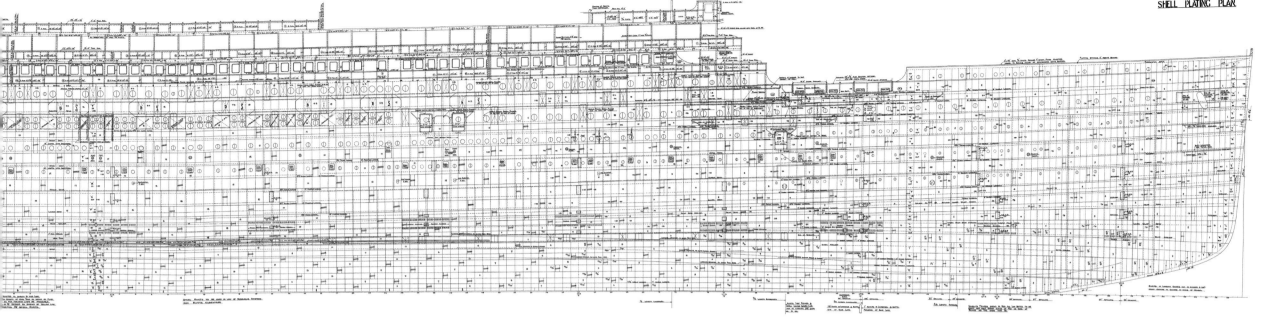

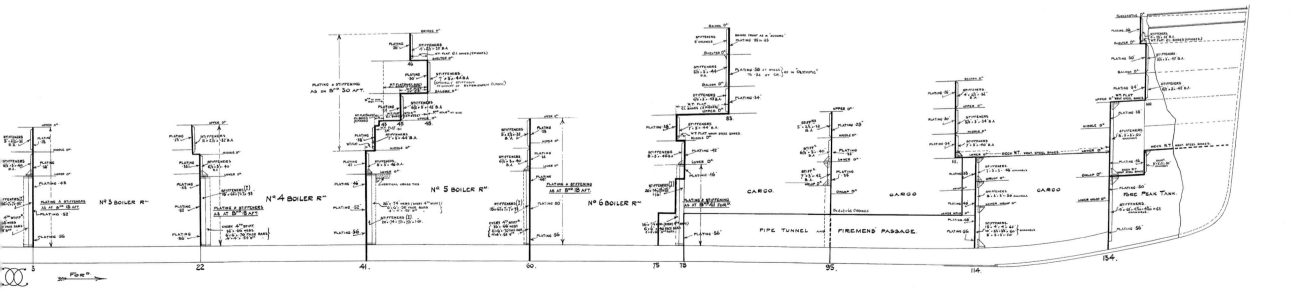

(7)   The sitting room on P side next forward 1st Entrance to be Louis XIV style in Oak, that on the S side to be Régence similar to s.s. 401.   The sitting rooms at fore end No.2 Boiler casing to be Georgian style painted white.

ABOVE: *References to the* Olympic *crop up several times in the* Britannic's *specification book, but the* Titanic *is referenced only once. Even then the ship was acknowledged only by her yard number; the mere mention of the name* Titanic *had become taboo in the shipyard.*

LEFT: *The size of the gantry davits made it possible for some of the lifeboats to be transferred from one side of the ship to another if an excessive list made it impossible to lower them on the higher side.*

BOTTOM LEFT: *The* Britannic's *aft well deck would be enclosed, resulting in a major external difference to the original design. At the B deck level second- and third-class would each gain additional open deck space, beneath which third-class would have their own covered promenade and a gymnasium for the second-class passengers.*

to the level of the promenade deck. On the port side of the boat deck, where there had been only open space in the *Olympic* and *Titanic*, an additional deckhouse was included in the *Britannic*, effectively mirroring the gymnasium to starboard. In terms of size, the two rooms were identical, but the deckhouse on the port side had an altogether different purpose, serving instead as a playroom for the first-class children.

For the highest paying passengers, White Star continued with the concept of the parlour suites, which had proved so successful in the *Olympic* that the *Titanic*'s two B deck suites had been expanded to incorporate their own private promenade. It was a feature that looked set to continue in the *Britannic*, but while the general

arrangements indicate that the layout of the port-side suite would be practically identical to that in the *Titanic*, questions arise as to the final configuration of the *Britannic*'s starboard suite. Despite the conflicting evidence, however, the specification book does at least describe the layout of the two parlour suites in the most intricate detail:

'*The suite on the port side to consist of two bedrooms and a sitting room, with lavatory accommodation and wardrobe rooms arranged between the bedrooms; the sitting room being at the fore end of the suite next 1st Class Entrance. The after bedroom to be decorated and furnished by H & W, the walls being Oak panelled and the furniture of Oak in French style; this room to contain two cot beds one 6'9 x 2'9" and one 6'6" x 4'3"; a settee with an oval table in front; a two-basin washstand; a 3'0" dressing table with chair; and an electric heater; the floor to be laid with blue carpet. The forward bedroom to have two Brass cot beds of same size as above, the other articles of furniture being as enumerated for the after bedroom, but the decoration of the room and style of furniture to be to approval by A. Heaton & Co. The sitting room by A.H. & Co. to have round table in the centre of the room, with two armchairs and two ordinary chairs, a sideboard, a cabinet, a corner* writing table with chair, two other lounge chairs, a fireplace and an octagonal coffee stool; the panelling, decoration and style of furniture to be to approval. The lavatory accommodation to consist of a bathroom and W.C.; the bathroom containing bath with shower, an open washbasin, a hinged grating seat and electric heater. The floor of the bathroom, W.C. and communicating corridor between the bathrooms to be laid with Lino tiles. A wardrobe room for each bedroom to be arranged with hat and coat hooks and suitable chest of drawers.

The suite on the starboard side to consist of two sets of rooms each comprising bedroom, wardrobe room, bathroom and W.C. Each set to be separately entered from the fore and aft passageway through a vestibule and private athwartship corridor. Between the two sets of rooms a Saloon and Veranda to be arranged each separately communicating with the bedroom of either set of rooms. The Saloon to have a small Pantry at the fore end, and a servant's bedroom to be arranged adjacent to the forward set of rooms, with an entrance from the main fore and aft passageway. Each bedroom to have two cot beds, one 4'6" and one 2'6" wide; a settee with small round table in front; an arm chair, writing table and chair; a combined dressing table

BELOW: *The Britannic's first-class children's playroom was an additional feature to the original design and mirrored the gymnasium on the port side.*

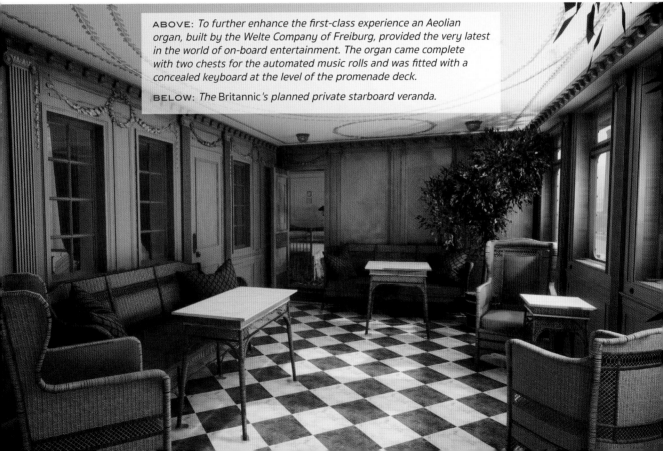

ABOVE: *To further enhance the first-class experience an Aeolian organ, built by the Welte Company of Freiburg, provided the very latest in the world of on-board entertainment. The organ came complete with two chests for the automated music rolls and was fitted with a concealed keyboard at the level of the promenade deck.*

BELOW: *The* Britannic's *planned private starboard veranda.*

and washstand, with chair; an electric heater. The Saloon to have round table in the centre constructed so as to extend for the accommodation of four persons; four chairs to be supplied for the dining table; a sofa bed; four arm chairs; a corner writing table and chair; a small square table and chair; a sideboard, and a fireplace. Bathrooms to contain bath with shower, washbasin and hinged seat. The Veranda to have three settees with small square tables in front, two round backed chairs, two arm chairs, and two small round tables. The servants' rooms to be finished in dark mahogany and fitted with bed having

Pullman over, sofa, wardrobe, folding lavatory, electric heater and a red carpet.'

In terms of on-board facilities, it was also evident that the working arrangement of the *Titanic*'s modified Turkish bath had proved far more amenable than that in the *Olympic*. As a result, the *Britannic*'s Turkish bath largely mirrored that of the *Titanic*, and once again the specification book is able to detail the fixtures and fittings in the most precise detail:

RIGHT: *The* Britannic's *Turkish bath was practically identical to the layout in the* Titanic.

BELOW: *The* Britannic's *B deck parlour suites, with the modified layout on the starboard side.*

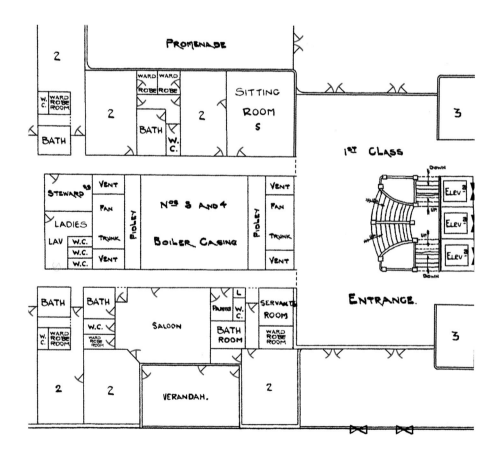

COOLING ROOM

To be fitted with five couches, six canvas chairs, five small square tables, and a weigh chair. To have three dressing boxes at one end, and a small box for valuables. The floor to be covered with Lino tiles on Veitchi. To have two entrance doors, one from the Main Staircase approach, the other from the athwartship passage next to the swimming Bath, each Entrance having a vestibule.

ELECTRIC BATH ROOM

To be fitted with reclining light bath and to have a tiled floor, the wall next the vestibule to have a steel dado with glass panels above having steel astragals.

SHAMPOOING ROOM

The access to be from the fore and aft passage through two curtained doorways. The floor to be tiled and an 8" waterway to be arranged along the fore and aft walls. To be fitted with two marble slabs, two sinks, two showers and drinking fountain.

TEMPERATE ROOM

The walls and ceilings to be lined and the floor insulated. To have six canvas chairs and three couches, and to be screened from the hot room by a curtain.

STEAM ROOM

The access to be from the temperate room through a vestibule with an insulated door, the inner door of the vestibule to be fitted with a 'Blount's' spring. The roof to be insulated with 2" Magnesia. The walls to be lined and the floor insulated.

HOT ROOM

The walls to be lined and the floor insulated; roof to have 2" Magnesia insulation. To be fitted with two canvas chairs and one couch.

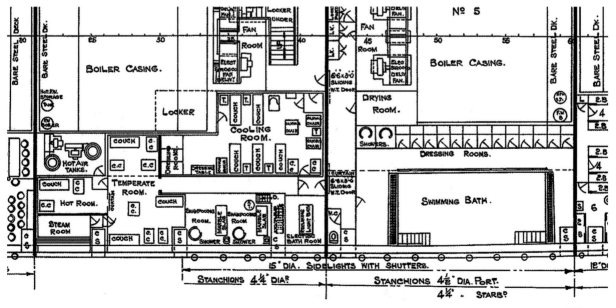

HOT AIR TANKS

A room for these to be arranged on S side of No. 4 Boiler casing and access to be had from the temperate room through a vestibule. The roof and walls to be insulated with 1½" Magnesia.

There was, however, no comparison between the actual swimming baths. The pools in the *Olympic* and *Titanic*, although undeniably popular with the travelling clientele, were on the whole reasonably utilitarian, whereas the pool destined for the *Britannic* would be an altogether more magnificent affair. Gone were the functional tiles and bare metal walls. The flamboyance of the Pompeian-style swimming pool on Hamburg America's SS *Imperator* had

BELOW: *The* Britannic*'s projected Roman swimming bath when completed.*

not gone unnoticed by the White Star Line, and in true commercial fashion they responded in the only way they could. As a result, the *Britannic*'s elaborate Roman-marbled swimming bath provided an appropriately grand riposte to the German ships.

For the less energetic passengers, the *Britannic*'s dining arrangements also differed somewhat when compared to her two sisters. The à la carte restaurant had proved so popular in the *Olympic* that by the time the *Titanic* was entering service the decision had already been taken to expand this particular on-board experience to the port side of the ship. The deckhouse structure had also been expanded to the starboard side of the ship, but while the area had been incorporated into the separate Café Parisien, the *Britannic*'s layout would once again be significantly different. This time there would be no Café Parisien, the à la carte restaurant instead extending across the full width of the bridge deck.

CHAPTER TEN

GOODBYE TO THE OLD WORLD

On the whole, 1913 would be a successful year for the *Olympic* as she quickly regained some of the popularity she had lost following the sinking of the *Titanic*. As the ship quickly settled back into her established routine, Captain Haddock's log once again dealt with the more run-of-the-mill issues that any captain might experience on the North Atlantic ferry, rather than collisions with tugs, armoured cruisers, icebergs and industrial strife.

The first two voyages passed without incident, as indeed did the vast majority of the *Olympic*'s crossings that year, but on the third westbound crossing, two days out of Southampton Robert Cameron was found on board, cowering under a bunk in glory hole 9. With no ticket and little prospect of even being able to pay his way, Cameron had no option but to admit to being a stowaway, although in this case his luck was in when his passage was unexpectedly paid by an unnamed clergyman after the ship arrived at New York on 20 May. Second-class passenger Alexander Rafter was less fortunate when in the early hours of 18 May he died from heart failure after passing out during an attack of acute alcoholism. In line with the practices of the time, as the ship was still two days from New York, Rafter was buried at sea at 11pm that night.

Stowaways and deaths on board may have been routine occurrences in the early 20th century, but it didn't necessarily follow that dying on board ship would automatically consign you to a watery grave. During one eastbound crossing on 7 May 1913, second-class passenger Thomas Hutchings died in the ship's infirmary from acute pulmonary phthisis, better known as pulmonary tuberculosis but often referred to at the time as the 'White Death'. On this occasion, Hutchings was travelling with his cousin, and with the *Olympic* only a day from Plymouth his body was landed the following day. Nor did stowaways always find themselves being automatically handed over to the legal authorities. One particular example can be found in a log entry on 22 January 1914, when shortly after leaving Queenstown Albert Hammond and Thomas Bradley were discovered on board without tickets. Both admitted to being stowaways but, interestingly, on 4 February Hammond would sign on as a trimmer for the return trip from New York. For sheer audacity, however, you almost have to admire the bare-faced cheek of Bradley, who, when reporting to the ship's master-at-arms on 28 January to retrieve some clothing, promptly went below and stowed away a second time.

By the time the *Olympic* returned to Southampton on 20 December, having safely completed another dozen round trips that year, attention was once again starting to turn to Belfast. While the *Olympic* was busy re-establishing her reputation on the North Atlantic, work on the *Britannic* had been quietly progressing, the Harland & Wolff engineering

department recording that the framing had been completed on 27 February 1913 and that the hull was fully plated by 20 September. Compared to the *Olympic*'s construction schedule it was undeniably slower, but if you stop to consider the *Britannic*'s larger and more elaborate hull, combined with the fact that IMM was not giving as much priority to the construction of the *Britannic*, then the additional five months on the slipway are not difficult to justify. Certainly, if you consider that the *Britannic* spent only one month longer on the slipway when compared to the *Titanic*'s

BELOW: *The* Britannic, *ready for launching on slip no 2.*

less hectic construction schedule, it would seem that progress on the third ship was largely unaffected by the *Titanic* disaster.

By 26 February 1914 the *Britannic* was finally ready to take to the water. As was his practice, Lord Pirrie was at the shipyard as early as 5am to oversee the final preparations, before the Belfast Steamship Company's SS *Patriotic* arrived alongside Belfast's York Dock later that morning, carrying the hundreds of officials, guests and members of the press invited by the White Star Line to witness the great event. Way ahead of them, thousands of observers, braving the drizzle and squally conditions, were also assembling along both banks of the Lagan river to see Harland & Wolff's largest ship to date finally take to the water.

Despite the significance of the occasion, once again there was little ceremony on show apart from the customary signal flags and White Star burgee adorning the Arrol Gantry. One of the Queen's Island workers, clearly unimpressed by the lack of ritual, was later moved to observe 'They just builds 'er and shoves 'er in', but for all the absence of formality there can be no doubting that by the time they were ready to launch the *Britannic*, Harland & Wolff had refined their process of launching the largest British-built steamers. As the yard foreman kept a close eye on the rising tide, at 11.10am the first red rocket shot into the air, signalling any nearby vessels to stand clear as the last of the supporting shores were dislodged from beneath the hull. Moments later, the full weight of the 24,800-ton hull was supported only by the sliding ways that had been specially built for the occasion; five minutes later, a second rocket served as a signal for the pressure to be released in the hydraulic cylinder of the launch triggers as, without the need for any assistance from the launch jacks, the *Britannic* slowly began to slide backwards towards the water's edge.

The width of the Lagan river allowed for a launch run of up to 2,350 feet and the three equally spaced anchors laid on the riverbed on either side of the ship, ranging from 5½ to 8 tons, along with the same 80 tons of anchor chain used to launch the *Olympic* and *Titanic*, controlled the speed of the hull perfectly. Additional wire ropes secured to eye plates riveted to the shell helped to bring the *Britannic* to a complete halt so efficiently that it took only 81 seconds from the moment the hull began to move to the vessel being afloat. During the launch, the *Britannic*'s hull attained a maximum speed of 9½ knots, which, compared to the 62 seconds and 12½ knots recorded on the day the *Olympic* was launched, clearly shows that the heavier *Britannic*'s launch had been far more controlled.

With the *Britannic* safely afloat, it was still business as usual as the workers immediately set about clearing slip 2 for the construction of what would be Yard No 469, the Red Star liner *Nederland*. In the meantime, Yard No 433 was quietly towed downstream by the tugs *Hercules*, *Herculaneum*, *Huskisson*, *Hornby* and *Alexandra* to the same deep-water wharf where the *Olympic* and *Titanic* had undergone their own metamorphosis. The *Britannic*'s own transformation from empty shell to a floating palace, however, would not proceed so smoothly. It could be said that the White

Star Line's ambition to have the ship in service by the autumn of 1914 was overly optimistic, although certainly feasible had the *Britannic* been given the same priority as that given to the *Olympic*, but four months later it was clear that the schedule had begun to slip, so much so that on 2 July 1914 it was announced that *Britannic* would not be ready for her maiden voyage until the spring of 1915. The reason for the delay was due in no small part to the fact that Harland & Wolff was now working at full capacity, which had not been the case when the *Olympic* was being completed, but to further complicate matters, issues with supplies and industrial relations were only helping to intensify the problem. Added to that the fact that IMM already owed Harland & Wolff the not insignificant amount of £585,000, combined with rumours of the combine also being in financial difficulty, the *Britannic* not surprisingly found herself slipping further down the list of priorities at Belfast.

In the meantime, the *Olympic*'s resumption of service following her winter overhaul indicated that Harland & Wolff could still learn valuable operational lessons that could be incorporated into the *Britannic*. Problems began to occur

BELOW: *Following the launch, the* Britannic's *draught when afloat was 15 feet 4½ inches forward and 25 feet 7 inches aft, corresponding to an overall launch displacement of 24,800 tons.*

WHITE STAR LINE R.M.S."BRITANNIC"-50,000 TONS.
LAUNCHED FEB. 26TH 1914.

ABOVE: *White Star publicity postcard for the* Britannic *based on the 1914 oil painting by Charles Dixon.*

as early as the first voyage of the year. On 4 February 1914 the *Olympic* had departed from New York on what everyone expected to be a routine voyage home, but three days later, and without any warning, nine of the sidelights on the port side of the ship suddenly shattered. Although such incidents were not completely unknown when at sea, bearing in mind that the *Olympic* was at the time in what was later described in the Board of Trade paperwork as only 'moderate weather', as opposed to the severe conditions reported in the press, with the hull neither rolling nor pitching to any great extent, it was clearly grounds for some concern. The passengers seated in the dining saloon, especially those showered with broken glass either from the eight broken dining saloon sidelights (the ninth was in the potato wash room on E deck) or from the stained-glass windows, would certainly have found little reason to disagree.

Curiously enough, the incident only came to the attention of the Board of Trade's principal ship surveyor in London when he read about it in the press, prompting an immediate memo to their Southampton office to obtain more details. Intriguingly, the response indicated that none of the broken sidelights were of a size or design approved by the Board, but perhaps of greater concern was the revelation that this was not the first time the problem had occurred. In this case the damage was made good after about an hour, during which time the *Olympic* had slowed down to make the task easier for the repair crew, but while there seemed to be no threat to the ship on this occasion, the mishap was clearly of enough concern to the Southampton ship surveyors to require an increased number of spare deadlights or wood plugs to be carried in the spaces concerned. However, with additional support being considered for the sidelights in question, the surveyor's recommendations that some structural provision be made to deal with the pivoting ports on D deck were already being acted upon.

For the most part, the following voyages had less of the drama associated with shattering portholes, but from the human perspective it was sometimes a lot harder. There were the inevitable problems with stowaways, but in this respect the third voyage of the year proved to be especially eventful, with no fewer than five stowaways being discovered at various stages of the voyage – three of them before the ship had even reached Queenstown. Iris Emmwise was the first to be found on board without a ticket, but due to her incoherent and irrational behaviour she escaped the worst of Captain Haddock's wrath and was instead placed in the care of the ship's surgeon. Josiah and Samuel Winglay, on the other hand, were not accorded the same consideration and were promptly handed over to the company's Queenstown agent for prosecution. Then again, not all stowaways ended up in the hands of the authorities, a perfect example being Percy Fleming and Gilbert Parker, who on the return voyage informed the chief steward that they were stowaways. Rather than face the legal

consequences, upon arriving at Southampton on 4 April they were evidently persuaded to pay for their passage and were subsequently allowed to land with the other passengers. Two voyages later Frank Rhoades had the same misfortune to be found on board without a ticket, but with no means of paying his way he was handed over the authorities at Queenstown for prosecution.

Dealing with stowaways was part and parcel of everyday life on an ocean liner and in this respect the *Olympic* was little different to any other vessels on the North Atlantic, but the recording of passenger deaths in the ship's log was never easy. The first fatality of the year came on 5 March 1914, when only one day out of New York and bound for Southampton, a third-class Italian passenger named Egisto Cesare Suzzi died from a combination of tubercular disease, bronchopneumonia and heart failure. Seventeen days later another third-class passenger, Pedro Vernal, succumbed to pneumonia, obliging Captain Haddock to conduct yet another funeral at sea, but perhaps the saddest note to be made in the logbook came on the return journey, when eight-month-old Franciszek Matusik, while being treated for convulsions, died from acute tubercular meningitis. The jinx continued into the following month when on 10 May first-class passenger José Maria Panèda, a Spanish merchant from Havana, succumbed to tuberculosis after being admitted to hospital with haemorrhaging lungs.

Issues with the crew were also relatively uncommon, but not unheard of. A log entry for 27 May 1913 records Quartermaster J Phillips being demoted to ordinary seaman for being insolent to the third officer when told to be more attentive at the wheel, but tragedy struck on 7 March 1914 when Senior Seventh Engineer William Costley fell into bunker 5, suffering a depressed fracture of the vault of the skull and lacerations to the brain. Following an emergency operation, Costley failed to respond to treatment and on 9 March he died in the ship's hospital. Three months later, on 18 June, trimmer Henry Savage, suffering from inflamed kidneys, found himself being rushed to hospital in New York, where he would die only a few hours later. Fortunately, not all events on board ended in tragedy, although sometimes it came perilously close. On 16 June 1914, fireman Arthur McMullen found himself laid up in the ship's infirmary, suffering from a scalp wound and a bruised hip courtesy of fireman John Hughes, who for no apparent reason had struck him with a metal bar and then kicked him.

Inevitably, there were also cases of petty larceny to record, one noticeable incident coming on 27 March when steward Michael Cunningham was found to be in possession of an overcoat stolen from a third-class passenger. The coat was subsequently handed over to the company agent in New York to be returned to its owner, but it is interesting to note that the name crops up again in the ship's log six months later, when on the afternoon of 26 September 1914 an M Cunningham was found stowed away on the ship when bound for Glasgow. Evidently, his knowledge of the ship, if indeed it is the same person, was of little use in helping him to remain hidden.

By the late summer of 1914, however, the old world was fast disappearing, not that anyone would have realised it at the time. While the *Olympic* was re-establishing her reputation on the North Atlantic, the competition was quickly catching up. HAPAG's *Imperator* had already entered commercial service in the summer of 1913, but the spring of 1914 brought the double whammy of the German line's second and even larger vessel *Vaterland* entering service on 14 May, followed on 30 May by Cunard's *Aquitania*. The stage was well and truly set for a gargantuan struggle as the four largest ships in the world vied with each other for the all-important passenger traffic for which they had been created, but it was not to be. Less than a month after the *Aquitania* made her maiden voyage from Liverpool to New York, the old world for which they had been created would suddenly be changed for ever, in a previously inconceivable way.

On 18 July 1914, the *Olympic* entered the Solent in the final stages of an eastbound crossing from New York. Dr John Beaumont remembered how the sight of 59 ships of the Grand Fleet anchored off Spithead had so impressed one of the American passengers that he was moved to comment that if the Kaiser could see such an array of ships he would think twice about going to war. While the sight may indeed have been awe-inspiring, sadly the Kaiser had other thoughts. Germany's violation of Belgian neutrality on the continent meant that Great Britain had finally sided with France and Russia against Germany and Austria-Hungary and shortly after 11pm (midnight Central European time) on 4 August the Admiralty sent the official telegram 'Commence hostilities against Germany'.

The outbreak of war found the *Olympic* in the final stages of a westbound crossing to New York, relatively safe from any prospect of being attacked by a German surface raider. Nevertheless, Captain Haddock increased speed and any early-rising passengers on the morning of 5 August would have been bewildered to see the ship's crew preparing the necessary wartime blackout procedures. The *Olympic* arrived safely at her western terminal later that morning and would remain there for the next four days, during which time the crew was kept gainfully employed by blacking out the windows and painting the white superstructure a dull grey colour. The scheduled departure date of 8 August came and went, but on Sunday 9 August the *Olympic*, carrying neither passengers nor cargo, quietly pulled away from Pier 59 to return to England. However, once she was through the Ambrose Channel the planned destination would be very different. With Southampton appropriated by the military authorities in order to transport the British Expeditionary Force to France, Captain Haddock instead set a course around the north coast of Ireland, arriving safely and without incident at Liverpool six days later.

Despite the uncertain future, there were still passengers needing to cross the Atlantic. Westbound it was mostly a matter of transporting Americans home from Europe, while the eastbound trade consisted largely of British nationals returning to the mother country in its hour of need, all of them eager to join up before the show was over. With so many smaller vessels being requisitioned for national service, the *Olympic* therefore remained more important than ever to the White Star Line, and as a result they were still able to maintain a credible makeshift weekly IMM service out of Liverpool by utilising the *Olympic*, *Adriatic*, *Baltic* and Red Star liner *Lapland*. Liverpool, however, proved to be less than ideal. A combination of no safe place to anchor and inadequate docking facilities meant that the *Olympic*'s second departure from her home port on 16 September would also be her last.

For the next two months the *Olympic*'s European terminal would be Greenock on the Clyde, even though from an administrative point of view the arrangement brimmed with difficulties, especially with the imminent expiry of the ship's passenger certificate, proving that bureaucracy thrives even in wartime. Ongoing surveys were normally carried out by the surveyors at Southampton at the end of each voyage, and while the company already planned to have the *Olympic* laid up before the end of November the checks still needed to be carried out, even if it meant doing it while the ship was lying at anchor and with steam up. The arrangement was far from ideal, but the unsatisfactory and exposed anchorage at Liverpool left the company managers with little alternative. Nevertheless, on 3 October the *Olympic* arrived at Greenock to prepare for what would turn out to be her only scheduled voyage from that port. With only one more round trip scheduled for the remainder of the season – such as it was – at 10.50pm on 9 October the *Olympic* was once again westbound for New York, where, while maintaining her established high speed and following a now obligatory zigzag course, she arrived safely seven days later.

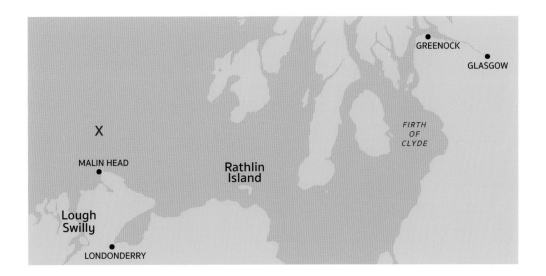

GREENOCK

GLASGOW

FIRTH
OF
CLYDE

X

MALIN HEAD

Rathlin
Island

Lough
Swilly

LONDONDERRY

ABOVE: *The loss of the HMS* Audacious.

In view of what occurred next, it is perhaps ironic that the White Star Line ever considered Greenock to be the 'safer' option. The same perhaps could be said of the admirals who, concerned by the inadequate submarine defences of the Grand Fleet's main base in the Orkney Islands, had temporarily moved their base of operations to Lough Swilly on the north Irish coast until Scapa Flow could be properly secured. It was into these now hazardous waters that the *Olympic* steamed on the last leg of her voyage home. After departing for her final crossing of 1914 on 21 October, the following six days at sea had followed a fairly routine pattern with no unusual sightings or alerts; by the morning of Tuesday 27 October the *Olympic* was less than a day from the Clyde when the voyage was suddenly and dramatically interrupted. In her path lay the British 2nd Battle Squadron, which while out for a spot of gunnery practice had unwittingly steamed into a German minefield. Suddenly, and without warning, at 8.50am the 25,000-ton

British battleship HMS *Audacious* had struck a mine off Tory Island.

Lieutenant Thomas Galbraith was on the bridge at the time and recorded that the battleship had almost completed a turn to starboard when the bridge suddenly shuddered. Moments later, Captain Cecil Dampier came dashing up the bridge ladder in a great hurry, asking, 'Who fired that gun?' Galbraith quickly confirmed that no gun had been fired and as the battleship took a sudden roll to port the order was given to close the watertight doors. With the signal hoisted to confirm that the *Audacious* had been damaged by a mine or a torpedo, the rest of the fleet immediately dispersed while the light cruiser HMS *Liverpool* and a number of smaller vessels were instructed to stand by to assist the damaged battleship. Meanwhile, Captain Dampier turned the ship's head into the swell to reduce the rolling. With

135

the *Audacious* slowing noticeably, the crew set about preparing the boats for lowering, only for the onboard power to fail almost immediately; with the main engines now dead, there was no choice left but to attempt to tow the *Audacious* to safety.

Right on cue, the *Olympic* appeared on the horizon at 10.30am and straight away the captain of the HMS *Liverpool* ordered Captain Haddock to assist with the evacuation of the *Audacious*'s crew. Galbraith later recalled that, with the sun having finally appeared, the *Olympic* and four destroyers coming towards the battleship at full speed made for a wonderful sight, and within two hours all but 250 of the crew had been taken off. As soon as the *Olympic*'s lifeboats had been recovered, the destroyer HMS *Fury* succeeded in attaching a 6-inch hawser between the *Audacious* and the *Olympic*, and at 2pm the tow commenced. At first everything looked to be in hand as the convoy steamed steadily westwards, but when Haddock altered course to SSE towards Lough Swilly, the situation quickly began to deteriorate. With the battleship's steering gear already out of action, the combination of the heavy seas and the wind on the *Audacious*'s superstructure caused the wire to part as the battleship swung around and turned back into the wind. A second attempt was made at 3.30pm when the *Fury* succeeded in attaching a second towline to the *Liverpool*, but after only 15 minutes it became fouled in the cruiser's propellers, so at 4pm the *Fury* took over a third and, as it would turn out, final cable to the collier *Thornhill*. Unfortunately, it too gave way just as it was being tightened.

Once again Captain Haddock was ordered to stand by and be ready to make another attempt, but with the conditions deteriorating the decision was taken to first disembark all but the executive officers and 40 seamen. The increasingly heavy swell only served to impede the process and by 5pm the *Audacious*'s quarterdeck was awash, forcing the decision to abandon the battleship until the morning, when tugs from Belfast would make another attempt at towing her to safety. Thomas Galbraith would be in the last boat to leave the side of the battleship while Captain Dampier remained on board, wandering round the upper deck and seemingly paying no attention to the calls for him to enter the boat until the last minute, but by 6.30pm the *Audacious* was abandoned and adrift. Fortunately, the decision to evacuate would ultimately prove justified when, at 8.55pm, there was a massive explosion in the vicinity of the forward magazine serving A and B turrets. Moments later the battleship capsized and sank stern first.

As the flotilla dispersed the *Olympic* was escorted to Lough Swilly, where the rescued crew of the *Audacious* could be disembarked. For security reasons she still had to remain out of sight of the fleet so that the passengers would not be able to observe any military activities, but with a number of German-born Americans on board having witnessed the demise of the battleship, it was clear they could not be relied upon to keep their silence. Unfortunately for the British they were now neutral American citizens, so it was impossible to arrest or intern them, although they could still be detained for questioning when the passengers were disembarked; needless to say, the interrogations would not be rushed.

In the meantime, Captain Haddock was faced with the task of keeping his passengers occupied while they were marooned on board with no communication with the shore. The White Star Line was in no particular hurry to risk their flagship in the mine-infested waters as she was due to be laid up anyway, but equally the military authorities could not allow the passengers to disembark at Lough Swilly. The only people permitted to leave the ship were the rescued crew of the *Audacious*, Chief Surgeon John Beaumont, who was being transferred to the *Celtic*, and Charles M Schwab, head of the Bethlehem Steel Corporation, who had urgent business with the Admiralty in London. Not surprisingly, Beaumont would do everything in his power to help the British authorities cover up the loss of one of their most modern and powerful vessels, always denying any knowledge of the sinking when questioned by the press two weeks later at New York. Until the end of the war he would be known as 'Audacious' Beaumont, and it would not be until after the Armistice in November 1918 that Beaumont – and indeed the Admiralty – would acknowledge that the *Audacious* had been sunk, admitting that he had always felt it his duty to 'lie like a gentleman'.

On the afternoon of 2 November, Captain Haddock was finally allowed to depart Lough Swilly for Belfast, where the *Olympic*'s final voyage of the season would terminate, and where her small complement of passengers would finally be allowed to disembark the following day. For the foreseeable future, however, the *Olympic*'s war was over.

BELOW: *The* Olympic's *lifeboats transferring the crew of the HMS* Audacious *to safety.*

CHAPTER ELEVEN

THE CALL TO ARMS

By the winter of 1914 both the *Olympic* and *Britannic* were mothballed at Belfast, representing over 90,000 GRT of British shipping of no use whatsoever to the war effort. With the majority of available raw materials also diverted to shipyards with Admiralty contracts, Harland & Wolff also found themselves with little opportunity to carry out any substantial work on any civilian contracts.

To further compound their problems over 6,000 skilled workers laid off by the shipyard had rushed to enlist, so that when the need for increased tonnage became more vital to the war effort – and inevitably it would – the loss of so many skilled labourers would prove difficult to replace. Even so, by early September the *Britannic* could at least be placed in the graving dock to have her propellers fitted, but once the first Admiralty orders began to arrive at Belfast the following month, all work on any non-military contracts came to a complete halt.

The White Star Line also had problems of its own. The drop in passenger revenue was to a certain extent offset by the fact that the *Oceanic*, *Celtic*, *Cedric* and *Teutonic* had all been requisitioned as armed merchant cruisers, while the *Laurentic* and *Megantic* had been allocated to trooping duties. With the Admiralty paying for the use of these ships there was less pressure on the company finances, but the inability to find any use for the *Olympic* and *Britannic*

was causing something of an embarrassment, with the Admiralty reluctant to use the larger ships because of their operational limitations and cost. The collision between the *Aquitania* and the Leyland liner *Canadian* on 22 August, combined with the grounding and ultimate loss of the *Oceanic* in the Shetland Islands on 8 September, had proved just how unsuitable the larger ships were for use as armed merchant cruisers, which combined with the exorbitant cost of running them meant that by the spring of 1915 the *Olympic*, *Britannic*, *Aquitania* and *Mauretania* were all surplus to requirements.

Of the larger ships, only the *Lusitania* remained in commercial service, but the status quo was not set to last for much longer. At the end of April, the commencement of the Allied Gallipoli offensive, combined with the sinking of the *Lusitania* on 7 May 1915 by the German submarine *U-20*, would dramatically change the picture. Within days, Cunard had agreed to charter the *Mauretania* to the Admiralty as a

ABOVE: *September 1914: The* Britannic's *propellers are finally fitted, the original four-bladed centre turbine propeller configuration having been re-established.*

troopship at the rate of 15/- per gross ton per month, which although a long way short of the £46,000 that the Admiralty would have had to pay under normal circumstances, reflected the business realities of the time. The simple truth was that the Cunard directors either agreed to an advantageous rate on their larger ships or risked losing more of their smaller but infinitely more useful vessels instead. Sure enough, on 11 May the *Mauretania* was duly requisitioned as a troopship.

In truth, the Admiralty's Transport Division was not exactly thrilled at the prospect of using the larger ships either. True, they could accommodate large numbers of troops and their high speed was a decided advantage in a

war zone, but the risk of submarine attack due to their size and the lack of harbour facilities caused no little concern. In terms of hard cash, however, it was unquestionably cheaper to convert a single ship of the *Olympic*'s size than a larger number of intermediate-sized vessels. In the end, the financial incentives must have helped to sway the Admiralty's decision and on 18 June 1915 the *Aquitania* was finally requisitioned as a troopship.

As work was progressing on the *Aquitania*, discreet enquiries from the Admiralty had also

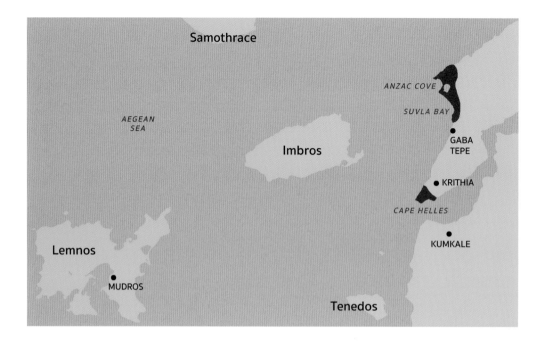

ABOVE: *Mudros and Gallipoli.*

begun to arrive at the White Star head office in Liverpool concerning the capacity, range and speed of the *Olympic*. Data provided by Harland & Wolff confirmed that berths could be arranged for anything up to 7,000 troops, while the bunker capacity would allow the ship to maintain 21 knots from Southampton to Mudros and at least as far back as Gibraltar, but because the *Olympic* had spent the last seven months laid up in dirty water she would need to be dry-docked before assuming any military duties. The tides at Belfast also meant that it would be impossible to use the Thompson Dock before the end of June, and with the *Aquitania* already occupying Liverpool's Gladstone Dock the options were limited. On 22 June the Transport Division decided that for the time being they could make do without the *Olympic*, but it would only be a temporary reprieve. By the autumn of 1915 the Mediterranean casualty

figures had grown so alarmingly that both the *Mauretania* and *Aquitania*, by now both converted into hospital ships, had resulted in a lack of trooping capacity for reinforcements. The answer to the conundrum was lying idle at Belfast and on 1 September 1915 an official telegram arrived at the Belfast Divisional Transport Office advising: 'S.S. *Olympic* required for urgent Government service. Owners have been requested to prepare her and you should render any assistance required.'

After ten months languishing at Belfast, the *Olympic*'s call to arms had finally come. Scrutinising the terms of the ship's charter to the Admiralty in closer detail, in order to ensure parity with Cunard Harold Sanderson had agreed to the existing terms of 10/- per gross ton per month, which, in the case of the

Olympic, amounted to a little over £23,000 per month. The discussions over the actual value of the vessel, however, would prove to be a thornier issue. The government was undertaking to reimburse the company in the event of her total loss, whether through accident or military action, but while the Admiralty valued all chartered ships on a first-cost basis, they made no allowance for any subsequent improvements made to improve the earning potential of the vessel.

On 28 September, Sanderson wrote to the Director of Transports stating that allowing for depreciation in value, the first cost of the *Olympic* was £1,459,542, but that this figure included an additional £156,501 incurred due to the extensive alterations completed after the company's 'unfortunate experience with the *Titanic*'. Because this expenditure had been made for safety reasons, rather than to increase the vessel's earning power, he argued that White Star was justified in including the additional expenditure for insurance purposes, but while the Admiralty was prepared to agree the extra cost in the final quantum, they were still unable to accept the White Star figure. Sanderson had allowed for an annual depreciation in value of 4 per cent, whereas the Admiralty calculated the depreciation value of any vessels in government service at 5 per cent. On this point the Transport Division simply would not budge and it was only by insuring the difference – a sum that eventually worked out at £76,279 – on the insurance market at White Star's own expense that the matter was eventually resolved.

Meanwhile, the *Olympic*'s conversion continued apace. Once the ship's fixtures and fittings had been landed, enough space could be made for some 6,000 men, largely by removing the third-class interchangeable cabins on E deck and converting the public rooms to mess deck and hammock arrangements. Even then it was not possible to complete everything at Belfast, so for the first time in over ten months the *Olympic* departed from that port on 12 September in order to be dry-docked at Liverpool. On the surface, everything seemed to be on schedule as far as the conversion was concerned, but the issue of her captain remained unresolved. Harold Sanderson had always intended to have Herbert Haddock reappointed to his old command, but unfortunately the Admiralty considered his role as Commodore of the Special Services Squadron at Belfast – a fleet of dummy warships created in order to deceive the enemy – to be more important. Sanderson's second choice, however, presented no such problem and on 16 September Captain Bertram Fox Hayes was appointed in his place.

Although an experienced RNR officer, Hayes's first meeting with the Principal Naval Transport Officer at Liverpool got off to a less than promising start, the official seemingly less concerned with the utter confusion on board but rather more irked by the fact that Hayes was out of uniform. Nor did matters improve when Hayes also insisted that his assistant commander should be given a rank higher than sub-lieutenant, otherwise he would allow him to wear his company uniform at sea to give him more authority over the higher-ranking military officers. Despite the personal friction, by the time the *Olympic* vacated the Gladstone Dock

ABOVE: *Captain Bertram Fox Hayes.*

her conversion was complete, and at 10am on 24 September the newly designated Transport 2810 left Liverpool on her first trooping voyage to Mudros.

On board were some 6,000 troops of the Southern Counties Yeomanry and contingents from the Welsh Horse Division. Throughout the voyage, Captain Hayes tried to maintain an air of normality, including a hunt dinner for the 42 Masters of Hounds who were on board. He even had a Welsh regimental choir helping with the entertainments throughout the voyage, but on 1 October the normality was interrupted off Cape Matapan when lifeboats were sighted in the water directly ahead. Hayes immediately stopped the ship so that the survivors of the French steamer *Provincia* could be rescued, but while his rescue of the seamen would later earn the grateful thanks of Admiral Dartige du Fournet, who recommended that Hayes

should be awarded the Médaille de Sauvetage en Or, British Admiral Sir John de Robeck saw things in a different light. Thirty-three French lives may well have been saved by Hayes's actions, but during this time the fully loaded *Olympic* had been a sitting target, which any lurking submarine would have found all but impossible to miss. To be fair, de Robeck did have a point; indeed, two hours after resuming course a surfaced submarine was observed off the starboard bow, but with the *Olympic*'s best defence always being her high speed, Hayes immediately turned away, resuming his original course after dark.

The following day the *Olympic* arrived at Mudros, where the *Provincia* survivors were transferred to the SS *Aragon*. It would not be until the evening of 11 October that the ship was ready to depart, but although the *Olympic* was now empty the homeward leg would be equally hazardous. Requiring additional fuel and water to complete the journey back to England, the voyage would take the ship to the northern Italian port of La Spezia, but although the waters of the Ligurian Sea were nowhere near as hazardous as those of the eastern Mediterranean, as the *Olympic* slowly approached the breakwater the sight of an Italian destroyer suddenly closing and firing her guns was not at all what anyone had anticipated. The situation was clarified when it transpired that the destroyer was only firing to ensure that the *Olympic* didn't stray into a minefield, before signalling Hayes to follow astern as the destroyer guided him safely into port. It would be a further eight days before the voyage to England could be resumed, a journey not made any easier by the fact that the drinking water had become contaminated, so that by the time the *Olympic* arrived back at Liverpool on 31 October many of her crew were either ill or recovering from stomach problems.

Fortunately, it would be another two weeks before they were due to depart for the Mediterranean again, allowing plenty of time for the crew to recover, and shortly before dawn on 15 November the *Olympic* was once again bound for Mudros. Arriving on 22 November after an uneventful voyage, the process of disembarkation remained as slow as the first visit, but this time the proceedings on board were more eventful when, after four days in port, Private J Howarth of the North Lancashire Regiment locked himself in one of the lavatories on E deck and attempted to cut his throat

with a razor; it was only the prompt action of another soldier, who heard him groaning and forced open the door of the cubicle, that saved Howarth's life. The following day, Dr John Garland of the RAMC confirmed at an inquiry that the wound was self-inflicted, while Howarth himself admitted that he had been feeling depressed after seeing his girlfriend with another man before leaving for Mudros. When asked why he did it, Howarth simply replied, 'I was fed up!'

The voyage home was once again uneventful, and after making the established call at La Spezia for coal and water the *Olympic* arrived safely back at Liverpool on 21 December. This time, however, an old friend was there to welcome the ship back from her second trooping run to the eastern Mediterranean.

LEFT: *Reinforcements and equipment for the Gallipoli front piled up in the* Olympic's *forward well deck.*

CHAPTER TWELVE

THE MOST WONDERFUL HOSPITAL SHIP TO EVER SAIL THE SEAS

Considering the high attrition rate in the eastern Mediterranean, it should come as no surprise that by the autumn of 1915 even the *Mauretania* and *Aquitania* were insufficient to handle the increasing volume of casualties.

As if the Turkish and German bullets were not already taking a large enough toll on the beaches at Gallipoli, disease – most notably typhoid and dysentery – was decimating the Allied forces. On top of that, the always unpredictable military activity in France was such that in October 1915 even the Inspector General of the British Expeditionary Force had written to the Admiralty on the necessity of being prepared at short notice to meet an evacuation estimated at between 5,000 and

BELOW: *Section of 1915 starboard profile of the HMHS* Britannic.

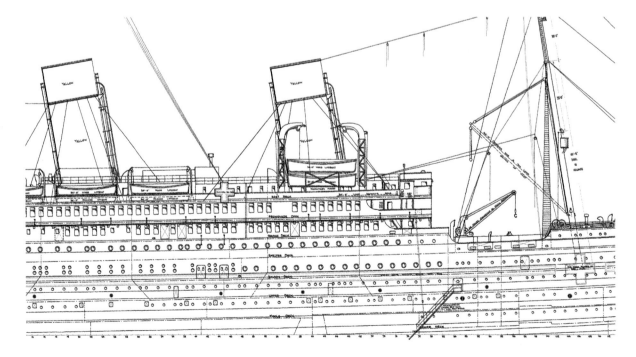

ABOVE: *Additional Welin davits along the mid-ship section on either side of the previously open boat deck helped to make good the shortfall in the number of lifeboats due to the three missing sets of girder davits, with additional floats stationed amidships to further augment the* Britannic's *lifesaving equipment.*

6,000 cases a day. The Transport Division, ever mindful of the financial cost of maintaining an unspecified number of hospital ships on indefinite standby, reasoned that as there were already 64 hospital ships in service there would in all probability always be some in home ports and available for emergency use, but before long even their reluctant eyes were turning towards Belfast as they once again began to think the unthinkable. Sure enough, on 13 November 1915 the *Britannic* was finally requisitioned for service as a hospital ship.

With the *Britannic* at last taking priority, Harland & Wolff started to weigh up the options for completing the ship as quickly as possible. On the one hand, the interior of the vessel was still very far from complete, with much of the wooden panelling and customary White Star fixtures and fittings still waiting to be installed, although the potential this offered for much larger wards would ultimately prove extremely beneficial in the layout of a military hospital

ship. On the other hand, she was already seaworthy, having completed the mooring trials of her engines six months earlier.

Externally, the *Britannic* also required considerable work. Twenty-one months after being launched only five of the planned eight sets of davits had been installed, but while this was still enough to provide for 27 lifeboats, six additional sets of Welin davits still needed to be installed on either side of the boat deck, along with two more on the poop, in order to make up the numbers. With each Welin davit handling one rigid and one collapsible lifeboat, the revised arrangements would increase the number to 55. The paintwork would also need a complete overhaul, the dingy two-year-old grey

ABOVE AND BELOW: *As per the requirements of The Hague Convention, at night the electric red crosses on the boat deck and a string of green lights beneath the promenade would signify the* Britannic *'s protected status as a hospital ship.*

paint being replaced by the internationally recognised colours of a hospital ship, namely a white hull with a green band painted from end to end. In the *Britannic*'s case the green band was broken by three large red crosses on either side, while the funnels were finished in a bright mustard yellow. By day there could be no mistaking the nature of the ship, which in theory would render her immune from deliberate enemy attack; in addition, a line of green electric boxes beneath the promenade deck, combined with two large red electric crosses mounted on either side of the boat deck, would ensure that the nature of the ship would be unmistakeable even at night.

Internally, the *Britannic*'s layout would

bear little similarity to her commercial design. For the most part the doctors and nurses would occupy the staterooms on B deck, while spaces on the incomplete lower decks would be allocated to the remaining medical orderlies. The first-class dining saloon would continue to serve in its originally intended purpose as the patients' mess, even if the fittings would not be quite so grand, but for the most part the lower public rooms and cabins would be given over to open ward space. By the time the conversion was complete there would be space on board for 3,309 casualties, with ship's surgeon Dr John 'Audacious' Beaumont later describing the completed *Britannic* as '...the most wonderful hospital ship that ever sailed the seas'.

Not surprisingly, all this work came at a colossal cost to the war effort. It had taken £68,000 to fully equip the *Mauretania* and a further £63,000 to convert the *Aquitania*, first into a troopship and then into a hospital ship;

BELOW: Britannic's *modified poop, with a purpose-built mortuary on the stern. The ship would fly the flag of the Admiralty Transport Division – a blue ensign with a yellow anchor in the fly side.*

with another £90,000 having been spent on the *Britannic*, these three ships alone accounted for a total expenditure in excess of £220,000. Even so, the Admiralty bean counters had little option but to acknowledge the fact that it was still considerably cheaper and more practical to fit out three big ships rather than a larger number of smaller vessels, which could be more gainfully employed elsewhere. The Admiralty would still be getting a good deal. The *Britannic* was chartered at the same rate as the *Olympic*, namely 10/- per gross ton per month, but with a GRT of 48,158 tons, thus making her capacity some 4 per cent larger than the *Olympic*, the final total would still amount to over £24,000 per month. There could also be no dispute over depreciated value as the *Britannic* was brand new, and with the Transport Division assuming full responsibility of insuring the vessel, Harold Sanderson did at least have some grounds for satisfaction.

Despite this, he still could not have the captain he wanted. Having failed seven weeks earlier to get Herbert Haddock reappointed to the *Olympic*, Sanderson decided to try and have him appointed instead to the *Britannic*, describing him as '...the very best man in our employ'. On this point, however, the Transport Division remained unmoved; Captain Haddock would remain in his post at Belfast. Once again Sanderson had to consider his options and it did not take him long to find the right man for the job: Captain Charles Bartlett, formerly the commander of the *Cedric*. Since January 1912 Bartlett had been White Star's marine superintendent at Liverpool, during which time he had been able to monitor the *Britannic*'s

ABOVE: *Captain Charles Alfred Bartlett, White Star's Marine Superintendent at Liverpool and captain of the* Britannic.

construction and fitting out at Belfast. Following the outbreak of war, he had been assigned to patrolling duties in the North Sea, so there was little doubt that he would be available.

The diplomatic bureaucracy also continued right up until the last minute. After receiving confirmation that the *Britannic*'s trials were imminent, on 6 December 1915 the Admiralty

BELOW: *Starboard profile of the* Britannic *as a completed hospital ship.*

officially informed the German government, via the established neutral channels with the American government, of the *Britannic*'s protected status as a hospital ship; two days later Colonel Henry Concanon, one of the White Star managers at Liverpool, officially entered the ship in the Liverpool register. That same day, under the command of Captain Joseph Ranson, the *Britannic* finally steamed into the Irish Sea to undergo her engine trials. As in the case of the *Olympic* and *Titanic*, everything proceeded satisfactorily and after returning later that evening to a particularly foggy Belfast Lough, representatives of the White Star Line officially took delivery of the *Britannic*. Unlike the *Titanic*, however, there would be no quick departure as the Gladstone Dock was still occupied by the battleship HMS *Barham*. It was only three days later that the *Barham* was ready to vacate the dock and on the evening of 11 December, a little over four years after the laying of her keel, the *Britannic* finally left Belfast to proceed across the Irish Sea to her home port of Liverpool.

On the morning of Tuesday 14 December Captain Bartlett finally arrived from Aberdeen to assume command of the *Britannic*, but it would still be another eight days before the outfitting was complete. By the morning of 22 December the conversion was finished and at 11am the *Britannic* finally cast off in readiness to depart from the Gladstone Dock. This maiden voyage, however, would be a very different affair to those of her two sisters, and the *Britannic*'s initial progress would seem to be disappointing at best. At this stage, none of the medical staff on board had even the faintest idea as to their ultimate destination, but no one had expected the ship to proceed barely a mile before dropping anchor once again in the Mersey. The mystery was quickly resolved when word went around that the Royal Army Medical Corps (RAMC) orderlies were late in arriving from Aldershot, and that the delay would only be temporary. It would still be another 12 hours before the orderlies were on board but, shortly after midnight on 23 December, the *Britannic* was finally ready to head out into the Irish Sea.

Even after departure, military secrecy meant that only a chosen few on board knew their ultimate destination. If the speculation was to be believed then the ship was headed for Australia, but either way it made little difference to the on-board routine. The captain and senior medical officer usually had a degree of flexibility in how they ran things on board, but for the most part they were required to adhere as closely as possible to the approved Admiralty guidelines. Patients would be woken at 6am, after which the wards and passageways would be cleaned; patients' breakfast would then be served between 7.30 and 8am, after which the tables, benches and WCs all had to be cleaned and ready for the captain and senior medical officer's rounds at 11am. Lunch was at 12.30, after which the wards would again be swept out and the hospital areas disinfected, before tea was served at 4.30. The patients would then be expected to be in bed by 8.30pm before a ship's officer and a medical officer made the final rounds half an hour later.

For the next few days, however, the routine would not have been too arduous as there would be no patients on board until the ship arrived at her destination. Fortunately, this allowed time for the RAMC landlubbers, many of whom were laid low by the stormy waters of the Bay of Biscay, to find their sea legs, but the nurses were not so fortunate. With over 3,000 cots to be made up, they already had their work cut out just to have everything ready for the invalids when they came aboard, and woe betide them if any failure on their part exposed them to the wrath of matron! If this arrangement resulted in a well-coordinated and methodical system, at

ABOVE: *Lieutenant Colonel Henry Stewart Anderson, the* Britannic's *Senior Medical Officer.*

least from the military perspective, 'Audacious' Beaumont had little doubt what he thought of the arrangement. Never having been a fan of the 'red tape fiend', to him the best interests of the patient seemed to be nothing in comparison to the military's strict adherence to their bureaucracy and regulations.

Although the *Olympic* and *Britannic* were both assigned to the eastern Mediterranean, their routines were very different. As a troopship, the *Olympic* was fully loaded on the outward voyage, meaning that she would travel non-stop to Mudros and then refuel at La Spezia on the homeward leg. The *Britannic*, on the other hand, was usually empty on her outward journey, so instead Captain Bartlett was required to refuel en route to Mudros; once the wards were full, he could then make his homeward run without stopping. The procedure made sense in a variety of ways as it not only helped to keep the troops or patients on board for as short a time as possible, but it also saved considerably on the ships' coal consumption when anchored; according to the Transport Division calculations, every day the *Olympic* remained anchored with a full complement of troops on board would burn an additional 25 tons of coal. So that the coaling facilities of La Spezia were not overwhelmed, the *Britannic* would instead take on coal and fresh water at Naples, where she duly arrived on the hazy morning of 28 December. A chosen few were given passes to go ashore that afternoon, but for most there was little to do but admire the distant view of Mount Vesuvius and watch the coaling process. With the ship not due to depart before the following afternoon, Lieutenant Harold Goodman, having joined the RAMC barely one week before being posted to the *Britannic*, took full advantage of a morning pass to go ashore for lunch with a few colleagues, but it would only be the briefest of visits. By 4pm the *Britannic* was once again headed south into the Tyrrhenian Sea, en route for her final destination, which everyone had by now worked out would be Mudros. So much for Australia...

On the morning of 31 December, Dr Goodman accompanied Captain Bartlett, Colonel Henry Anderson and Commander Harry Dyke on their final rounds before the ship was due at Lemnos at 4pm. Of the bay itself, Goodman's first impressions were of a hilly and utterly barren landscape, covered with tents and encampments, but while no one had anticipated anything happening until the following morning, especially as Captain Bartlett and Colonel Anderson had gone ashore, at 7pm the hospital ships *Assegai* and

ABOVE: *Dr Harold Goodman enjoying a moment of relaxation on the boat deck while en route to Mudros.*

Egypt suddenly arrived alongside. Due to the huge scale of the *Britannic*, the patients – for the most part walking wounded – found themselves boarding at the level of D deck via gangways from the smaller vessels below, the unrehearsed embarkation process taking some four hours before the last of the invalids had

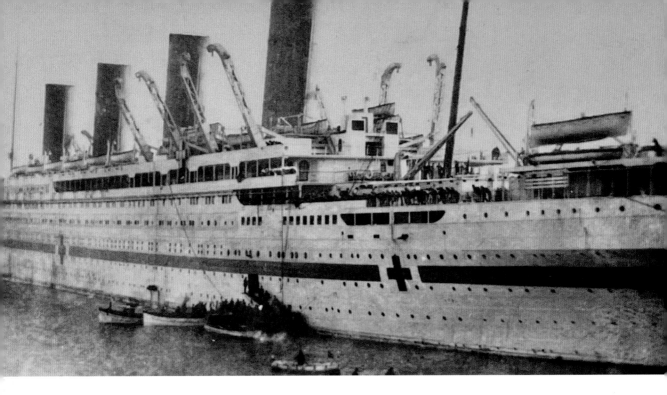

been assigned to their wards. By 10pm the men had all been allocated to their wards and given a light dinner of chicken broth, at which point the medical staff enjoyed a brief respite to have their own dinner, only to be loudly interrupted at midnight when Mudros suddenly exploded into a cacophony of noise as every vessel in the bay sounded its whistle to welcome in the New Year.

The first day of 1916, sadly, proved to be little different to the last day of 1915. Throughout the morning the patients continued to come aboard from the *Egypt* and *Assegai*, followed the next day by invalids from the *Asturias* and *Killman Castle*. On top of that, a constant procession of barges from the shore-based hospitals accounted for another thousand patients. The task was made easier by the fact that the wounded had already received emergency treatment, but even so the walking wounded – categorised as non-cot cases – still needed to be issued with hospital suits (blue trousers and jackets with brown facings) before they would be allowed up on deck. Their military uniforms would be stored in the invalids' effects room until the ship returned to England, just as any officers who had retained their personal firearms were obliged to hand them over for storage in the ship's strong room; once the pistols had been secured, the keys would then be kept by Captain Bartlett until the ship was back in England. Despite the volume of men, the process worked smoothly and efficiently, and after landing the body of Private Arthur Howe, who had died on board from tubercular disease, at 3.35pm on 3 January the *Britannic* was westbound for Gibraltar.

On the whole, life for a patient on a hospital ship was reasonably comfortable. Depending on their particular ailments, the patients' diets could vary considerably, so at 6pm every evening Colonel Anderson would present Claude Lancaster, the *Britannic*'s purser, with a list of provisions needed for the next day. The ship's chief chef would personally supervise the preparation of any special meals, while the wounded officers, as long as their medical cards allowed it, were even permitted a ration of wine or spirits at dinner. The final accounts would later be sent to the Admiralty for settlement. The catering arrangements on a troopship, however, were less flexible, so that when the White Star Line tried to supplement the troops' rations on the *Olympic*'s first trooping voyage it had resulted in an overall loss of £2,713.17.10. On 20 January 1916 Harold Sanderson would even write to the Admiralty in an attempt to negotiate a new victualling rate, suggesting 6/-6d per head per day for officers, 3/- for NCOs and 1/- 9d for other ranks, but once again the Admiralty refused to treat the *Olympic* as a special case. Even so, they did acknowledge that the rising cost of food would necessitate a revision of the overall rates.

As a serving hospital ship, deaths on board would have been seen as inevitable, but a most intriguing entry in the *Britannic*'s log occurs less than two days after the ship had departed from Mudros, when at 6.39am on 5 January a report was rushed to the bridge that a man

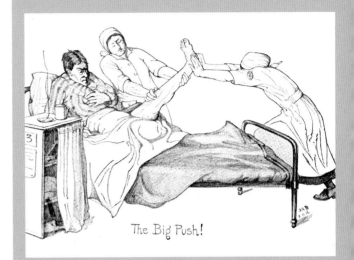

The Big Push!

The Ministering Angel.

A Little Bit of Fluff?   KAMARAD!

TOP AND MIDDLE: *A brighter look at life in a military hospital.*

RIGHT: *The Voluntary Aid Detachment (VAD) nurses were often on the receiving end of the Tommy's sense of humour. The VAD acronym was occasionally re-worked to 'Victim Always Dies', but the nurses got their own back, equating the RAMC acronym to 'Run Away Matron's Coming'!*

had either jumped or fallen overboard. The regulations did not allow for a military transport ship to stop in a war zone, as Admiral de Robeck had so forcefully reminded Captain Hayes after the *Provincia* incident, so all that could be done was to try to find out who the unfortunate man was. After the ship had been searched, it was found that Samuel Lloyd Jones, a seaman in the Royal Naval Division's Drake Battalion, was indeed missing but the inquiry held at 3pm that same day was unable to determine whether he had jumped or fallen. In the end, the only conclusion they could agree on was that it was '...reasonable to assume that he is dead'.

And so the *Britannic* continued homeward, the routine briefly interrupted at Gibraltar where Captain Bartlett's sailing orders required him to transmit a breakdown of patients into categories, including naval or military, cot cases and walking wounded, as well as the number of dysentery and enteric cases on board. It was the only time that a hospital ship was allowed to use its transmitter, but the information was crucial as it gave the medical authorities three days to assemble the required number of ambulances or hospital trains at Southampton. Meanwhile, the remaining time at sea ticked away. At midday on 7 January the daily run was logged at 506 miles, with the figure dropping slightly to 478 miles the following day, but by the evening of 8 January the time had come to return the patients' uniforms before the ship arrived back at Southampton the following day.

Progress during the last stage of the voyage would be painfully slow as the escorting minesweepers stationed off the Needles lighthouse guided the *Britannic* through the

mist, along the Solent and into Southampton Water, so it was not until 3pm on 9 January that the business of disembarkation could finally begin. The process usually started with the officers, who were nearly always placed on one of the hospital trains bound for London, after which it would be the turn of the other ranks, destined instead for one of the five provincial medical centres. Whenever possible, they would be sent to hospitals that were closer to their homes to facilitate visiting, but the immediate priority was usually to deliver them to hospitals specialising in treating their specific ailment. The last to be landed would be 21-year-old Private Charles Vincent, a rifleman with the Hampshire Regiment who had died earlier that morning of tuberculosis. Being so close to home, Captain Bartlett was spared the necessity of a burial at sea and Vincent would instead be interred in the nearby military cemetery at Netley.

Shortly before noon on 20 January, the *Britannic* was once again headed for the Mediterranean after only 11 days in port, but although her maiden voyage had been an unqualified success, with the last Allied foothold at Gallipoli now abandoned it also meant that after a single voyage the *Britannic*'s military future was already in doubt. For the next five days, however, the crew would have been oblivious to these important developments. By the evening of 25 January, having taken on 2,510 tons of coal, Captain Bartlett signalled that he would be ready to depart from Naples the following morning in order to be at Mudros by dawn on 28 January, only to receive orders later that evening to remain in port and await

the arrival of the hospital ship *Grantully Castle*. The *Grantully Castle* was not due to arrive for another 36 hours, but any thoughts of additional shore passes came to naught with the arrival of the American cruiser USS *Des Moines* on 26 January, providing Sidney Churchill, the British consul at Naples, with an ideal opportunity to demonstrate to a neutral power that the *Britannic* was a legitimate hospital ship. Orders quickly arrived on board from the consulate instructing Captain Bartlett and Colonel Anderson to invite the American captain on board, while the cruiser's medical personnel were also invited to inspect the *Britannic*'s facilities. Two days later Thomas Nelson Page, the American ambassador to Italy, who just happened to be on holiday in Naples, was also happy to accept Churchill's invitation, even taking his wife and daughter with him.

ABOVE: *The USS* Des Moines *provides the only recorded visit to the* Britannic *by representatives of a neutral power to verify the ship's non-combatant status.*

Shortly after lunch on 27 January the *Grantully Castle* finally arrived alongside the *Britannic* and the task of transferring her 438 invalids got underway. The process was actually completed within three hours, but any thoughts of an early respite were dashed when the hospital ship *Formosa*, carrying another 393 patients, arrived alongside at 5.25pm. After the departure of the *Formosa* on 28 January things once again quietened down, but it would not be until 30 January that orders would finally arrive directing the *Britannic* to return to Southampton as soon as the hospital ships *Essequibo*, *Nevasa* and *Panama* had transferred their patients. Sure enough, the following morning the *Essequibo* was alongside with another 594 invalids and 24 hours later it was the turn of the *Nevasa* with another 493; the *Panama* finally arrived on the morning of 4 February with 319 more, and at 3.15pm that same day the *Britannic*, having taken aboard a total of 2,237 invalids, was once again westbound for Gibraltar.

The *Britannic* was back at Southampton on 9 February, where she would languish for the next six weeks. The evacuation of the Gallipoli beaches, combined with the resulting decrease in the number of casualties from the Mediterranean, had left the Transport Division struggling to find any justification to keep the vessel in service, and the rumours of the *Aquitania* having brought home only 1,500 wounded on her last voyage did not help the case for retaining the larger transports indefinitely. With little prospect of the *Britannic* being put to any practical use for the foreseeable future, on 22 February she was quietly moved to an open anchorage off Cowes in order to vacate the berth at Southampton for more important vessels.

However, even though the *Britannic* was now out of sight, she was by no means out of mind. On 1 February 1916, during the extended stay at Naples, a representative of the Neapolitan Sanitary Authorities had gone aboard in order to inspect the medical procedures and precautions, after which the Italians subsequently raised official concerns regarding the use of Naples as a base for transferring patients due to the potential 'dangers of infection'. The more secluded Sicilian port of Augusta was suggested as an alternative, at which point an Admiralty transport officer was quickly dispatched from Malta to examine the facilities there. His initial prognosis was not encouraging – aside from the dearth of coaling facilities at Augusta, he also concluded that the small number of jetties would make the transfer of casualties more difficult – but while the transport officers from Malta were speaking, the Transport Division in London didn't seem to be listening. Captain Bartlett was more sanguine about the prospect, noting that while Augusta was by no means ideal, the *Britannic* could anchor in 10 fathoms of water if need be. With the port being open to the south-east, the anchorage would be exposed to strong winds from that quarter, which would not only make the transfer of invalids more difficult but would also make it advisable to have steam up and ready for immediate use at all times, but despite these drawbacks, Bartlett's letter was positive enough to set the minds of the Transport Division at rest.

By the afternoon of Monday 20 March, after a lay-up of almost six weeks, the *Britannic* was finally headed for her new Sicilian terminal. One man destined not to be on board for the third voyage, however, would be Dr John Beaumont, forced to leave the ship the day before sailing after contracting paratyphoid B fever on the previous voyage. In his place went David Stevens-Muir, who had been on the *Arabic* when it was torpedoed seven months earlier, and he could not have picked an easier voyage on which to start his tenure on the *Britannic*. Despite the wet and foggy conditions in Britain, by the time the ship arrived at Naples on 25 March the weather was glorious; two days later, having taken on coal and water as usual, the ship was once again

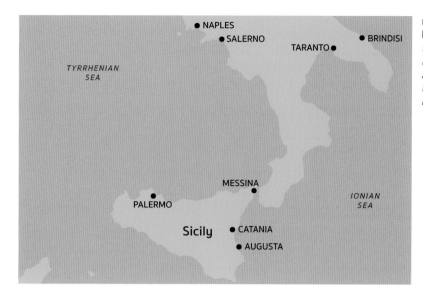

● NAPLES
● SALERNO
TARANTO ●
● BRINDISI

TYRRHENIAN SEA

MESSINA ●

IONIAN SEA

●
PALERMO

Sicily   ● CATANIA
● AUGUSTA

LEFT: *The Britannic's terminals at Naples and Augusta in the central Mediterranean.*

headed south for the Strait of Messina.

Dr Harold Goodman later recalled that as the *Britannic* entered the bay of Augusta on the morning of 28 March, several hospital ships were already awaiting their arrival. The transfer procedure was not helped when, upon dropping anchor, the *Britannic* was quickly surrounded by numerous boats selling oranges, but by 10.15 enough space had been cleared on the port side for the *Dunluce Castle* to go alongside. By 12.15 things were also clear enough on the starboard side for the *Egypt* to begin disembarking her passengers, while further aft a Canadian field hospital was busy transhipping their equipment.

By the following morning, Wednesday, the pace seemed to have settled down. The aft cranes were still busily hauling the Canadian equipment on board while the embarkation of patients from the *Glengorm Castle* and *Valdivia* had slowed to a trickle, allowing Dr Goodman time to join one of the ship's launches going

ashore to collect sand for cleaning the decks – something for which Captain Bartlett, sometimes referred to by his crew as 'Holystone Charlie', had a particular liking. After being piggybacked to the shore by the local boatmen, Goodman and a ship's officer went for a stroll through the orange and lemon groves to a local farm, while the deckhands collected Captain Bartlett's precious sand, but it would only be the briefest of sojourns with everyone ordered to be back on board in time for lunch. After that it was once again business as usual when the hospital ship *Formosa* arrived alongside, although by this time Goodman had been called away from his embarkation duties to clear L, M and N wards of any patients in order to make space for the orderlies of the 1st London Field Ambulance. It was only when he became aware of the vibration of the *Britannic*'s engines at 3pm that he realised the ship's one and, as it turned out, only visit to Augusta was over.

Skirting the south-east corner of Sicily, on

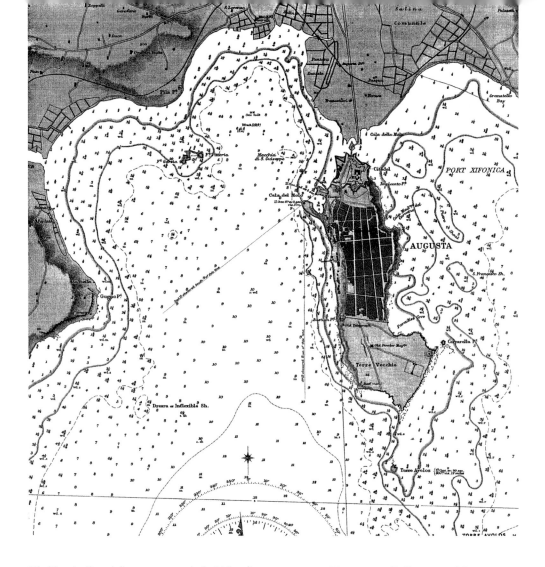

ABOVE : *The eastern Sicilian port of Augusta.*

31 March the daily run recorded 444 miles in the 21 hours to midday, but the following day the ship was headed into a strong north-westerly, so that when Gibraltar was passed at about 9.30pm on 2 April the daily run had been reduced to 442 miles. The rest of the voyage would be largely routine, save for the death of Private Robert Pask of the 8th South Wales Borderers, succumbing to diabetes in the early hours of 4 April, but with the *Britannic* by this time so close to home, his body, like that of Private Vincent on the first voyage, would be landed for burial at Netley.

By 11am on 4 April, the *Britannic* was once again safely in the White Star Dock, but this time the welcome-home committee had included Surgeon General Benjamin Franklin and several Russian princes, who had gone aboard for lunch. It was a sure sign that something was afoot, and with the ship being nowhere near full to capacity, few on board would have been too optimistic regarding the *Britannic*'s ongoing viability. The *Mauretania* had already been paid off on 1 March, with the *Aquitania* due to follow her on 10 April, so it therefore came as no surprise when later that day the expected news was confirmed: the *Britannic* would be laid up and the ship's medical staff dispersed to other duties. Declining Colonel Anderson's offer of an immediate transfer to the hospital ship *Dover Castle*, Harold Goodman chose instead to remain with the *Britannic* for one more week to complete the itemising of the ship's remaining inventory, even though the huge vessel was becoming increasingly deserted. On 6 April the nursing staff disembarked for the last time, while Goodman remained to oversee the landing of the remaining stores over the next five days, but even though he was thrilled by the fact that his manifest showed a surplus on practically all the supplies that had been issued, his enthusiasm was crushed when one of the NCOs told him, 'It doesn't matter a damn!'

At 4pm on 11 April 1916, Harold Goodman,

along with Colonel Anderson and doctors Urwick and MacClagan, stood at the end of the quay to watch the *Britannic* as she pulled away from the White Star Dock to her new anchorage off Cowes. All that remained to be done was to make the necessary payments to the Southampton customs officers regarding the Chianti he had bought in Naples, after which he returned to Guildford for seven days' leave. His next posting would be to the 76th Field Ambulance in France, but in the case of the *Britannic* there was no such certainty. After only three voyages, the ship was already surplus to requirements.

BELOW: *A medical officer snaps the nurses playing a game of deck cricket on the promenade deck.*

CHAPTER THIRTEEN

A YEAR OF
LIVING DANGEROUSLY

The end of the Gallipoli campaign had resulted in an uncertain future for the larger hospital ships; by the end of January 1916 the future employment of all four of Great Britain's largest liners was in increasing doubt. Lord Kitchener's decision to abandon the beaches of Gallipoli, although a welcome relief to the increasingly pressed Allied forces in the eastern Mediterranean, meant there was also no longer the need for large numbers of reinforcements to be sent to Mudros.

Due to the secrecy of the evacuation it would still take a while for the full effect of the withdrawal to filter through the system, even though the numbers of reinforcements had already started to be reduced for the winter as early as September 1915. The complete abandonment of the Gallipoli beachheads at Suvla Bay and Anzac Cove on 20 December left

BELOW: *The* Olympic, *now in the guise of Transport 2810, armed with a 12-pounder gun on the foc'sle and two 4.7" guns on the poop deck.*

only the original Cape Helles beachhead, and by 9 January 1916 even that had gone, yet five days earlier Captain Hayes had still received sailing orders to return to the Mediterranean.

Sure enough, at 8.30am on 4 January the *Olympic* was once again bound for Lemnos, minus storekeeper Thomas Watts, who had been dismissed from duty the previous day after

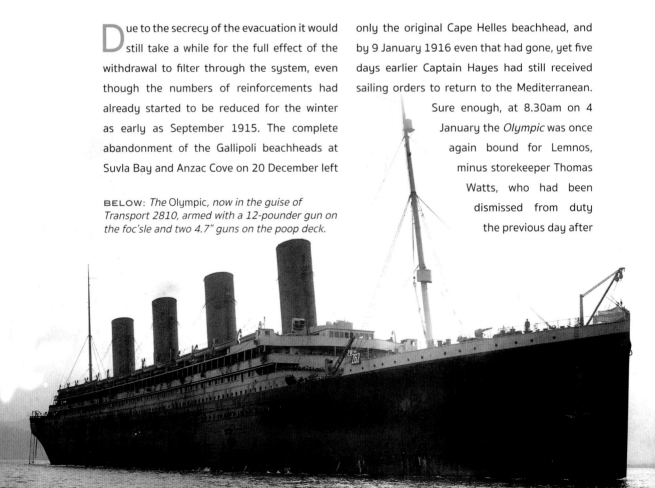

being caught selling stores from the ship's canteen.

The journey itself went without a hitch and by 31 January the *Olympic* was safely back at Liverpool, awaiting instructions for the next voyage. It was while the ship was secured in the Mersey that Captain Hayes decided to experiment with a notion he had been considering for some time. Reasoning that whenever the was in home port the number of crew absent from duty had soared, Hayes assembled his entire stokehold crew in the forward well deck and proposed that they consider taking what he called 'disembodied leave'. His idea was that by granting generous leave while in home port, although the men would not be paid while they were away from the ship, considering the high cost of any fines levied on those who did abscond from duty this was probably no great loss to them. The scheme certainly struck the right note with the black gang, and for the next ten days it seems logical to assume that they took full advantage of the generous new arrangement.

By 11 February the *Olympic* was once again outward bound, one assumes with a relatively complete and happy stokehold crew, this time bound for Southampton where, over a five-day period, she would embark troops. She would remain tied up in the White Star Dock for six days, enjoying another brief reunion with the *Britannic*, having returned three days earlier from her second voyage to the Mediterranean, but by the morning of 17 February the *Olympic* was once again outward bound for Mudros. By now, the routine was running like clockwork. Disembarkation of the troops at Lemnos had

been quicker than ever and by 27 February the ship was already on her way home. The voyage was not quite as uneventful as the previous one, however, when only one day out of Mudros a submarine was observed shadowing a small unidentified steamer, but perhaps mindful of Admiral de Robeck's earlier reprimand, Captain Hayes simply alerted the local patrol vessels and continued at high speed to La Spezia. The coaling process at the Italian port seemed to proceed as slowly as ever, but this time the master-at-arms found himself dealing with a more unusual on-board situation. Pilfering by the crew on any ship was not uncommon, but three days after arriving in port the theft turned out to be not quite so petty when a stock check revealed a significant number of items missing from the forward canteen, the final list consisting of one tin of sausages, 12 bottles of Bovril, two tins of sweets, nine tins of cocoa and milk, 42 lb of tobacco, 65 pairs of drawers, 72 singlets and 700 cigarettes. The ship was searched from end to end without result, but the following day a large pile of the missing stores, including 72 singlets, 60 pairs of drawers and 600 cigarettes, mysteriously reappeared in the main companionway on E deck. The pilfered food was never recovered, nor, unsurprisingly, the 42 lb of tobacco.

By the time the *Olympic* arrived back at Liverpool on 13 March, her future as a military transport was as uncertain as that of the *Britannic*, but while the *Olympic* was still fitted out as a trooper there was no immediate rush to lay her up. Certainly, the Transport Division had been considering their options as early as January, even toying with the notion of using the *Olympic* to convey troops to India, but the potential logistics of such a voyage only served to illustrate once again just how limited the use of the larger ships could be. Gallipoli had proved beyond doubt that the speed and size of the *Olympic* made her ideal for carrying large numbers of troops over great distances, but the logistics for a voyage to the subcontinent would prove to be particularly daunting. Even maintaining a speed of only 19 knots the ship would consume an estimated 550 tons of coal per day, meaning that some 8,760 tons would be needed just to reach Cape Town, but with the ship's maximum bunker capacity of 7,430 tons this would only be a realistic possibility if the ship stopped to refuel at the Cape Verde islands. The ever helpful White Star management even suggested the possibility of cutting through the bulkhead between holds

2 and 3 to increase the ship's reserve bunker capacity, but the downside of this proposal was that the ship's draught would be 38 feet 6 inches – 4 feet more than her designed load draught. When fully loaded, this would require the *Olympic* to be anchored 1,200 yards from the dock entrance at Cape Town, where the number of available coaling lighters was already limited, while at Bombay the logistics would have required her to anchor 2 or 3 miles out to sea. Trincomalee, although offering a less exposed anchorage, also did not have coaling facilities to accommodate a vessel of her size. The officer investigating the proposal had no doubt what he thought about the logistical nightmare, writing: 'The whole matter appears to bristle with difficulties from a coaling point of view. I hesitate to say that the proposal is an impracticable one...'

BELOW: *The* Aquitania *and* Olympic *at Mudros.*

Not surprisingly, on 8 February the Transport Division decided to shelve the plan altogether, the net result being that the *Olympic*'s future as a trooper remained as uncertain as ever. There seemed to be little doubt that she would be paid off or laid up along with the *Mauretania*, *Aquitania* and *Britannic* when, right on cue, the Canadian government suddenly stepped in to save the day. Vessels were urgently required to transport the increasing number of Dominion troops from the North American continent to Europe, a task for which the *Olympic* was tailor-made, and with the Dardanelles now abandoned she could be made available almost immediately. The following month the *Olympic* was officially chartered to the Canadian government and at midnight on 22 March 1916 Captain Hayes, for the first time in almost 18 months, pointed the *Olympic* westwards across the North Atlantic towards her new North American terminal at Halifax, Nova Scotia.

The *Olympic* made her maiden arrival at Halifax on 28 March, the ship's log sadly having to record the death of one James Donovan the previous day from cardiac failure, but on arrival Captain Hayes immediately found himself with huge concerns over the Canadian navy's strategic thinking. There was no issue about getting the troops to sea as quickly as possible, but the notion of having the ship travel as part of a protected convoy was more concerning, particularly when he learned that the convoy's speed would be limited to only 12 knots. Travelling at such a reduced speed would have made the *Olympic* an irresistible target for any self-respecting U-boat captain, and he urged the Canadians to allow him to sail unescorted, relying instead on the ship's high speed, which had always been her best defence against submarines. Fortunately, the Canadians were prepared to listen and it was agreed that the *Olympic* would be allowed to sail alone, especially as none of the escorts had either the necessary range or speed to keep up with her for the entire crossing. By 9.15am on 5 April the embarkation of the Canadian troops was complete as Hayes once again set course for Liverpool, but the voyage got off to an ominous start before the ship had even reached the open sea. Everything seemed to be going according to plan until the *Olympic* stopped to rendezvous with a patrol vessel as it came alongside to take off the pilot, when, as the smaller vessel began to roll in the choppy seas, its mast carried away lifeboats 24 and 26 on the *Olympic*'s aft port side, damaging one of the Welin davits in the process. Fortunately, no one had been hurt in the accident and the rest of the crossing passed uneventfully, with the *Olympic* arriving back at Liverpool on 11 April.

On the whole, 1916 would be a good year for the *Olympic*, successfully completing ten voyages between Halifax and Liverpool. Throughout these voyages Captain Hayes had to record only two losses in the log, the first on 5 May when Private JG Stephen of the Canadian Expeditionary Force's 51st Battalion died of cardiac syncope and was buried at sea that same day, the second on 7 June, when Private Oswald Peto of the 88th Battalion died of pleurisy at the end of the third voyage. The two most serious occurrences in the log took place in the autumn, the first at 8am on 29 October when the *Olympic* temporarily grounded off

New Brighton while swinging at anchor in the Mersey. For nearly four and a half hours the vessel was beached, raising fears of possible structural damage to the keel, but a thorough sounding of the hull after she had floated off again could detect no sign of any damage; less than 24 hours later, the ship was once again westbound for Canada, where she arrived safely on 5 November. The arrival, however, was not without incident, with the log recording a serious fire that day in the third-class galley flue, taking two hours to bring under control. By the time the flames had been extinguished, the area – located mostly inside the dummy funnel – had sustained extensive structural damage, but with the ship already due her annual refit at the end of the year they were able to make do with temporary repairs.

More than anything, it was the day-to-day crew matters that took up most of the time on or off the ship, and it seems that even during times of national emergency the *Olympic* was not exempt from the occasional industrial dispute. On 17 May, while secured at Liverpool, Captain Hayes had mustered his crew to inform them that they would no longer be receiving their £1 monthly war risk bonus from the Admiralty, but that the White Star Line would instead be paying an extra £1 on top of the wages normally paid to the crew. In effect, the wages would remain unaltered, but while the crew accepted the revised arrangement under protest, Joseph Cotter, General President of the National Union of Ships' Stewards, Cooks, Butchers and Bakers, saw things differently. His members did not earn as much as some of the other grades on the ship and he argued

that as his members had been guaranteed an Admiralty bonus in the ship's articles, it should therefore still be paid. The discussions were not helped when someone rather tactlessly hinted that if the men failed to accept the new terms, they might be dismissed from the ship, the implication being that with military conscription having been introduced in January 1916, the dissenting crewmen risked being called up for military service if they failed to find another vessel within two weeks of leaving. Perhaps in an effort to find a face-saving way to dig himself out of the hole he had created, Cotter suggested a compromise whereby the crew could be re-signed under a new agreement, but while the Admiralty had no problem with the proposal, they remained adamant that the disputed war bonus would not be paid beyond 1 May.

A more ominous incident occurred later that year, revealing a potential threat to the troops on board when, in October 1916, the Superintending Aliens Officer at Southampton received an anonymous tip-off informing him that there was not only a baker on board the *Olympic* who was of German descent, but that his father had been interned in one of the camps on the Isle of Man. The information was vague at best, but the Senior Naval Officer at Southampton was nevertheless instructed to look into the matter. His investigation revealed that Frederick Repphun, although having been born in Liverpool, was indeed the son of a German expatriate who had lived in England for 30 years. Although his mother was English, Repphun admitted that he had been forced to go to sea after experiencing difficulty in obtaining work on land following the loss of the *Lusitania*, due to his German ancestry. The issue of his parentage had never come to light because the Board of Trade only asked for details of nationality, and as he was a British national he was therefore a legitimate member of the crew. In normal circumstances this would have been enough for the matter to be dropped, but during the investigation it transpired that Repphun was also suffering from a rather severe case of venereal disease, which, because it would take up to two months to cure, forced him to leave the ship for medical reasons. And so the entire matter quickly blew over – well, almost. A few days later, an official at the Admiralty requested that a letter be sent to the *Olympic*'s company doctor, asking him to explain how and why someone suffering from venereal disease had been passed as fit to serve as a baker on one of His Majesty's troop transports.

On 30 December the *Olympic* returned to Liverpool, having completed ten round trips to Halifax. Tired and long overdue for a refit at Harland & Wolff, on 12 January 1917 she duly arrived back at Belfast, where for the next three months she would undergo a complete overhaul, but by this time fate had already dealt the White Star Line yet another heavy blow. Of the three great ships first envisaged by Joseph Bruce Ismay and Lord Pirrie nearly ten years earlier, only the first now remained.

BELOW: Olympic with Returned Soldiers at Halifax *by Arthur Lismer (1919).*

CHAPTER FOURTEEN

BRITANNIC RECALLED

As the *Britannic* lay idle at Belfast throughout the summer of 1916, the war continued at an unabated pace, but while the military situation in the Mediterranean had settled down, the British Somme offensive in France had resulted in ruinous casualties. During the week ending 9 July alone, a total of 151 hospital trains had left Southampton carrying over 30,000 casualties, while the reconditioning of the *Aquitania* and *Britannic* for commercial service had continued uninterrupted.

BELOW: *In spite of the large advance paid by the Admiralty to recondition the ship for commercial service, minimal work seemed to have been carried out on the Britannic during the summer of 1916, save for the appearance of an additional deckhouse on the starboard poop.*

The war at sea had also taken a dramatic turn. The long-awaited clash between the British Grand Fleet and German High Seas Fleet on 31 May would also lead to a decisive change in the conduct of the war, although perhaps this would not have been immediately appreciated.

While the German fleet had more than held its own during the clash, the Battle of Jutland had proved to the German admirals once and for all that they could not hope to win a large surface action. In the weeks to come, the emphasis of the German sea campaign would instead focus less on the construction of battleships and more on the rapid expansion of their submarine fleet.

As the summer wore on, the flow of casualties from the Mediterranean also started to rise. Gallipoli may have been abandoned, but since October 1915 an Allied force had been established at Salonika in northern Greece in order to frustrate a potential supply line between Germany and Turkey. The opening of a new Allied offensive at Salonika against Bulgaria in September 1916, combined with two ongoing British offensives against the Turkish armies in Palestine and Mesopotamia, meant that the hospital facilities at Mudros were under intense pressure as disease once again reared its ugly head. This time it was malaria rather than typhoid or dysentery doing the damage, and by the late summer the situation was once again critical. No doubt the War Office belatedly realised their short-sightedness in paying off the *Britannic* altogether, rather than keeping the ship laid up at half-rate, but as the *Aquitania* was already at Southampton and occupying badly needed harbour facilities, on 21 July the Cunard flagship was once again requisitioned as a hospital ship. In the end it didn't really matter which ship was called up first, when, on 28 August, news also arrived at White Star's Liverpool office advising that the *Britannic* was again being requisitioned as a hospital ship.

ABOVE: *VAD nurse Vera Brittain, a passenger in transit to Malta on the* Britannic*'s fourth voyage and later a famous pacifist.*

It's hard to see how much work may have been carried out on the *Britannic* over the previous three months, although it is clear that some work had been done as on 20 October the White Star Line informed the Transport Division that for insurance purposes the vessel's first cost had risen by over £27,000. Even so, any internal work that had been carried out would probably have been quickly undone as the Belfast workforce set about re-establishing the ship's original military specifications. They must have made double-quick time as by 9 September the *Britannic* had not only left Belfast but had also taken on new medical staff, equipment and stores at Southampton, before returning to her former anchorage off Cowes. In terms of the senior medical staff, Lieutenant Colonel Henry Anderson was reappointed as the ship's senior medical officer, while on 1 September the formidable Elizabeth Dowse was transferred from Lakenham Military Hospital in Norwich to assume the position of ship's matron. On 4 September, Charles Bartlett, who had returned *pro tem* to his civilian duties at Liverpool, was also reappointed to command the ship, but even though the senior personnel were back in post, the following weeks would seem like something of an anticlimax.

While everything may have seemed calm in the waters off Cowes, in Whitehall the *Britannic*'s return to service had provided the War Office with an ideal opportunity to transport large numbers of RAMC medical personnel and Voluntary Aid Detachment nurses to their foreign postings. The VAD nurses were duly ordered to report aboard the *Britannic* on 23 September and among their number was 22-year-old nurse and later famous pacifist Vera Brittain. Vera would never forget her first sight of the distant *Britannic* as the tender proceeded down Southampton Water, describing her as '...a great white monster with four funnels and three large red crosses painted on her side'. Once on board, her first impressions were confirmed: 'To us who have never been on a liner before, her size was almost terrifying, especially when I looked over A deck after night had fallen and noticed her height from the water.' Sadly, Vera would be quite disappointed with her accommodation

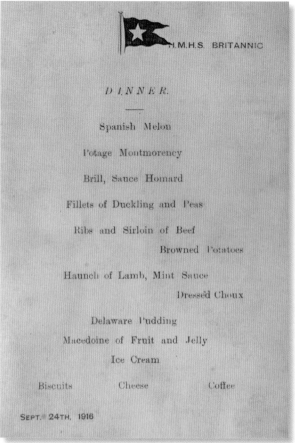

ABOVE: *The first dinner at sea after the Britannic's return to service.*

– an inner cabin without a porthole – even though it was a lot cosier than the wards into which the later arrivals would go. Sunday 24 September found the *Britannic* still anchored off Cowes, allowing the opportunity for any last letters home to be taken off by the pilot, but by 5.40pm the ship, escorted for the first stage of the journey by a destroyer and several seaplanes, was finally on her way back to the Mediterranean.

Once again Biscay lived up to its fearsome reputation, cutting a swathe through those members of the medical staff who had yet to find their sea legs. Even those who did brave the dinner tables didn't stay for long, but by the following day the waters were considerably calmer and on the morning of Friday 29 September the *Britannic* entered the Bay of Naples for the first time in six months. By Sunday evening the last of the coaling had been completed and the ship was once again bound for the Aegean on the final and most hazardous part of the voyage to Lemnos, clearing the three rows of mines protecting the Bay of Mudros by the afternoon of Tuesday 3 October. The embarkation of patients began almost immediately from the seven hospital ships that already lay in the harbour, one of the first alongside being the *Galeka*, which by 9pm had been emptied of its patients and was ready to embark the nurses who had been posted to Malta. This time Vera's experience of life on a hospital ship was less agreeable, no longer finding herself in a comfortable cabin, but instead in one of the *Galeka*'s lower wards, which offered little in the way of privacy and only the most primitive sanitary arrangements. Not only that but it had only just been vacated by the convalescing troops, so it comes as no surprise that by the time the *Galeka* reached Malta, 16 of the VAD nurses, including Vera, would be suffering from a serious fever.

By 11 October the *Britannic* was safely back at Southampton, the voyage home largely uneventful save for the death that same day of Corporal Joseph Seddon of the 1st Battalion Manchester Regiment. Despite the four-month lay-up, the *Britannic* had slipped effortlessly back into her old routine and the following

voyage, beginning only nine days later, would be much the same. The outward journey went like clockwork with the ship arriving at Naples on 25 October, and at Mudros during the early hours of 28 October. Over the next two days a total of 3,022 casualties would be taken aboard from the hospital ships *Dunluce Castle*, *Glenart Castle*, *Llandovery Castle*, *Grantully Castle*, *Valdivia* and *Wandilla*, so that by 6 November all but one of the invalids had been safely returned to Southampton, the exception being Corporal George Firth Hunt of the RAMC, formerly of the 38th General Hospital at Salonika, who had died on 2 November of dysentery and heart failure. Three months later, Hunt's death would be pivotal in casting a giant shadow over the *Britannic*'s reputation in a way that few could possibly have imagined at the time.

Although the stormy weather that had accompanied the *Britannic* on her return to Southampton had subsided, damage to the *Aquitania*'s stern meant that her next scheduled departure would have to be delayed. However, with the hospitals at Mudros still under pressure, the Transport Division was unable to wait that long and in her fastest turnaround to date, at 2.23pm on 12 November, a calm and bitterly cold Sunday afternoon, the *Britannic* was once again headed down Southampton Water and back to Mudros – or so everyone thought.

For the next six days they made steady progress, passing through the Strait of Gibraltar around midnight on the 15th and arriving at Naples on the morning of Friday 17 November to take on coal and water. By late afternoon the preparations were well underway to put to sea again, until all hopes of a quick turnaround were

RIGHT: *A sketch by Rev John Fleming of one of the wounded soldiers aboard the Britannic.*

dashed when the stormy weather rendered the ship's passage through the harbour entrance too hazardous. There was nothing left to do except ride it out, but by the Sunday afternoon the storm seemed to have broken, giving Captain Bartlett the opportunity he needed to put to sea. Even then it turned out to be only a brief respite, with the seas beginning to rise again even before the harbour pilot had disembarked, but by the following morning the *Britannic* was safely through the Strait of Messina and in calmer waters.

On board, the activity was as frantic as ever. The nurses were still busily finishing making up the 3,000 medical cots while the store men were issuing the last of the medical equipment and preparing thousands of hospital suits for the patients, but Nurse Sheila Macbeth records that by the Monday afternoon the work was

complete, allowing the nurses time for their afternoon dip in the ship's swimming bath. Having entered the eastern Mediterranean, the *Britannic* was now in the most dangerous waters of the voyage, but if there were any concerns on board then no one seemed particularly keen to show it. That evening the usual church service, described by Private Percy Tyler of the RAMC as 'one of the best since the boat had been in commission', was held in the large dining saloon, with all on-board activities continuing as if there was absolutely nothing out of the ordinary.

Having safely skirted Cape Matapan the previous evening, by the morning of Tuesday 21 November the *Britannic* was approaching the Saronic Gulf, making a steady 20 knots. Everything was in readiness for the ship to arrive at Mudros at about lunchtime when shortly before 8am, after taking bearings off Angalistros Point on the nearby island of Makronisos, the *Britannic* assumed a course of N 48° E, bringing her into the Kea Channel. Ahead lay the Petali Gulf and the Doro Passage between the islands of Euboea and Andros, followed by a straight run to Lemnos. Up on the bridge, Chief Officer Robert Hume and Fourth Officer Duncan McTavish were standing watch, while, as eight bells sounded, lookout J Murray was up in the crow's nest relieving lookout J Conelly at the end of his watch. Down below, the ship's Presbyterian chaplain, Rev John Fleming, was in his starboard cabin gazing out of the porthole at the distant white-painted town of Ioulida, perched high up in the hills of the nearby island of Kea, while most of the nurses were enjoying their last breakfast before the patients came aboard. Further down in the

ship, RAMC orderly Private Percy Tyler, having already had his breakfast, was sitting on his bunk in barrack room 2 industriously polishing his tunic buttons and Private Thomas Jones was on duty in his allocated ward, busy with his final preparations in order to be ready to receive their first batch of wounded soldiers later that day.

At 8.12am the tranquillity was suddenly and unexpectedly shattered by the sound of a loud explosion, which Rev Fleming, who was just leaving his cabin to go up to breakfast, later described '...as if a score of plate glass windows had been smashed together'. Depending on where you were in the ship, the reaction to the

BELOW: *The blustery conditions at Naples would delay the* Britannic's *departure by almost two days.*

initial blast varied. Back in his ward, located amidships, Thomas Jones felt only a slight jar and did not think that anything serious had happened, whereas the ward's medicine dispenser was not as relaxed as he came rushing out of the dispensary.

'Come, on, Tom, lad!'
'What's up?'
'She's got something this morning.'

With that, two men were quickly headed for the boat deck.

Down in his barrack room, Percy Tyler recalled a violent bump that was enough to make him stagger momentarily until he once again found his balance, yet no one in the room seemed overly concerned. One orderly commented that they had probably hit something, but no one even seemed interested enough to go topside to find out what it was that they might have hit. On the other hand, there were others who were much closer to the impact. Fifth Officer Gordon Fielding recalled a more violent blow. He was shaving in his cabin, just aft of the bridge on the boat deck, and recalled that the force of the explosion was so great that he was forcibly thrown across his cabin and ended up sprawled across the floor with much of the cabin's contents landing unceremoniously on top of him. For the narrowest of escapes perhaps we need look no further than Private John Cuthbertson, who was alone in the RAMC forward barrack room down on G deck. Aside from the concussion of the actual explosion, the rush of water quickly washed him through the door and up to the level of E deck. Almost

certainly the closest to the blast was stoker Albert Smith, working down in stokehold 11 of boiler room 6. Having passed down the forward firemen's tunnel only moments earlier at the beginning of his watch, he felt not only the full effect of the blast but also the mass of cold water that was suddenly pouring into the tunnel. Somehow, he managed to fight his way to the escape ladder in the vestibule forward of boiler room 6, and moments later he was safely up on E deck, at the forward end of the 'Scotland Road' working passage.

Despite the mayhem below, at first the situation in the lounge remained calm. Sensing the nurses' apprehension, Major Harold Priestley of the RAMC immediately stood up and instructed the ladies to stay where they were as the captain had not yet sounded the alarm. As everyone returned to their breakfast in the suddenly tense atmosphere of the lounge, Matron Elizabeth Dowse left the room to investigate. Up on the bridge, however, it was more intense. Captain Bartlett, who had himself been sitting down to breakfast in his cabin when the explosion occurred, suddenly found himself rushing onto the bridge while still dressed in his pyjamas. Immediately ordering the engines to be stopped, an assessment of the damage quickly revealed that a huge explosion had occurred low down on the forward starboard side, in the vicinity of the bulkhead between holds 2 and 3. With only two compartments open to the sea, the *Britannic* should not have been in any great danger, but the explosion had also inflicted serious damage to the forward pipe tunnel running between the forward boiler room to the firemen's quarters higher

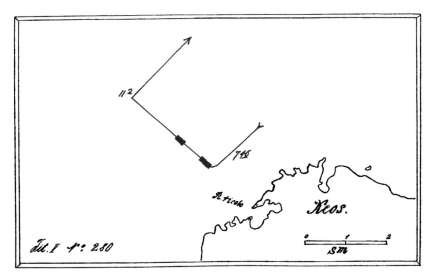

LEFT: *The war diary of the German submarine U-73, indicating the location of the two mine barriers laid by Kapitänleutnant Gustav Siess on the morning of 28 October 1916.*

up in the ship's bow. In theory, the external damage meant that only two or possibly three compartments were open to the sea, but with the watertight door between boiler room 6 and the pipe tunnel jammed open, combined with the open door between boiler rooms 6 and 5, within seconds tons of sea water was also surging into these undamaged compartments. Within two minutes, both of the forward boiler rooms had been evacuated, the only crumb of comfort being that the watertight door between boiler rooms 5 and 4 had definitely closed. Considering the White Star Line's confident claim that the *Olympic* could float with her forward six compartments open to the sea, this should in theory have been enough to save the ship; but nonetheless, moments later Captain Bartlett ordered a distress call to be sent, signalling that the *Britannic* had struck a mine off Port St Nikolo, and gave orders for the lifeboats to be uncovered.

As the alarm finally sounded throughout the ship, the previously subdued calm exploded into a deluge of frantic commotion as the crew reacted to their situation. Immediately after the explosion, Rev Fleming had returned to his cabin to snatch his lifebelt before heading for his assigned emergency station in one of the lower wards, but finding everything deserted immediately headed for the breakfast room. Major Priestley had already taken command of the situation, as nurse Ada Garland later recalled him standing up and saying in a calm voice, 'Ladies, go to your cabins, put on your lifebelts and go up to the boat deck.' Within seconds the nurses were all moving towards the exit in a hurried but orderly manner. Stewardess Violet Jessop, back with the White Star Line for her first voyage since leaving the nursing service herself, was in a nearby pantry when the alarm sounded, making up a breakfast tray for one of the nurses ill in her cabin. She later recalled that the men immediately 'dropped what they were doing and jumped over presses with the agility of deer. In seconds, not a soul was to be seen and not a sound had been uttered.'

CHAPTER FIFTEEN

CASUALTIES OF WAR

Within minutes the *Britannic*'s distress call had been picked up. Lieutenant Commander Henry Tupper, of the British destroyer HMS *Scourge*, was the first to hear the news at 8.15am, while standing by the beached Greek steamer *Sparti* after that vessel had struck a mine off the island of Phleva. The imprecise position given in the SOS didn't help, with several ports in the Aegean named after St Nikolo, but within minutes the destroyer was racing south toward Cape Sounion, while the slower French tugs *Goliath* and *Polyphemus* followed in her wake.

Fortunately, there was help even closer at hand, and more by luck than judgement they knew exactly where to look. The auxiliary cruiser HMS *Heroic*, on the mail run from Mudros to Salamis, had actually passed the *Britannic* less than an hour earlier, the *Britannic* making no small impression on the *Heroic*'s officer of the watch, Lieutenant R Paget, wishing he was on board the fine steamer himself. At 8.28am the *Heroic* had just turned north into the Saronic Gulf when the *Britannic*'s distress signal was received and without hesitation the ship's commanding officer, Lieutenant Commander Percival Ram RNR, turned hard about and headed quickly back towards the Kea Channel.

Unaware of the approaching rescue due to

BELOW: *HMS* Scourge.

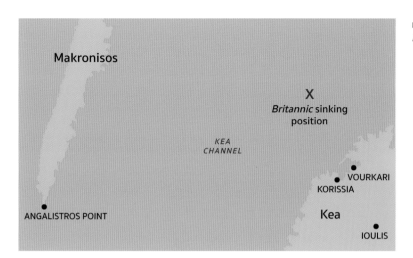

a fault with the *Britannic*'s damaged wireless receiver, Captain Bartlett quickly decided that his best chance lay in beaching his command on the nearby island of Kea. It was only a matter of 3 or 4 miles at most, but the manoeuvre was complicated by the fact that the ship's steering gear had apparently failed; in the end it was only by using the engines that he was able to successfully turn the ship towards the shore. Meanwhile, the evacuation of the ship was continuing for the most part in an orderly manner. An initial rush by a group of stewards on two of the boats under the aft port gantry davits was quickly brought under control by Fifth Officer Fielding, while down below, at the aft end of the promenade deck, cooler heads prevailed as the RAMC orderlies lined up in true military fashion for a roll call to be taken. As soon as the nurses had been taken up to the boat deck, Matron Elizabeth Dowse personally counted them all into the boats, before finally stepping in herself; the orderlies would then follow in groups of 50.

The apparent safety of the lifeboats, however, was just an illusion. Because the *Britannic* was still moving, the order had not yet been given to send them away, but simply to uncover and lower them over the side. Nurse Sheila Macbeth later recalled that, with her lifeboat suspended only a few feet above the churning surface of the water, they were kept hanging for what seemed like an eternity until the ship came to a complete halt. On the port side aft it was no different, where Fielding also kept his first two boats dangling 6 feet above the surface, much to the annoyance of its occupants. Further aft on the poop, however, the discipline momentarily lapsed when Assistant Commander Harry Dyke was forced to temporarily leave his post at the aft starboard gantry davits to call back a group of firemen who had launched from the stern without permission, before ordering them to rescue any swimmers who had jumped overboard.

All the while, the *Britannic* was still moving forwards, but as news arrived on the bridge of the flooding in the forward boiler rooms, combined with an increasing list to starboard,

the ship was also becoming increasingly unmanageable. Fifteen minutes after the explosion the portholes on E deck, normally 25 feet above the waterline, were already beneath the surface; to make matters worse, some of them had been opened earlier that morning by the medical staff to ventilate the lower wards before the ship arrived at Mudros later that day. It was not until 8.35am, 23 minutes after the explosion, that Fifth Officer Fielding finally heard the order to stop the engines so that the boats could be sent away, but the lowering procedure was further complicated by the fact that his forward set of girder davits jammed inboard almost immediately after lowering only one boat. Fortunately, he was still able to lower two more in quick succession from the aft set, including

one of the 5-ton motor launches, under the command of First Officer George Oliver, who had been ordered to co-ordinate the rescue of survivors in the water. After that, Fielding was only able to send away one final lifeboat, and even then with great difficulty, before the ship's increasing list to starboard made the launch of any more boats from the higher port side all but impossible.

It was at about this time that the events leading up to the great tragedy of the day would be set in motion, although based on the survivors' accounts there remains considerable doubt as to what happened. According to Fielding, two of the lifeboats under the forward Welin davits, being lowered by Third Officer Francis Laws, had apparently released their automatic lowering gear without authority before dropping into

LEFT: *Immediately after the alarm was sounded the RAMC orderlies would assemble in their parade ground in the enclosed aft well deck before being taken up to the boat deck.*

RIGHT: *A post-sinking sketch of the* Britannic's *compromised forward compartments.*

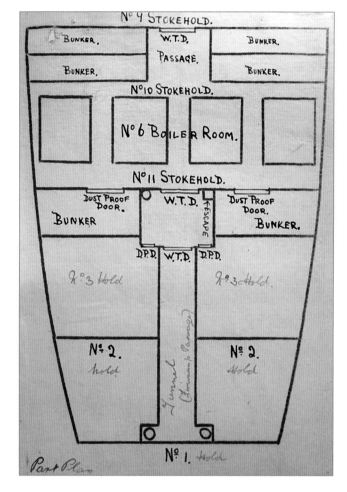

the water, but perhaps the greatest authority on what happened would be Violet Jessop. Immediately after the initial explosion, she had left the pantry where she was working to assist the nursing sister who had been lying ill in her cabin. After helping her to dress and sending her up to the boat deck, Violet then returned to her own cabin to retrieve a few of her most treasured possessions, including a ring, a Bible, an alarm clock and – remembering her dire need of one after the sinking of the *Titanic* – a toothbrush. Violet's own recollections

would seem to leave us in no doubt that the unfortunate boats were not launched without the knowledge of the third officer as, upon her arrival on deck, an unnamed officer was surprised to see a woman still on board, having assumed that all the nurses had already gone. Violet herself wrote that she could even see the boats pulling away while the *Britannic* was still moving, before taking her place in another lifeboat – number 4 on the forward port side – and awaiting her turn to be lowered over the side.

Violet recalled that as lifeboat 4 bounced and scraped down the port side of the listing ship, the boat caught on the brass rims of the open portholes, splintering the glass of the green electric light boxes running beneath the promenade deck, before finally hitting the water with a terrible impact. As the boats clustered along the *Britannic*'s side struggled to extricate themselves, the forward movement of the ship began to tell. All might have been well, but due to the combination of the increasing list to starboard and the *Britannic* now being heavily down by the bow, the huge port propeller was by now working well above the surface. As the lifeboats drifted aft, they were being drawn relentlessly towards the huge turning blades. At first Violet was oblivious to what was happening, until she realised that for some reason everyone in her boat was suddenly leaping into the water. Turning to see the huge

blades slicing through another lifeboat and its crew trying helplessly to escape, she knew that her only option was to jump, even though her childhood fear of drowning meant she had never learned to swim. She almost made it, but not quite; no sooner was she in the water than the blades were upon her as she was pulled under by the suction and spun around by the propeller before being shot back to the surface, hitting her head on the keel of the smashed lifeboat. By some miracle, however, although badly dazed and with a deep gash in her thigh, she was still alive and away from the ship. Moments later the propeller stopped turning, allowing Captain T Fearnhead just enough time to push against the now stationary blades as his

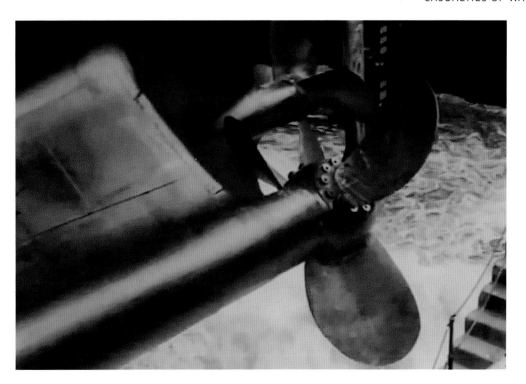

ABOVE: *The* Britannic's *port propeller, responsible for all thirty of the casualties on the day of the sinking.*

own lifeboat drifted clear, but in the meantime 30 men in the two smashed boats had paid the ultimate price. Violet Jessop would be one of the lucky survivors, and even then her injuries appeared to be mercifully light compared to others who had been unable to escape the turning propeller.

For a period of about ten minutes the *Britannic* lay motionless in the Kea Channel, during which time as many boats as possible were lowered into the water, but Colonel Anderson, collecting survivors in the port launch with First Officer Oliver, recalled that at 8.45am the ship's engines were restarted, and that as she once again began to move forwards she seemed to move in a wide circle

to the right. From his bridge, Captain Bartlett had noticed that the ship seemed to have stopped settling a little and with the situation apparently stabilised he had passed word to stop lowering boats in order to make a final attempt to work the *Britannic* towards Kea, now less than 3 miles distant. But it was not to be; the forward momentum once again increased the rate of flooding and whatever slim chance still remained disappeared when word finally arrived from below that the water had risen above D deck. With no further delay, the order went down for the engineers remaining in the engine room to come up top, and for those remaining on board to abandon ship.

Even now, during the last moments of the *Britannic*'s life, dozens of people still remained on the boat deck. Among the last to leave was Private Percy Tyler, in the second-to-last boat, after having made several trips below to fetch

179

ABOVE: *A lucky survivor from one of the smashed lifeboats, Stewardess Violet Jessop in her VAD uniform prior to returning to civilian service with the White Star Line.*

ABOVE: *Major Harold Edgar Priestley, RAMC.*

additional lifebelts. Also in the boat was one of the ship's sea scouts, who had to be thrown 'rather forcibly' into the boat just to get him to leave the ship, along with Rev Fleming, who had also been ordered in by Major Priestley. The good major would decline a seat himself, instead taking a final look around to make sure that everyone was safe, but minutes later he stepped into the last boat to be lowered, along with Claude Lancaster, the *Britannic*'s purser, who carried with him the ship's papers and – according to legend – even a spare uniform!

Fifth Officer Fielding, along with half a dozen of his remaining seamen and some 30 medical orderlies, also remained on board practically to the last, frantically throwing as many of the collapsible liferafts and deckchairs overboard as they could find, secure in the knowledge they would be using those very same rafts themselves only a few minutes later. Ordering the remaining RAMC orderlies over the side, Fielding was about to report to the bridge when he spied Sixth Officer Herbert Welsh beside one of the few remaining lifeboats, about to go overboard with his remaining crew. After much manoeuvring – badly burning his fingers with a running rope in the process – Fielding and his men got the boat over the side and managed the control brakes as the boat was lowered safely into the water; moments later, he followed the two remaining brakemen down the falls and into the boat. As the lifeboat pulled away, it seemed to Fielding as if the huge 53,000-ton *Britannic* was about to topple over right on top of them, with the forward superstructure by now so low in the water that Captain Bartlett, Commander Dyke and Chief Engineer Robert Fleming were practically able to walk off the bridge and into the water. Meanwhile, further aft he spied the assistant chief engineer and several of the remaining engine room officers sliding over the lofty stern of the ship, before rowing over to pull them from the water.

The *Britannic*'s remaining life could now be measured in seconds. As the ship continued to heel over to starboard, one by one the funnels crumpled at their bases before giving way under the strain. Across the water the survivors, keeping their distance as the ship went down, could only watch and listen to what sounded like a rumbling noise, thought by some to be

the boilers exploding inside the hull as the cold water rushed into the open funnel casings. By 9.07am – only 55 minutes after the initial explosion – what little stability remaining to the ship had gone as the *Britannic* completed her roll to starboard. Nurse Winifred Greenwood's last glimpse of what had been her home was nothing but a little bit of her stern through a cloud of smoke, which for a moment had become so thick that she was no longer able to see through it; by the time it had cleared, the *Britannic* had gone. As Winifred would later recall in her journal, 'The sea looked smooth almost as a mill pool, and the sun was shining down in splendour on the very spot where our ship was last seen.'

BELOW: *A photograph from nurse Sheila Macbeth's scrapbook, alleged to be the last of the* Britannic.

A MODERN GREEK TRAGEDY

Despite the horrific injuries caused by the *Britannic*'s propellers, the conditions in the Kea Channel compared to those in the North Atlantic after the *Titanic* had sunk over four years earlier were considerably easier. In April 1912 the *Titanic*'s survivors had found themselves stranded hundreds of miles out to sea in pitch black and freezing conditions, with most of the passengers having little idea as to when – or even if – their rescuers might arrive at the scene. With the *Britannic*, it was completely different. The survivors may have seen few positives, having just seen their ship most violently sunk, but the fact that the *Britannic* had gone down in broad daylight and barely 3 miles from the shore, along with the fact that the funnel smoke of the approaching rescue ships could already be seen on the horizon, was more than enough to reassure the dazed survivors. More importantly, in the case of the *Britannic* the lifeboats had gone back for survivors. Having managed to swim to one of the emergency floats, Captain Bartlett was quickly coordinating as many of the rescue activities in his immediate area as was possible, while the military discipline of the RAMC orderlies also paid dividends; before long the two motor launches, each towing another lifeboat, were headed towards Port St Nikolo on Kea, carrying as many of the seriously injured as possible. Matron Elizabeth Dowse had also seen to it that enough nurses were transferred into the boats going ashore, where they could assist with the injured; indeed, Sheila Macbeth later recalled that their brandy flasks proved invaluable, while other personal items, ranging from aprons to pillowcases and even parts of a lifejacket, served a far more practical purpose as slings and bandages.

Several local Greek fishing vessels had arrived on the scene almost immediately to assist with the rescue, but the *Heroic* and *Scourge* were also fast approaching from the west. The first on the scene was the *Heroic*, sighting the first of the *Britannic*'s lifeboats at 9.30am. By 10.15 the *Scourge* was also lowering her boats and over the course of the next two hours carried out a systematic search in the Kea Channel, rescuing 494 and 339 survivors respectively. By 11.30 both ships were full to overflowing

BELOW: *Port St Nikolo today.*

when the second wave of rescue vessels began to arrive. By 11.45 HMS *Foxhound*, under the command of Lieutenant Commander William Shuttleworth, was also at the scene and quickly proceeded into the harbour of St Nikolo where some 170 casualties, many seriously injured, had already been landed. As Shuttleworth arranged to take aboard the survivors, the scout cruiser HMS *Foresight* was making one

ABOVE: *The* Britannic *'s two motor launches proved invaluable in towing the seriously injured to the nearby island of Kea.*

final search in the channel in the faint hope of finding any more survivors, but by 2pm this vessel was also anchored in the harbour. *Foresight*'s staff surgeon, Dr Henry Braithwaite, was already there, having preceded them in the ship's steam cutter, so that by 2pm all the

wounded had already been taken aboard the *Foxhound*. Fifteen minutes later, Commander Shuttleworth weighed anchor and set a course for Salamis.

Throughout the afternoon, the three rescue vessels arrived alongside the ageing battleship HMS *Duncan*, flagship of Rear Admiral Arthur Hayes-Sadler. The *Heroic* was first to arrive, at 3.30, followed by *Scourge* some 45 minutes later, each ship quickly offloading the survivors who were then swiftly dispersed around the fleet. The nurses and medical staff found themselves being taken ashore to hotels in Piraeus and Phaleron while the ship's crew was scattered around the fleet, with some on the *Duncan* and some on the ships of the French Third Squadron, as well as the French depot ships *Kanaris* and *Marienbad*. Last to arrive was HMS *Foxhound* at 5.30; as soon as the uninjured survivors had been transferred to the *Duncan*, the destroyer proceeded alongside an old grain wharf where Major Priestley was overseeing the final transfer of the seriously injured to the

BELOW: *By the end of 1916 King Constantine of Greece was caught between rival political factions supporting the cause of the Central Powers or the Allies, as the country trod an increasingly difficult path to maintain its neutrality.*

THE PERSUADING OF TINO.

Russian Hospital in Piraeus. It was to be a long process and it would be past midnight before the *Foxhound* was finally ready to proceed out of the harbour and return to her patrol line.

ATHENS INTERLUDE

Dawn on 22 November 1916 found the *Britannic*'s crew with the unenviable task of having to bury four of their comrades who had not survived the previous day's ordeal. Private Arthur Binks of the RAMC and trimmer Charles Phillips had both died of their injuries on board the *Heroic*, while fireman Joseph Brown, although alive when picked up in the water by the crew of the French tug *Goliath*, had failed to recover. The final casualty would be lookout George Honeycott, who had died during the night at the Russian Hospital, but all four would be laid to rest in the cemetery of Drapetsona that afternoon. Unbeknown to the survivors, however, the political situation in Athens was such that the British naval authorities were particularly keen to have them repatriated as quickly as possible. The nurses, secure in the comfortable surroundings of the Aktaion Palace Hotel in Piraeus, were fortunate that their hotel manager was sympathetic to the Greek prime minister Eleftherios Venizelos, a strong supporter of the Allied cause, whereas the medical officers found themselves billeted in another hotel where the staff were more sympathetic to the Greek king Constantine's apparent wish to keep Greece neutral. The deteriorating political situation would culminate in the armed confrontation of the Noemvriana on 1 December, so the repatriation of the

Britannic survivors was becoming increasingly urgent. Before that could happen, however, the British naval authorities needed to complete their own investigation into the loss of the ship, not made any easier for HMS *Duncan*'s commanding officer, Captain Hugh Heard, who was faced with the task of obtaining as much information as possible from the 1,032 survivors scattered around Piraeus.

Compared to Lord Mersey's seemingly limitless resources available to the 1912 Titanic inquiry, Heard, assisted by Commander George Staer, *Duncan*'s senior engineer, had only three days and miniscule resources. Their final 725-word report was a model of military brevity, but after summarising the layout of the damaged compartments and the nature of the damage, it is the 144 words of the final paragraph that deal with the crucial issue of mine versus torpedo:

9. Question of mine or torpedo.
The water was deep, probably over
100 fathoms and there is a current
through the Zea Channel. This against
the mine theory.

Three persons gave good evidence of
having seen

(a) A Periscope

(b) The wake of a torpedo immediately
before the explosion and in its direction.
This man F. Walters, Deck Steward having
been an Officers Steward in the Navy had
seen torpedo practice. He did not pretend
to have seen the torpedo.

(c) The wake of a torpedo on port side
apparently missing aft. It is to be noted
that the sea was glassy smooth.

On other hand there is no evidence of a column of water having been thrown up outside the ship.

The effects of the explosion might have been due to either a mine or a torpedo. The probability seems to be a mine.

Those last seven words say it all. Only one week earlier, the French troop transport *Burdigala* had run foul of another German mine in the Kea Channel, but the survivors had been so convinced they had seen the periscope of a submarine that one gun crew had even opened fire on the mysterious target. As a result, the reports of a torpedo had been taken at face value and no subsequent search of the area had been made. Had the French authorities conducted even a basic sweep of the Kea Channel then maybe – just maybe – the *Britannic* could have avoided her own fatal rendezvous only one week later. All too late, by 22 November the possibility of mines was now being taken far more seriously when, later that day, the *Scourge* and *Foxhound* both returned to the Kea Channel to carry out the more systematic search that should perhaps have been made a week earlier.

In the meantime, the survivors remained in Piraeus until transport had been arranged for their hurried repatriation. On the afternoon of 24 November, the ship's uninjured officers and crew went aboard the auxiliary transport *Ermine* for the first stage of their repatriation to Mudros, where they arrived shortly before midnight on 25 November, allowing Vice Admiral Cecil Thursby additional time to personally interview some of the survivors aboard his flagship, HMS *Lord Nelson*. In the end, Thursby could collate no additional information of any great worth and by 3.30pm the following day the surviving crew had been transferred aboard the transport *Royal George*, departing the following morning on a five-day voyage to Marseilles. After three days at that port the crew then found themselves having to endure a 50-hour train journey north to Le Havre, and it was only on the evening of 7 December that the exhausted, frozen and half-starved survivors finally went aboard the troopship *Caesarea*. By the time they awoke the next morning, they were finally back at Southampton, almost one month after departing from that port on 12 November.

For the medical staff, the voyage home was no less arduous, going aboard the hospital ship *Grantully Castle* on 27 November at the start of a three-day voyage to Malta. After that, the men would be shipped home in batches, with the majority of the medical orderlies departing for Marseilles on 10 December aboard the transport *Huntsend*, before having to endure the same hellish train journey that the *Britannic*'s crew had suffered only a week earlier. In all, the nurses probably had the best of it, being held back on Malta in order to spare them the hardships of the overland train journey to Le Havre, but on 17 December they were suddenly ordered aboard the hospital ship *Valdivia*. They finally arrived back at Southampton on Boxing Day, but while they had by then missed Christmas Day at home, at least they were permitted to return home on indefinite leave and await orders.

CHAPTER SIXTEEN

PICKING UP THE PIECES

The loss of the *Britannic* did not signify the end of the line for Ismay and Pirrie's
original concept of a three-ship express service between Southampton and New
York, but with the *Titanic* and *Britannic* both gone, combined with the country's
shipyards being fully committed to the war effort for the foreseeable future,
there was no prospect of revisiting the concept before the end of the war.

BELOW: *The* Britannic *takes
on wounded at Mudros.*

From the White Star Line's perspective, the only positive news was that the British government was accepting the full insurance liabilities for any vessels sunk while on government service through enemy action, ensuring that the *Britannic*'s construction costs would eventually be recovered in full. Sure enough, on 23 January 1917 the Admiralty made an initial down payment of £1,750,000 to the company until the final accounts could be completed, although by the end of May 1917 the balance was still outstanding, as were additional payments for the loss of the *Laurentic* and *Afric*. All told, the Admiralty owed White Star £600,000 for these three ships alone and on 31 May Harold Sanderson wrote again to the Transport Division on the matter. The Admiralty would subsequently advance a further £100,000 to the company in mid-June, but it would still be many months before the accounts were cleared in full.

The Admiralty, however, had more pressing concerns. The *Britannic* was gone but her legacy lived on, and if the Germans were to be believed then the British had every reason to be concerned. It had all begun on 13 October 1916, when the Transport Division had asked the Admiralty for permission to accept a request from the War Office to transport 501 officers and men of the RAMC, 161 nurses and 311 tons of medical stores in the *Britannic* on her next voyage to Mudros. Three days later the Board of the Admiralty determined that any future requests to transport medical personnel in hospital ships should not be approved, except perhaps for nurses who would be unlikely to raise any concerns about legality,

but because the request had been received prior to this decision it was agreed that on the grounds of expediency it would be treated as a special case. As a result, on 17 October the RAMC was duly instructed to have their stores alongside the ship and ready for loading the following day. When the *Britannic* departed on her fifth voyage on 20 October, along with her usual complement of medical staff she also had on board an additional 483 medical personnel destined for various theatres of war including Egypt, Malta, Salonika and India, as well as almost 3,000 packages of medical stores.

Up until the ship's arrival at Mudros on 28 October the transport arrangements would not have been of any great concern to anyone, until the hospital ship *Wandilla* arrived alongside two days later. Among the *Wandilla*'s passengers was Adalbert Franz Messany, a 24-year-old Austrian opera singer who had been interned in Egypt at the outbreak of the war and later transferred to Malta in December 1914. When he contracted tuberculosis, the medical authorities on Malta agreed to his repatriation to Austria and on 24 October he was placed aboard the *Wandilla* for transport to Mudros. While waiting to transfer to the *Britannic* for the next stage of his journey home, Messany had several days to observe the activities, including the ongoing transfer of the medical personnel and packages from the *Britannic* to other hospital ships, before being isolated in the *Britannic*'s mortuary for the voyage to England. The situation would become even more complicated on 2 November when Corporal George Firth Hunt of the RAMC died from dysentery. In accordance with the standard procedures, Hunt's body was placed in the mortuary before burial at sea later that evening, at which point Messany was moved to a bunk in one of the wards, where he would remain for the next four days. For the rest of the voyage Messany was therefore able to speak freely with his fellow patients, including two British servicemen named Reginald Taplay and Harold Hickman, before being landed at Southampton and taken to Dartmouth Hospital, where he would await his final repatriation to Austria at the end of December.

After Messany's return to Vienna, the British authorities had no further interest in the matter, or so they thought, until on 29 January 1917 the German government published a document listing 22 cases of alleged Allied abuses in the use and operation of hospital ships. Conspicuous in the list of allegations were a number of observations given by Messany to the Austrian authorities in Vienna on 5 January 1917, implying a more sinister motive to the alleged activities aboard the *Britannic*. According to Messany, he claimed to have seen men in military uniform and materiel being transferred to the *Britannic* at Mudros, that Taplay and Hickman were translators being transferred to France, and that both had claimed that there were 2,500 men below being fed on different food to the hospital cases and who had been ordered to

7

Annex 11.

Minutes of the Divisional Court at Vienna.

Hearing of Witness.

A.M.   *Vienna, January 5, 1917.*

Present :

Examining Judge : Oberleutnant Dr. Erhard Schiffner.
Registrar : Heinrich Konarsa.
Witness before the Court : Franz Greipel.

The witness was warned, in reply to the questions addressed to him, to answer the absolute truth according to his best knowledge and belief, not to conceal anything, and to make his statement in such a manner that he could, if necessary, support it on oath.

He gave the following personal information :—

Name : Adalbert Franz Messany.
Place of birth : Vienna.
Age : 24 years.
Religion : Roman Catholic.
Condition : bachelor.
Occupation : opera singer.
Address : 109, Mariahilferstrasse, Vienna, VI.
Relation towards the accused, or to other persons involved in the penal case :—

"At the outbreak of war I was at Luxor, in Upper Egypt, and was put under observation by the British authorities; subsequently I was interned and taken to Malta, where I arrived on the 1st December, 1914.

"On the 24th October, 1916, I was placed on board the hospital ship 'Wandilla.'* The vessel left the harbour of Valetta at 11 o'clock A.M., proceeding in a northerly direction; she then changed course West, and, later, South-West, finally anchoring in a bay on the coast of Malta opposite the island of Gozo. There the ship remained for one and a half days, during the whole of which time cases were taken on board, with the contents of which I was not acquainted.

"On the 26th October, 1916, we proceeded in the direction of Mudros, where we arrived, I believe, on the 28th October, 1916. There I remained for three days, and was transferred on the 1st November,

* The "Wandilla" was notified as a hospital ship by the United States Embassy in Berlin in their note of September 21, 1916.

Annex 11.

The statements as to movements of "Wandilla" are correct up to her arrival at Mudros on the 28th October, but the subsequent dates, both in the case of this ship and of the "Britannic," are not all correctly stated. The cases were transferred from the "Britannic" to the "Wandilla" (not *vice versâ*), and consisted, as the orderly is stated to have said, of Red Cross stores only.

The "Britannic" had the following invalids on board—

Naval officers (non-cot)	..	2
„ other ratings (cot)	..	3
„ „ (non-cot)	..	19
Military officers (cot)	..	15
„ „ (non-cot)	..	144
„ other ranks (cot)	..	349
„ „ (non-cot)	2,490

and the Austrian prisoner of war, Messany, who was suffering from tuberculosis. Among the invalids, who included 629 dysentery and 15 enteric fever cases, were No. 7481 Private R. Tapley, R.A.M.C., suffering from dysentery, and No. 1715 Private H. O. Hickman, South Notts Hussars, suffering from malaria. Neither of these men was being sent home for the purpose of being employed as an interpreter in France, or for any other reason than sickness. A statutory declaration by each of them is appended.

As regards the khaki clothing worn by the men seen in the ship's hold, which is apparently thought to indicate that these men were not sick or wounded, it may be stated that paragraph 14 of the "Standing Orders and Instructions to Officers Commanding Hospital Ships" reads : "When on the Mediterranean service he will obtain from Ordnance Stores sufficient home-pattern khaki serge clothing, shirts, underclothing, &c., to fit out, on the homeward voyage, the maximum number of sick and wounded the ships are equipped to carry. Hospital clothing will be used for all cot cases." It has never been deemed necessary to clothe walking cases on hospital ships in hospital clothing, though a certain number of cases on board the "Britannic" on the voyage in question appear to have been so clothed. A very large proportion of these patients are always convalescent from dysentery, enteric, and malaria, and are quite able to walk about, though unfit for military service.

There are no restrictions on the movements of patients to the upper decks of British hospital ships other than those reserved for officers and nursing sisters. The food for all on board is the same, subject only to the medical requirements of cot or other special cases.

ABOVE: *The first page of the German allegations of the* Britannic *being misused as a hospital ship, with the British rebuttal in the second column. This document would help to cast a shadow over the vessel's reputation for the next eighty years.*

stay below deck. Messany also noted that when the ship reached Southampton on 6 November, he saw these men paraded on the quayside and marching away in military formation, although he did acknowledge that they were not carrying any weapons. On the other hand, this was not the case in regard to the wounded officers, some of whom had been allowed to retain their side arms for the voyage home.

The Admiralty wasted no time in gathering the evidence to disprove any German allegations of the potential misuse of their hospital ships. Taplay and Hickman were quickly traced, and when interviewed their recollections of the voyage were not surprisingly different to Messany's. It transpired that Taplay, a private in the RAMC, was being repatriated suffering from dysentery, having been transferred to hospital in Manchester after the *Britannic* returned to Southampton, before being discharged to sick furlough on 7 March 1917. Hickman, on the other hand, was a private in the Hussars and suffering from malaria; on his return to England, he had been sent to hospitals at Eastleigh and Nottingham before being discharged to sick furlough on 19 December, just in time for

Christmas. Both men recalled meeting Messany but denied ever claiming to be interpreters, although coincidentally they did both have an 'L' patch on their sleeves, a relatively common distinction that any soldier on the Salonika front would have had on their uniform if they spoke a foreign language.

Perhaps more damaging was the issue of the 2,500 men who were ordered to remain out of sight while on board, and who were marched away after the ship arrived in Southampton. A breakdown of the 3,022 patients on board for that particular voyage showed that only 367 were categorised as being 'cot cases', while the more numerous walking wounded were certainly on different rations compared to the more seriously ill invalids on board, whose diets often varied from patient to patient. Even so, there were no restrictions to any of the men being allowed up on deck, provided they were permitted topside by the senior medical

BELOW: *The Admiralty's concept of military camouflage was developed in 1917 in close collaboration with marine artist Norman Wilkinson, reasoning that the disruptive pattern would make it more difficult for a U-boat skipper to calculate a ship's type, size and course.*

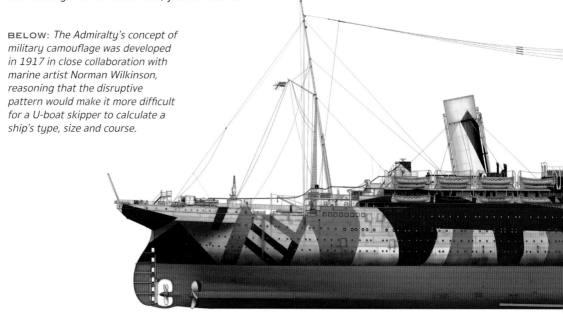

officer and wore the official hospital suits that were issued to them when arriving on board. As to the officers being allowed to retain their side arms, the British riposte to the German allegations stated that the conveyance of weapons belonging to wounded officers at one time was not thought to be in contravention of the Geneva Convention, although the practice was conveniently 'under consideration'.

In the end, all this effort made little difference. On 31 January 1917 Germany announced that from 1 February they would be reintroducing their campaign of unrestricted submarine warfare, for which the German High Command had been arguing for months. It would be a huge gamble on the part of the Germans and the resulting suspension of diplomatic relations between America and Germany probably came as no great surprise to anyone, although America would still not be drawn into the war for another two and a half months.

Olympic's Victory

While the diplomatic arguments over the *Britannic*'s bona fides continued, the *Olympic* had been quietly undergoing a complete transformation at Belfast during the first three months of 1917. In the interim, Captain Hayes had been placed in temporary command of the *Celtic*, during which time his ship had also run into a mine, while in the Irish Sea; 17 people on board were killed, but the *Celtic* remained afloat and the remaining passengers were transferred to the LNWR steamer *Slieve Bawn* for transportation to Holyhead. In the meantime, the *Celtic* was towed into Peel Bay, on the west coast of the Isle of Man, for temporary repairs before being taken to Belfast.

Captain Hayes would have been briefly reunited with his former command while at Belfast, where by the end of March the *Olympic* was finally nearing the completion of her refit. Over the previous three months the ship

had been transformed, but while she retained her drab grey and black colour scheme for the time being, by fitting six 6-inch guns the *Olympic* now had a far greater ability to defend herself. By 26 March the ship was back at Glasgow to take on her new crew and complete the process of fitting out, and it was here on 4 April 1917 that the White Ensign was officially raised for the first time as the *Olympic* was officially commissioned as one of His Majesty's transports.

It would still be another ten days before the *Olympic* was finally headed westwards to Canada, by which time America, pushed to its limits of patience by the unrestricted submarine warfare policy, had finally declared war on Germany. However, even this huge boost to the Allied war effort would be of little help in the short term. The United States army was nowhere near ready for war and it would be months before America was in a position to send over troops in anything like sufficient numbers, so for the time being the *Olympic* would remain on her established run to Halifax. Even so, the political reverberations were almost immediate and among Captain Hayes's first westbound passengers would be Arthur Balfour, British foreign secretary and former prime minister, on a diplomatic mission to the United States at the request of the American government. The *Olympic* arrived at her Canadian terminal on 20 April, at which point Balfour departed for Washington, and by 29 April the ship was once again eastbound for Liverpool. The return voyage, however, would involve an unexpected diversion when on 5 May, with submarines reported to be operating off the northern Irish

coast, the *Olympic* was once again forced to put into Lough Swilly. The visit was not destined to be a long one and by the morning of 7 May the ship was safely back at Liverpool, but it was an early indication that Germany was deadly serious in its intention to disrupt the flow of troops from the west.

While the trooping routine was quickly re-established, the *Olympic* also proved to be a useful diplomatic conveyance. Following in Balfour's footsteps, on the very next voyage Prince Ferdinando of Udine headed the Italian War Commission to Washington, but perhaps of greater interest is the fact that among the Italian delegation was none other than Guglielmo Marconi, the pioneer of the wireless that had done so much to help save the survivors of the *Titanic* disaster five years earlier. For the most part, however, the *Olympic*'s east–west shuttling between Halifax and Liverpool throughout 1917 became almost routine – that is, until December 1917, when Captain Hayes finally received orders to proceed to New York and embark American troops. On Christmas Day 1917, for the first time in over three years, the *Olympic* returned to her pre-war terminal and to a Hudson River that was so iced up she could not even be fully coaled for the return journey until 11 January. The American authorities were, if anything, even more eager to get their men over than the Canadians had been, but Hayes remained unconvinced with regard to their plans to transport 2,000 more troops than usual. Fortunately, his arguments prevailed about the risk of transporting such a large contingent in the event of the ship being attacked, to say nothing of the fact that the

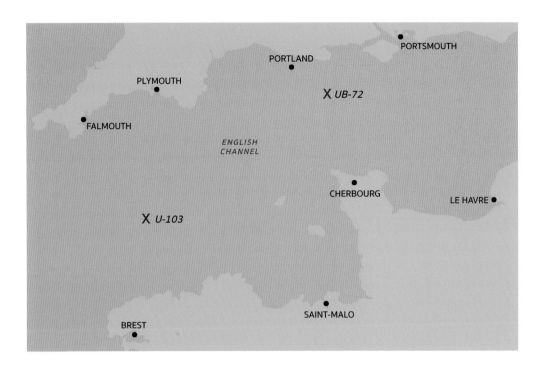

troops would not arrive in very good shape – especially good news for the men on board, which coincidentally included the son of Philip Franklin, the American president of IMM.

When the *Olympic* returned to New York again on 9 February, she carried with her a significant ghost from the White Star Line's past. On board was Lord Reading, formerly Sir Rufus Isaacs, about to take up the post of British ambassador to America. As plain old Sir Rufus, it was Isaacs who had represented the Board of Trade at Lord Mersey's *Titanic* inquiry in London five years earlier, but while the subject of the *Titanic* remained taboo, the *Hawke/Olympic* case, at which Isaacs had also acted for the Admiralty, seemed less sensitive. Lord Reading was curious to have Captain Hayes's opinion of the ruling and his quick response perfectly illustrates what a loss the *Olympic*'s skipper was

to the diplomatic service: 'The Admiralty must have had the better lawyer as they certainly hadn't the better case.' One point on which everyone could agree, however, was that the food on board the *Olympic* was far superior to anything that could be obtained in England at the time. In fact, the ship's food supplies were always purchased in Halifax so that the rationed supplies in England would not be depleted in any way, although due to the regulations any surplus food had to be destroyed, which in times of a national emergency seemed to make no sense whatsoever.

The next voyage also marked the *Olympic*'s return to the White Star Line's pre-war terminal at Southampton, stopping en route at Brest to disembark her cargo of American troops, but by 24 April 1918 the ship was once again westbound on what would be her 22nd trooping voyage. The crossing got off to a pretty lively start when a submarine was reported off the port bow, resulting in a depth charge attack by the escorting destroyers, but while the result of the attack was apparently inconclusive, it was an omen of things to come in the increasingly hazardous waters of the English Channel only 18 days later. By the early afternoon of 5 May the *Olympic* was once again eastbound, headed for her prearranged rendezvous point with the American destroyers USS *Davis*, *O'Brien*, *Conyngham* and *Porter*, where she would be escorted as far as the Lizard before being handed over to British escorts based at Plymouth for the final leg of the journey to Southampton.

On 11 May, the ship duly linked up with her American escort as planned; everything was on schedule for arrival at Southampton two days later when, at 3.55am on the morning of 12 May, while in the vicinity of 49° 16' N, 4° 51' W, the lookout at the ship's stem suddenly sighted a submarine off the starboard bow. The U-boat in question was the *U-103*, under the command of Kapitänleutnant Claus Rücker, a moderately successful skipper with some 174,655 GRT to his credit, although considered by his officers to be overly cautious. By the time Rücker had been called to the bridge, one of the escorting American destroyers ahead of the *Olympic* was even passing through the German submarine's wake, having missed the low profile of the U-boat against the darker horizon. Unfortunately for Rücker, the delay in flooding the submarine's stern tubes meant that he had missed his chance to get off an early salvo of

torpedoes, and with the *Olympic* now bearing down on the *U-103* before the tubes were fully flooded, the hunter had suddenly become the hunted. Immediately after the alarm had been raised, the *Olympic*'s starboard foc'sle gun quickly opened fire on the target, although by that time the *U-103* was so close that it was impossible to depress the gun enough. As a result, the opening shot flew harmlessly over its target. Suddenly aware that he had been spotted, Rücker tried to escape by heading at full speed for the oncoming *Olympic* before attempting to dive to safety once he was inside the ship's turning circle, but he was already too late. Up on his bridge Captain Hayes, having quickly decided that the best form of defence was to attack, had already altered course straight towards the enemy submarine. Judging the moment to perfection, he then ordered the *Olympic*'s helm to be swung hard to port. The 800-ton U-boat had no chance. A swinging blow backed up by the full force of the 52,000-ton liner did its job all too well and by the time the crippled submarine was passing the bridge Hayes could see that the U-boat was heavily down by the stern. Seconds later the liner's starboard propeller ripped into the *U-103*'s pressure hull as the crippled submarine drifted astern. The 6-inch guns on the *Olympic*'s poop deck also opened fire for good measure, but by then it was all over. Although at this stage the *U-103* could still just about manoeuvre, Rücker knew his chances of escaping were negligible and he signalled for the *Davis* to go alongside to take off his crew. The American destroyer lit up the sea to reveal the sorry sight of the *U-103*'s crew clinging to the conning tower,

ABOVE: *Kapitänleutnant Claus Rücker, commander of the* U-103.

it had been a costly morning for Germany, while Hayes had ridden his luck and the *Olympic* had emerged victorious from the encounter, in the process becoming the only liner ever to sink an enemy submarine in wartime. Even so, the ship had not emerged entirely unscathed from the action. On closer inspection at Southampton, divers confirmed that the *Olympic*'s starboard paravane chain had been torn away and, although the integrity of the hull remained largely unaffected, the ship's stem had been twisted some 8 feet to port.

Bertram Hayes would later be awarded the DSC for his actions that morning, while the lookout who spotted the U-boat received the DCM, along with the £20 bonus paid by the White Star Line to any seaman who sighted an enemy submarine from which their ship escaped. However, the lookout in the crow's nest, aggrieved at being overlooked in the post-sinking analysis, also laid claim to the cash, arguing that he had spotted the submarine at the same time and was in the process of telephoning the bridge. When Hayes asked him why he hadn't called out like the man on the stem, he replied, 'I thought he would hear me and go under again'. In the end the two men agreed to share the money, along with a share of the £1,000 reward from the Admiralty and Lloyd's of London, which would be divided among the ship's crew for the successful destruction of an enemy submarine.

the submarine's bow pointing into the air and her stern completely submerged, with black oil trailing in her wake. The *U-103*'s remaining time above the surface could be counted in seconds, but the *Davis* was still able to pick up a total of 35 survivors before she foundered, taking one officer and eight men with her.

Later that morning, the USS *O'Brien* handed over the escort duties to the British destroyers of the Devonport flotilla. The danger was not yet past as the *Olympic* was still headed into the increasingly hazardous waters to the west of the Isle of Wight, where only hours earlier the *UB-72* had also been torpedoed while lying in wait for a big troopship. With two U-boats lost,

After the action of 12 May, the remainder of 1918 would prove to be something of an anticlimax as the ship returned to her regular routine between Southampton and Halifax or New York. After the crisis on the western front in the spring of 1918, by mid-summer Operation Michael, the final German offensive in the west, had ground to a halt; the Allied counter-attack at Amiens on 8 August would mark the successful beginning of the Hundred Days Offensive that would see the German army pushed back almost to the borders of Germany, and by 8 October the Allies had even broken through the much vaunted Hindenburg Line. With American troops now flooding into Europe, all of a sudden there was a very real chance that the war really could be over by Christmas, but the end, when it came, would find the *Olympic* safely secured at Pier 59 in New York, having arrived at that port late on the evening of 10 November. By the time the passengers were ready to disembark the following morning, news of the Armistice had already gone around the world, and when the *Olympic* was ready to depart for Southampton five days later, instead of being packed with American troops she carried only a handful of passengers. The most noticeable difference on board was that for the first time since August 1914, the *Olympic* was finally able to run at night without having to observe any blackout precautions.

BELOW: *The* Olympic*'s damaged bow following the ramming and sinking of the* U-103.

CHAPTER SEVENTEEN

THE NEW *OLYMPIC*

For the next nine months, the *Olympic* continued with the task of repatriating the thousands of Canadian and American troops, their governments seemingly keen to get them home even though the Armistice had not yet resulted in a permanent peace treaty being signed.

There were also growing numbers of civilian passengers on board, not to mention filmmakers. On 2 July 1919, when the *Olympic* departed from Southampton bound for Halifax, among the first-class passengers was film producer Harry Heard, also known by his stage name Harry Lorraine. Before the war, Harry Lorraine had been a successful actor, famous for doing his own stunts and for having played British detective Sexton Blake in several films before the franchise was suspended in 1915 for the duration of hostilities. By July 1919 it was time for the series to be revived, although by now Lorraine had taken on the role of director and producer. *The Further Exploits of Sexton Blake: The Mystery of S.S. Olympic*, being filmed by Atlantic Pictures for Gaumont British, would instead feature Douglas Payne as Sexton Blake, Neil Warrington as his trusty sidekick Tinker, and Marjorie Villis playing the kidnapped female heroine. For added realism, many of the sequences were to be filmed on board the *Olympic*, where Sexton Blake would investigate and solve a murder on the ship and at the same time retrieve a valuable stolen industrial formula. Perhaps not surprisingly, the reviewer in the 21 August 1919 edition of *The Bioscope* observed that the main dramatic interest in the film lay in its daring stunts – a notable characteristic of the earlier Lorraine movies – which included a high-level chase sequence over the telegraph wires above Villiers Street near Charing Cross station and a motorcycle crashing through a sheet of plate glass. Sadly, though, he could not disguise his disappointment that the villain had been allowed to escape instead of being brought to justice. While the film's photography was considered to be 'on the whole satisfactory' and the staging 'good for a picture which does not purport to be more than a popular sensational melodrama', the scenes on the *Olympic*, which had apparently been 'borrowed' for the film, were described as 'especially effective'. Not

ABOVE: The Mystery of SS Olympic. *Filmed aboard the* Olympic *in August 1919, a sign that the world was finally returning to normal.*

only that, but to help the production company to faithfully recreate the ship's interiors, much of the panelling supposedly taken out of the ship when the *Olympic* was requisitioned was transferred by the White Star Line from Belfast to London. Whether or not this was true or just another piece of publicity hyperbole will never be known for sure, although if White Star did indeed provide Gaumont with any furnishings then it was more likely taken from the *Britannic*'s surplus panelling, which was being auctioned at Belfast by the Admiralty even as the *Olympic* headed west for Canada.

By 21 July, having completed seven repatriation cruises to Halifax and one to New York via Brest, the *Olympic*'s war service was finally done and on 16 August Captain Hayes headed across the Irish Sea to Belfast, where his now very tired ship would be restored to her pre-war glory. At only eight years old, the *Olympic* was still a relatively young vessel, although the previous four years of military duties probably equated to a decade of commercial service, the combination of maintaining high speed in a combat zone, anti-submarine warfare, groundings and even ramming an enemy submarine having all taken their toll. Perhaps the greatest surprise had come in February 1919, while the ship was being decommissioned at Liverpool. During a scheduled overhaul in the Gladstone Dock, an 18-inch dent had been discovered amidships, some 14 feet beneath the waterline on the ship's port side. Within this dent lay a 6-inch crack, which had caused a section of the double skin to flood, but because there was no way of testing the integrity of the watertight compartment

itself the damage had gone undetected. The mystery was further compounded by the fact that there was no record of any collision since the previous overhaul, leading to the inevitable conclusion that the *Olympic* had been hit by a torpedo sometime after May 1918 without anyone realising it.

The customarily efficient records of the German U-boat skippers offer a tantalising clue. The war diary of the *U-53*, under the command of Kapitänleutnant Otto von Schrader, contains details of an unsuccessful attack made on 4 September 1918, when a four-funnelled steamer of the *Olympic* type was observed in the Western Approaches of the English Channel. On this date the *Olympic* was certainly in the area, having departed Southampton the previous morning. The submarine's war diary records that the target was steaming at about 20 knots while maintaining a zigzag course of 230–270 degrees. Two torpedoes were fired at 6.05am, but with no apparent detonation von Schrader assumed that the torpedoes hadn't reached their target as the distance was greater than he had estimated. Oblivious to the fact that his ship had so nearly become yet another victim of the U-boat menace, Captain Hayes had continued merrily on his course while von Schrader set off in pursuit of another victim, little realising that he had come within an ace of sinking Britain's largest remaining passenger steamer. Later that day he would have more success, sinking the British steamer SS *War Firth* en route from Bilbao to the Clyde.

The damage to the *Olympic*'s port side, however, was only one of the items on Harland & Wolff's extensive to-do list. Not only did they

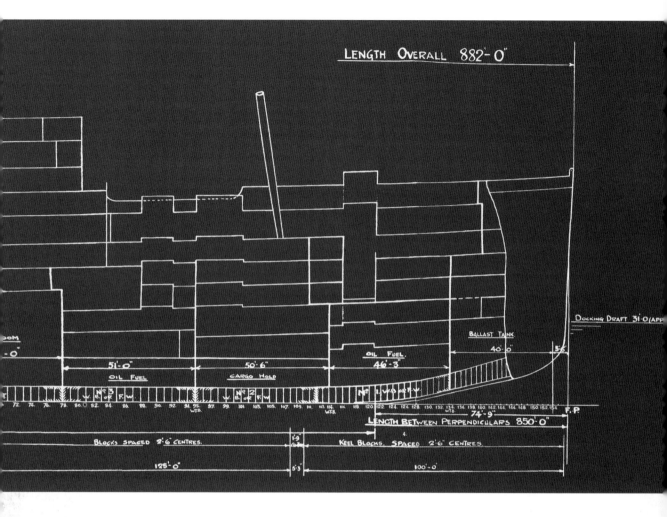

have to restore four years of military wear and tear but the White Star Line also had huge ambitions for updating their flagship to better equip her for the next ten years on the North Atlantic. The *Olympic* was about to undergo such a radical transformation that not only would the interiors be completely reinstated, but the process of updating the existing boilers and coal bunkers with new oil-fired machinery would result in a very different ship.

The initial tests on the thickness of the hull plating amidships and the inner skin plating

ABOVE: *The* Olympic's *internal modified bow allowed for the storage of additional oil fuel.*

were encouraging, revealing practically no issues, the only appreciable deterioration in the cellular double bottom being in the main traverse watertight bulkhead at the after end of the turbine machinery space. The problem was largely rectified by fitting ½-inch doubling plates in the affected areas, but the more visible battle scars also needed attention, the most obvious being the damage to the ship's bow

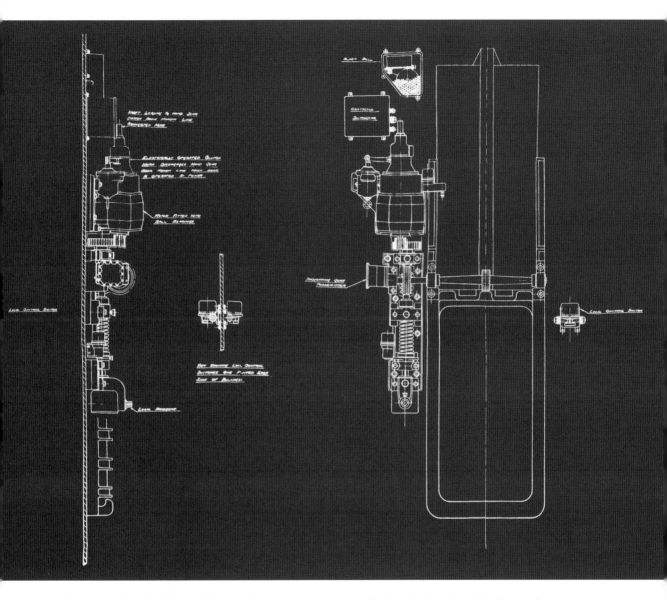

from the *U-103* collision. This would require the lower portion of stem to be faired, along with the replacement of six lower shell plates on the starboard side and three on the port side, while the mysterious torpedo damage would necessitate the replacement of some of the midship hull plates at the level of the O and P strake.

ABOVE: *Technical schematic of the improved electrically controlled watertight doors fitted in the* Olympic *after the war.*

The remainder of the repairs, with the exception of the bilge keels beneath boiler room 5, focused largely on the after part of the hull, including two plates being renewed at the level of the Z strake port and starboard between

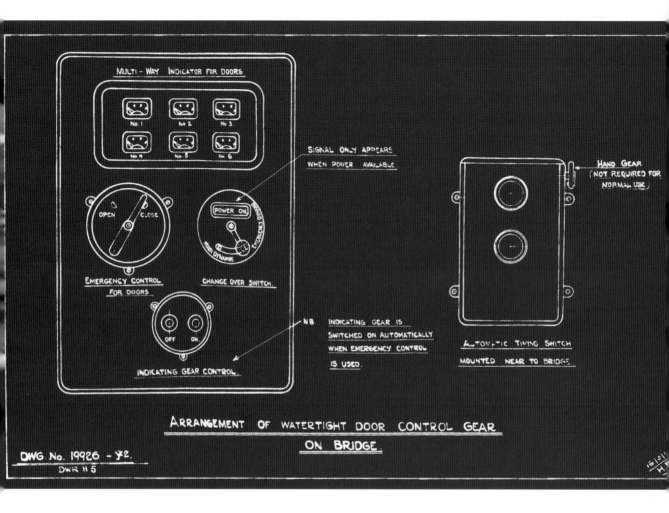

ABOVE: *The post-war bridge control panel for the watertight doors.*

frames 86 and 99 aft, another plate on the port side of the U strake between frames 142 and 148 aft, the aft N strake starboard and port plates, and the rivets requiring attention in the lower part of stern frame and scarph. Nor would the work be restricted simply to the fairing of the remaining shell plates, as the Q strake was earmarked for complete reconstruction along both sides of the ship between frames 107 forward and frame 56 aft. This was not due to any battle damage or structural issues, but rather to the new propulsion system that the

White Star Line was, at considerable expense, about to install.

In this instance, the oil-burning equipment of choice would be the 'White' system, manufactured by Messrs Brigham & Cowan of South Shields. Oil fuel was by no means a new innovation, but prior to the war it had been the high cost of the fuel when compared to coal that had deterred the mercantile shipping companies from installing oil-burning technology. The post-war economics, on the other hand, were very different to those of five years earlier. Oil fuel was still unquestionably more expensive, but it was also considerably more efficient and converting a large ship like the *Olympic* could reduce the usual refuelling time from days to a matter of hours. Not only that, but the number of engine room personnel, specifically firemen and trimmers, would be slashed by over 80 per cent. Although the actual refuelling of the ship would be a quicker, cleaner and much more straightforward process, it would still require strict adherence to laid-down procedures. It was important to refuel on each side of the ship simultaneously in order to maintain an even keel, the procedure requiring that the refuelling in each compartment begin with the aft tanks so that the rear trim of the ship would facilitate the drainage of any surplus oil into the overflow tank.

In terms of layout, there seemed to be little difference to the *Olympic*'s pre- and post-war machinery. There would still be 24 double-ended and 5 single-ended boilers, but the new arrangements meant that from 1920 onwards each furnace was heated by a single burner. To ensure that the oil flowed smoothly, numerous heaters were incorporated into the system to maintain a temperature of between 90° and 100° Fahrenheit (32–38° Celsius) while it was pumped through the system to the various burners at a pressure of up to 80 lb psi. While this all made for a more controlled working environment in the boiler rooms, for the Board of Trade surveyors the issue of fire control now took on a whole new meaning. The prospect

of uncontrolled heated oil spewing into the confined working spaces of a boiler room was too serious to ignore, so a raft of measures needed to be devised to ensure the utmost safety. Every possible precaution to contain the leakage of oil from any of the tanks or furnace fronts had to be considered, and measures taken to prevent it from spreading over the tank top or beneath the stokehold plates. This included making the furnace fronts oil-tight with asbestos tape and putty, through to gutters in the boiler rooms and drainage sumps. The boiler bottoms and sides were all insulated with a magnesia composition to provide additional protection for the oil tanks in the ship's double bottom and sides, while any wood flooring beneath the stokehold plates was removed altogether. To further ensure that any leaks were spotted more easily, not only was most of the tank top made more visible by removing the deep shield plates that normally ran alongside the boiler bearers, but the underside of the boilers were painted white and illuminated in the passage. But safety went further than just spotting oil leaks, with the ventilation system requiring considerable improvement in order to prevent the accumulation of any oil vapour. If, God forbid, a fire did break out, then all the exposed air pipes in the boiler rooms were covered in asbestos to prevent them being damaged by fire, while perforated steam fire-extinguishing pipes extended along and above all the gutterways beneath the boilers. In addition, steel bins in each stokehold containing 5 to 6 cwt of sand were readily to hand, while each compartment was equipped with two ordinary hose nozzles and one spraying nozzle, ample

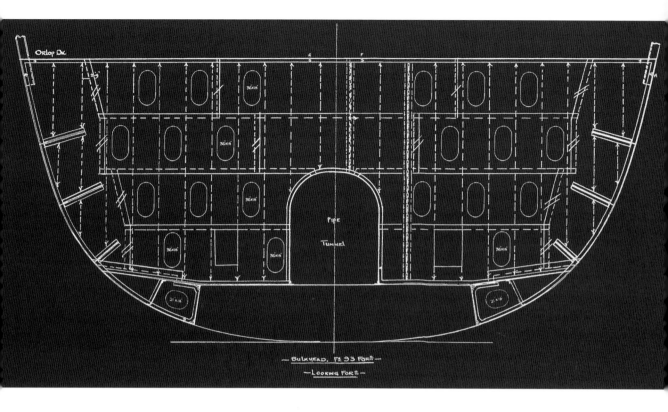

supplies of water, self-contained battery lights and fire extinguishers. In terms of fire safety, clearly no one was taking any chances.

Internally, the *Olympic* was being totally transformed, and to a certain extent this was reflected on the ship's exterior. Since 1913 the boat deck had been packed with additional lifeboats following the *Titanic* disaster, but because the White Star Line had chosen not to incorporate the girder davits later installed in the *Britannic*, the *Olympic*'s boat deck had appeared overly crowded by comparison. Stronger davits and larger lifeboats now enabled Harland & Wolff to clear away much of this post-*Titanic* clutter, but although the Board of Trade regulations required 26 sets of davits for vessels of the *Olympic*'s GRT,

ABOVE: *In November 1920 additional oil fuel carrying capacity was created by cutting through one of the forward bulkheads. This was primarily to reduce the need to take on oil at Southampton, where prices were considerably higher.*

bearing in mind the larger and stronger davits being installed this could only be achieved by positioning another set of davits on each side of the poop deck. While technically feasible, there were nevertheless concerns that the stern boats would be too close to the propellers for comfort. Even so, the final configuration of 24 davits allowed space for 3,428 persons – 13 more than the maximum total of passengers and crew – which in the end would suffice for the surveyors at Belfast.

THE POST WAR FLEET

As the reconstruction continued at Belfast, the White Star Line was also busy re-establishing its commercial activities in the post-war world. The 'Big Four' – *Celtic*, *Cedric*, *Baltic* and *Adriatic* – had all survived the hostilities, if not entirely unscathed, but none of them had anything like the service speed necessary to maintain a credible express service. At the same time, the loss of the *Titanic*, *Oceanic* and *Britannic* had left the company with few options but to contemplate replacement tonnage, despite the massive rise in the cost of shipbuilding over the previous five years.

Yard No 470 had actually been on the Harland & Wolff books since before the war, although her gross tonnage of 33,600 tons suggests a somewhat smaller vessel than the *Olympic*. The vessel was reportedly to be named *Germanic*, until subsequent events obliged the company to revise its nomenclature to *Homeric*. The war would ensure that in the end her keel would never be laid, and by the time the hostilities were finally ended White Star's need for new tonnage was greater than ever. However, it would not be until the signing of the Treaty of Versailles on 28 June 1919, whereby the Armistice agreed in November 1918 became nothing less than unconditional surrender for Germany, that an alternative way forward began to emerge. Crucially, it was Paragraph 1 of Annex III in the final document that would suddenly provide the White Star Line with an avenue that only weeks before had been inconceivable:

'The German Government, on behalf of themselves and so as to bind all other persons interested, cede to the Allied and Associated Governments the property in all the German merchant ships which are of 1,600 tons gross and upwards.'

With the division of the spoils agreed, on 17 November the British Shipping Controller was finally in a position to send a list of the prize tonnage to any of the interested shipping lines. Even at this stage the White Star Line was in a position of weakness when compared to Cunard's claim, not least because the future of the White Star vessels on the British registry was already a cause of concern at the Admiralty. Since 1902, the White Star Line had been a part of the American IMM combine, but in return for continued favourable treatment in the UK, the following year IMM had agreed that the vessels that had belonged to the previously British-owned constituent companies would remain on the British register for at least 25 years, continue to use British officers and always be available for British military, naval or postal service. The problem, however, was that any time after 27 August 1922 either party was at liberty to give five years' notice to terminate the agreement. Several years earlier, an internal memo to the First Lord of the Admiralty had also acknowledged that the IMM steamers, although under the British flag, were essentially owned by American interests, so the prospect of Great Britain's hard-won war prizes being allocated to White Star, only for them to be ceded to the Americans within a few years, was not one that the Admiralty was willing to contemplate. The

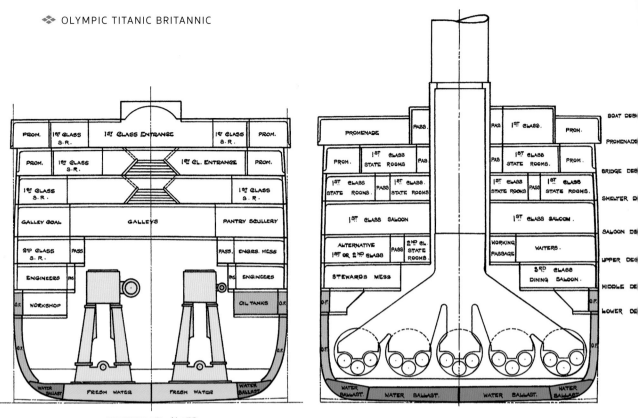

Sectional drawings of the new Olympic, *detailing the storage of oil fuel, fresh water and ballast tanks.*

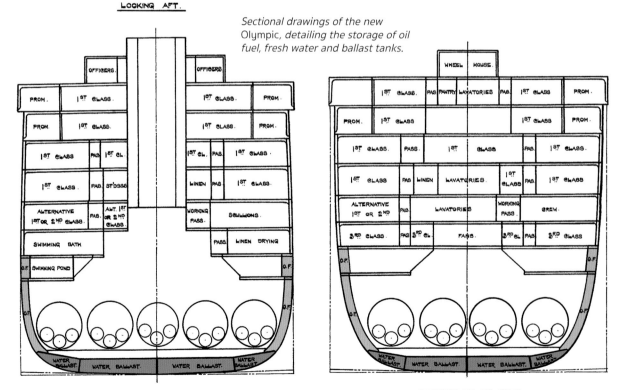

American-based IMM companies, on the other hand, already had access to a share of the war prizes allocated to the American government, but because of their existing agreement with the British government there was little chance of the White Star Line being able to avail themselves of the American quota.

The conundrum would finally be resolved on 2 September 1919 when IMM agreed to extend the original agreement for another 20 years. At a stroke, the anxieties at the Admiralty were eased and Harold Sanderson could finally start to cast his eye over the list of available tonnage. The list itself was impressive. The HAPAG liner *Imperator* had already been allocated to the Cunard Line, but with the incomplete 35,000-ton NDL liner *Colombus* lying at the Schichau yard in Danzig, and the even larger 56,551-ton HAPAG liner *Bismarck* still fitting out at the Blohm & Voss shipyard at Hamburg, it would still be considerably quicker and cheaper to base the reconstruction of the Southampton express service around these vessels, even though neither ship was likely to be ready before the end of 1921. However, with the *Columbus* being taken over and renamed *Homeric* and the *Bismarck* becoming the second White Star vessel to bear the name *Majestic*, it would no longer be necessary to build expensive replacements for the *Oceanic*, *Titanic* and *Britannic*.

Meanwhile, back at Belfast the restoration work on White Star's existing flagship was finally coming to an end. After two days open to public inspection, the proceeds of which were donated to Belfast's Royal Victoria Hospital, the 46,439 GRT oil-fired *Olympic* finally left Belfast for Southampton on 17 June to resume her place on the North Atlantic. That evening, a banquet was held on board to celebrate the return to service of the company's last big ship, being referred to by Harold Sanderson in his after-dinner speech as 'our one ewe lamb'. Bertram Hayes later recalled Field Marshal Sir William Robertson's suggestion that in view of the ship's war record, the word 'ram' would perhaps be more appropriate, but while the celebrations were continuing in the first-class dining saloon, below deck things were not running as smoothly as planned.

Among the passengers for the voyage to Southampton was Thomas Carlton, on board to observe the new oil-burning apparatus on behalf of the Board of Trade. For this particular voyage, the *Olympic* only needed to maintain a moderate speed and he noted that for the most part the trials were '...quite satisfactory excepting that a mishap occurred'. In the circumstances, the word 'mishap' seems like a colossal understatement. It began when an attendant in the forward stokehold turned one of the handles, believing he was opening one of the valves that regulated the flow of oil into the furnaces. What he did not realise was that the valve was already fully open, and that because of a design fault the handle continued to turn until it suddenly came away in his hand. Immediately, a jet of scalding-hot oil was sprayed at high pressure into the compartment, unfortunately at the exact same moment that another attendant was in the process of lighting the burner, so igniting the escaping oil as he drew the torch away from the furnace. Fortunately, the engineers were able to cut off the oil supply using a valve in

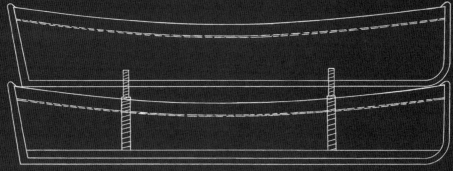

ELEVATION OF 28'-0" LIFEBOATS.
SCALE ½" = 1 FOOT.

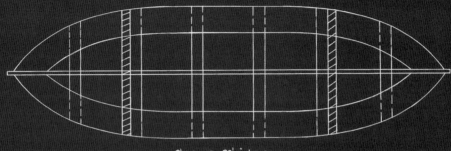

PLAN OF 28'-0" LIFEBOAT.
SCALE ½" = 1 FOOT.

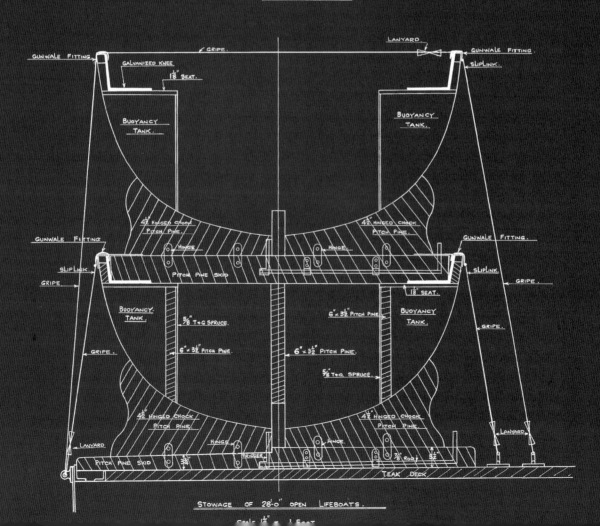

LANYARD

GRIPE.

GUNWALE FITTING.   GUNWALE FITTING.

GALVANIZED KNEE   SLIPLINK.

1⅛" SEAT.

BUOYANCY   BUOYANCY
TANK.   TANK.

4½" HINGED CHOCK   4½" HINGED CHOCK
PITCH PINE.   PITCH PINE.

GUNWALE FITTING.   GUNWALE FITTING.

HINGE.   HINGE.

SLIPLINK.   SLIPLINK.

GRIPE.   PITCH PINE SKID.   GRIPE.

1⅛" SEAT.

BUOYANCY   BUOYANCY
TANK.   6" x 3½" PITCH PINE.   TANK.   GRIPE.

GRIPE.   ⅝" T+G SPRUCE.

6" x 3½" PITCH PINE.   6" x 3½" PITCH PINE.

GRIPE.   6" x 3½" PITCH PINE.   ⅝" T+G SPRUCE.

4½" HINGED CHOCK   4½" HINGED CHOCK
PITCH PINE.   PITCH PINE.

LANYARD

LANYARD   HINGE.   HINGE.

TRIGGER.   ⅞" ROOT.

PITCH PINE SKID.   3¾"

TEAK DECK.

STOWAGE OF 28'-0" OPEN LIFEBOATS.
SCALE ½" = 1 FOOT.

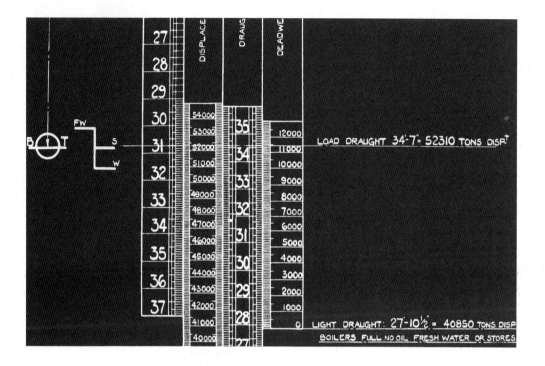

LOAD DRAUGHT 34'-7"= 52310 TONS DISP.ᵀ

LIGHT DRAUGHT: 27'-10½" = 40850 TONS DISP.
BOILERS FULL. NO OIL FRESH WATER OR STORES.

LEFT: *The post-war* Olympic *would be equipped with 24 sets of modified Welin davits, each handling two nested lifeboats. The full complement would include twenty-two 30' lifeboats, twenty 28' lifeboats, with two additional 28' motor boats, built by Gouk & Nisbet of Glasgow, fitted with a Marconi lifeboat transmitting and receiving wireless.*

ABOVE: *The* Olympic*'s revised load line, following the ship's conversion to oil.*

the next stokehold, but it would still be 15 minutes before the fire had been extinguished using a combination of sand, steam and carbon tetrachloride. Thanks to the new safety precautions the fire had been safely contained, but unfortunately John Hume, an employee of the oil installation patentee Brigham & Cowan, had not been so fortunate, sustaining serious burns to his face, back, arms and thighs. Hume would be transferred to hospital as soon as the *Olympic* reached Southampton on 19 June,

while the damage in the forward stokehold was quickly cleaned up and made good, but the fire was at least a useful opportunity for Carlton to note in his report to the Board of Trade: '...the occurrence will have good effect in showing the danger of an escape of heated oil and the necessity for keeping the stokehold clean and free from oil.' As to the initial cause of the fire, Carlton quickly attributed the accident to the defective handle design and over the next six days work was undertaken to replace as many of the defective oil valves as possible before the ship was due to sail. Those that could not be replaced in time would instead be secured by locking pins until the ship next returned to Southampton.

CHAPTER EIGHTEEN

THE ROARING TWENTIES

At midday on 26 June 1920, the new *Olympic*, now the largest oil-burning vessel in the world, pulled away from the White Star Dock for her first commercial voyage of the twenties, arriving at Pier 59 after an uneventful voyage of 6 days, 11 hours and 58 minutes, at an average speed of 20.7 knots.

WHITE STAR LINE

R.M.S. "OLYMPIC," 46,359 Tons
(The largest British Steamer)

The most interesting statistic of the ship's first oil-fuelled crossing was the data relating to the overall fuel consumption, which averaged 540 tons per day. The expectation was that the figures would improve on future crossings, as indeed they would, and the following year the *Olympic* would make her fastest ever crossing in only 5 days, 12 hours and 39 minutes.

By the early autumn, the *Olympic* had completed four voyages to New York with practically no operational issues of any great concern. The new oil-fired installation had the engines running with scarcely any variation in the number of revolutions, while the improvement was especially appreciated by the passengers, who no longer had to endure the sulphuric smell of burning coal or the hot

LEFT: *Although back in commercial service, this post-war colour postcard enabled the White Star Line to remind everyone of the Olympic's illustrious wartime record.*

embers – known as 'clinkers' – that could be blown into their faces while standing on deck. In the autumn there were, however, a couple of incidents on board that upset the routine. On 4 October, third-class passenger Mary Ruvald gave birth to a premature stillborn baby girl, and the return leg of that voyage would be no happier when, on 11 October, 53-year-old baker Charles Wilson from Vienna died of pneumonia. He was buried at sea at 5.30pm that evening, which was somewhat unusual as burial services were normally conducted later in the day when the passengers were more likely to be below decks or retired for the night. Perhaps the most unusual occurrence came right at the end of the year, when on 22 December the *Olympic* arrived at New York. As was customary, some of the crew were given leave to go ashore, but while trying to go through the gates of Pier 59 steward Arthur Dixon was stopped by the American customs officers and searched. They were almost certainly looking for alcohol as smuggling was not uncommon by members of ships' crews, particularly since the introduction of Prohibition 11 months earlier in America, as the European liners were an acknowledged source of illicit booze. In Dixon's case, however, alcohol was the last thing on his mind; by the time the customs officials were finished they were ready to charge him with illegally importing 98 wings and one whole Bird of Paradise! The only place Dixon would be spending his Christmas would be behind bars, although he was released on bail just in time

ABOVE: *Composer Irving Berlin with screen actress Norma Talmadge on an early post-war crossing.*

to rejoin the ship before the next scheduled departure on 29 December.

Nineteen twenty-one was only four days old when Captain Hayes suffered his first casualty of the new year, when first-class passenger Captain Llewellyn Nicholas succumbed to pleurisy in the ship's hospital. Deaths seemed to be part of the routine for the next few weeks, with Peter Nielsen also dying in the ship's infirmary on 16 April from acute gastroenteritis, but away from the day-to-day on-board minutiae, the real drama was now taking place ashore.

In May 1921, the United States government began to make its first serious attempt to restrict the inward flow of emigrants from

WHITE STAR LINE.

TRIPLE-SCREW R.M.S "OLYMPIC," 46,439 Tons.

ABOVE: *The rebuilt 46,439 GRT Olympic, now almost ten years old but looking as good as new.*

Europe through the introduction of the Dillingham Immigration Restriction Act, more commonly referred to as the '3 per cent Act'. In essence, this was an emergency measure limiting the number of emigrants entering the United States during the 12 months between 1 July 1921 and 30 June 1922 to 3 per cent of the foreign-born population of the United States, based on the national census of 1903. In actual fact, Congress had already taken the first steps to restrict immigration four years earlier, with a new requirement for all immigrants over 16 to be able to pass a basic literacy test. With most of the world at war and practically no westbound emigration to America during the hostilities, the tightening of the restrictions had gone largely unnoticed in Europe, but the restrictions contained within the 1921 legislation were more far-reaching. While pre-

war immigration into the United States had risen to in excess of 1,000,000 per annum, by the terms of the new legislation that annual figure would now be slashed to 360,000.

The implications for any vessels operating on the North Atlantic were all too evident. The extensive third-class business generated by mass migration had been a fundamental aspect in the development of the Olympic class liners, not to mention their counterparts in the Cunard and other European merchant fleets, but the impact on the volume of emigration movement, combined with the high building and operating costs of such large ships, meant that, in Harold Sanderson's own words, '...the building of further steamships of the monster type in

ABOVE: *The* Leviathan *and* Olympic *bow to stern at Southampton; two giants of the North Atlantic, already in danger of becoming floating relics.*

the near future is rendered problematical'. In view of the huge increase in shipbuilding costs, with the *Homeric* and *Majestic* still not scheduled to enter service until the spring of 1922, Sanderson was all the more grateful that White Star had not gone down the route of ordering two new ships to replace the *Titanic* and *Britannic*. With the prospect of additional American immigration restrictions in the future, even though they were still far less restrictive than the immigration policies of many other countries, the new immigration structure would have a considerable impact on the building programme of the North Atlantic steamship companies as they switched instead to more economical vessels of moderate size and speed.

Insofar as the day-to-day operations were concerned, for the *Olympic* it was still a case of business as usual as Captain Hayes contended with the customary issues of births, deaths and stowaways. Sometimes two came together, such as the birth on 19 July in the ship's hospital of Frederick Davison, only for the log to record his death and burial at sea three days later due to being premature. August 1921, however, would be far more unusual, when the first mysterious on-board disappearance occurred during an eastbound crossing on the afternoon of Wednesday 17 August. After lunch that day, first-class passenger Julius Smolin, en route to visit relatives in Germany, had been sitting in the open up on A deck with his son Nat. At some stage Nat had apparently dozed off, waking up at about 3.30pm to find his father gone. After an hour he began to get worried and went

to look for him, but it was not until 7pm that he finally reported him missing. The ship was thoroughly searched and the enquiries were by no means fruitless, with bath steward Frederick Jeffs apparently seeing Smolin near the lifts on E deck at about 5.30 to 5.45pm, while lift attendant Leslie Brown recalled taking him up to A deck at about the same time. A first-class passenger named Wheeler also remembered seeing Smolin standing by the aft crane on A deck shortly afterwards, but no one had noticed anything at all unusual in his demeanour. Nat Smolin did say that his father suffered from neurasthenia, the symptoms of which can include fatigue, headache and irritability and could be associated with emotional disturbance,

but whether Julius Smolin's disappearance was an accident or suicide would never be conclusively proved.

The mysteries continued on the very next voyage. The *Olympic* had departed from Southampton at midday on 24 August, bound as usual for New York via Cherbourg; by 8pm on 30 August, the ship was only hours from her American terminal. Second-class passenger Annie Thompson would allege it was at this time that she had found a letter on her bed, along with the pen, purse, ring and knife of her fiancé, Thomas Brassington. Thompson later claimed that the contents of the letter had so alarmed her that she immediately destroyed it before going to look for him, but from memory she recalled the content as being 'I Thomas Brassington leave all my personal belongings to Annie Louisa Thompson, 635 Haight Avenue, Alameda, California. My troubles at home and the thought of Ellis Island are more than I can bear.' However, Annie's story now becomes that much more intriguing because she then went up on deck, where she apparently found Brassington and tried to cheer him up by reassuring him that Ellis Island would not be so bad, and that they would be married in March the following year. After returning his belongings to him Brassington said that he was going to bed, at which point he made a sudden move forwards, causing Annie to faint; by the time she had recovered, she was alone. After the ship was searched, no trace could be found of Thomas Brassington, although steward W Girard did recall seeing him at 8.45pm, when he asked him for some baggage tags. Brassington was also seen in his cabin ten minutes later by a passenger named Pratt, with whom he was sharing. Pratt confirmed that Brassington was looking upset at the time, but when he asked him if he was tired he had simply left the room, never to be seen again.

On a more pleasant note, visits from Hollywood royalty were not uncommon and included in the eastbound passenger list was none other than Charlie Chaplin, returning to England for the first time in almost nine years. Chaplin's decision to make the trip had been so sudden that shooting on his latest film, *Pay Day*, had been suspended with barely 350 feet of film (about six minutes) in the can, but a combination of factors including overwork, a bout of influenza and even a steak and kidney pie in New York with British-born author Montague Glass had increased his feeling of nostalgia for England. With *The Kid* also doing the circuits in London, it seemed like the ideal time to return home, with Douglas Fairbanks and Mary Pickford on hand to wave him *bon voyage*. By 3 September the *Olympic* was once again eastbound for Southampton. Perhaps inevitably, the press correspondents travelling on board made it impossible for Chaplin to truly relax, as they wired incessant reports on how he made use of the ship's gymnasium, Turkish bath and swimming pool, along with the fact that he took great interest in the card games in the smoking room, if not actually taking part in them himself. Although naturally shy, the "Little Tramp" was happy to appear in a ship's concert as the proceeds were being donated to a seamen's charity, his famous shuffling walk as he exited producing the loudest cheers of the evening, but even the cavernous interiors of the largest British ship could afford no sanctuary from the determined reporters who had swarmed aboard at Cherbourg to grab an interview. It would probably have been even worse at Southampton's civic reception when the ship arrived back on 10 September, but as luck would have it the *Olympic*'s arrival was delayed by fog; by the time the ship finally docked, the crowds had shrunk significantly.

The year end was also not without incident when, on 12 December, the *Olympic* ran into heavy weather on her final eastbound crossing of the year. Already running at reduced speed, at 3.44am the ship was suddenly hit by such heavy seas that a number of galley ports were smashed and the travelling ladder was carried away, forcing Captain Hayes to heave to while the damage was plugged. Five hours later the starboard portholes of the reception room received similar treatment and the forward tackle of the starboard emergency boat was even unhooked by the water, but worse was to come at 2.05pm, when the ship suddenly gave several quick rolls. The motion played havoc with the clasps securing some of the sliding watertight doors, with third-class passenger John Onsik having his left foot trapped in door 33 as it slammed shut. The result was a compound fracture above the ankle, but although Dr Beaumont recommended amputation below the knee, Onsik would not agree to undergo the operation for a further three days. Another third-class passenger, Domenico Serafini from

Pisa, was killed outright when door 28 suddenly slammed shut, the force of the impact being so great that it dislodged a vertebra, causing a massive compression of the spinal cord.

With the damage patched up, by 21 December the *Olympic* was westbound for her final voyage of the year, notable for the fact that Captain Hayes would be in command for the last time. It would not be the happiest of voyages when on 27 December first-class passenger Alice Bickel gave birth to a stillborn baby in the ship's hospital, but by New Year's Eve the ship was once again homeward bound, arriving back at Southampton on the morning of 7 January. Here, after more than six years in command, Hayes – now made commodore of the line – would finally take his leave of the ship in order to travel to Hamburg, where he would take command of the *Majestic*.

Nineteen twenty-two would also mark a significant change for White Star. On 15

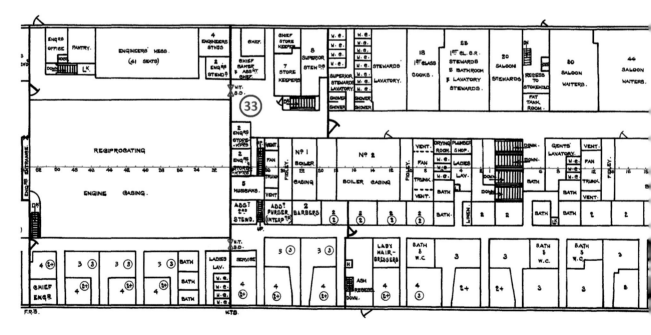

February the *Homeric* had finally joined the company's Southampton to New York service, while the 16,789 GRT *Arabic* (formerly the NDL liner *Berlin*, which coincidentally had laid the mine that sank HMS *Audacious*) had already made a single voyage from Southampton to New York before taking her place on the company's New York–Mediterranean route. By the end of March 1922, the *Majestic* was also ready to be handed over at Hamburg, after numerous delays while fitting out. The original nine-month completion estimate had been considerably extended by a mysterious on-board fire in 1920, along with White Star's prudent decision to have the ship converted to oil-firing before entering service, but on 12 April the *Majestic* was finally ready to be handed over. On 10 May 1922, White Star's brand-new flagship finally left Southampton on her maiden voyage to New York, nearly eight years after being launched.

Another sign of the changing times was the renaming of the company's Southampton terminal. Since commencing their express service between Southampton and New York, the Olympic class vessels had always been berthed in the White Star Dock, but with other shipping lines – most notably Cunard and Canadian Pacific – now making regular use of the facility, the port authorities had decided that the name 'Ocean Dock' would instead be more appropriate. Along with the change in the American immigration regulations, the *Olympic* would be competing with these ships for slices of an increasingly small third-class pie on the Southampton to New York route, which prior to the war had been a virtual White Star monopoly.

BELOW: *The watertight doors at either end of the Scotland Road companionway, where the two accidents occurred during the storm of 12 December 1921.*

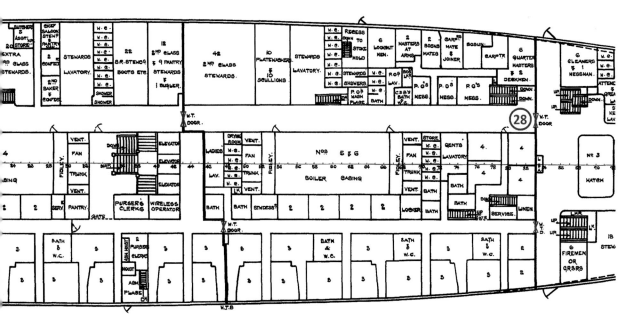

ABOVE, LEFT AND RIGHT: *The crack in the* Olympic*'s sternpost would be the first indication of a longer term maintenance issue for the White Star Line.*

On 7 January 1922, Captain Alexander Hambleton of the *Adriatic* was appointed to command the *Olympic*, having been on board during Hayes's last voyage in order to familiarise himself with the ship – being referred to as 'Hayes' pupil' – so that the transition in command was practically seamless. Fortunately for Hambleton, 1922 would prove to be largely uneventful, but interestingly the ship's performance while at sea may have been showing the first indications of a more long-term problem. The *Olympic*'s departure from New York on 15 July had been quite routine, with the ship averaging a creditable 22.6 knots as she headed east. The *New York Times*, however, later reported that while in the English Channel the ship had maintained a speed of 27.81 knots for several hours. If this news was to be

believed then it was a level of performance that eclipsed even the *Mauretania*, which in normal circumstances might have raised more than a few quizzical eyebrows, but few would have linked this alleged turn of speed to the fact that the *Olympic*'s next scheduled departure, on 2 August, would have to be abandoned. The indications are that the two events may well have been connected, even if no one realised the significance of the problem at the time. During the enforced lay-up at Southampton, a number of stern repairs were undertaken at the Harland & Wolff ship repair facility, caused by the appearance of a crack in the sternpost. Surveys in February 1922 had already confirmed that the turbine remained in good condition and that the ship's oil-firing system was working satisfactorily, but this was the first indication that the centre turbine propeller was generating a transverse vibration. The full extent of the problem would not become apparent for a while, but the stresses had still been great enough to result in a crack across the top of the scarph on the starboard side of the sternpost. With the necessary repairs completed, the *Olympic*'s next scheduled departure on 23 August went without a hitch, but while the ship would continue to perform with her accustomed reliability for the remainder of the year, the sternpost would need to be watched more carefully in the future.

By the end of January 1923, Captain Hambleton, having reached the mandatory White Star retirement age, relinquished command to Captain Hugh David, who like his predecessor had been transferred from the *Adriatic* and was on board for Hambleton's final voyage. This time, however, the handover would not be so seamless. On 10 January the *Olympic* had departed from Southampton as scheduled, when barely a day into the voyage Captain Hambleton suddenly collapsed on his bridge. The medical prognosis indicated that he was suffering from gastrointestinal bleeding, which was serious enough for him to be placed in the ship's infirmary while the ship's assistant commander, Captain Eustace White, automatically assumed command, but by the time the *Olympic* departed from New York Captain David had officially taken over as captain. In the meantime, Hambleton remained in a Manhattan hospital until 10 February, when he was fit enough to return home aboard the *Cedric*.

Hugh David's tenure of command would also be largely uneventful, save for his first westbound crossing when at 8.40pm on 4 February 1923, while still three days from New York, steward J Bartholomew smelt burning while walking down the port-side corridor on C deck. A fire on any ship was always a serious prospect, but fortunately Bartholomew was passing at a time when the crisis was still in its early stages. Further investigation revealed that the smoke emanating from behind one of the wooden panels outside cabin C68 was the result of a short circuit in the cabin bell wires, but fortunately the flames were quickly extinguished by the engineers without any undue alarm, the only outward evidence being some minor water damage to the wood panelling. Even so, it had been a lucky escape.

By and large the number of passengers carried in the *Olympic* throughout 1922

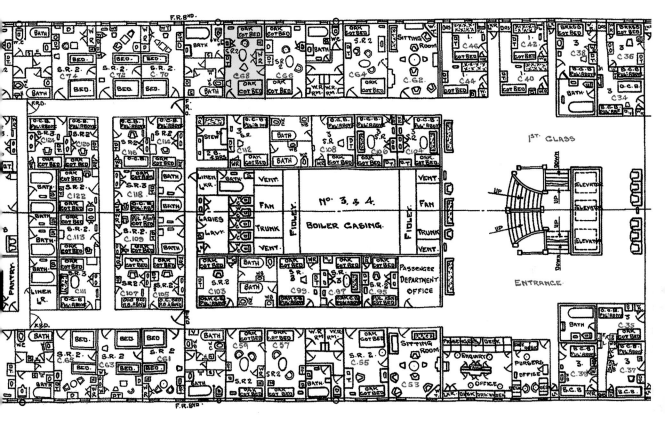

ABOVE: *Cabin C63, where an electrical short circuit was discovered just in time to avoid a major fire at sea.*

and 1923 showed a small decrease, most significantly in third class where the impact of the new American immigration laws was beginning to be felt, but on the whole the vessel remained mechanically sound and financially profitable. On 21 November 1923 Captain David ceded command to Captain Francis Howarth, who would take command for the last voyage of the year, and by 8 December the *Olympic* was once again safely back at Southampton before departing that same evening for her annual overhaul at Belfast.

Nineteen twenty-four, however, would mark an important turning point on the North Atlantic. With the 1921 American immigration restrictions further extended to the point where the number of immigrants allowed to enter the United States would henceforth be limited to 2 per cent of the foreign-born population according to the census of 1890, the new quotas would allow for only 160,000 immigrants per year, a figure that was a long way short of the pre-war annual figure of 1,000,000. For vessels of the *Olympic*'s ilk, each heavily dependent on steerage passengers to pay their way, the implications were sobering; if the ship was going to continue to thrive then the White Star Line would need to change its strategy.

The decision to scale back on the con-struction of larger ships had already been taken soon

ABOVE: *The* Olympic *and* Homeric *in the Ocean Dock at Southampton on 7 August 1923. The* Aquitania *occupies the Trafalgar graving dock.*

after the war. The focus was now very much on ships of a more moderate size and speed, with less ornate public rooms yet with the existing standards of comfort being maintained for first-class passengers, along with improvements in both the second- and third-class facilities. Mindful of the close family links between Europe and America, Harold Sanderson remained optimistic that there would always be a significant number of passengers on the North Atlantic, but with particular attention going to steamers of the cabin- and third-class type, which were becoming increasingly popular in the more democratic twenties. The intention, therefore, was to develop a new branch of travel

that would serve to offset any restrictions on emigrant traffic, so in the coming years the *Olympic*'s accommodations would be adapted to reflect the changing times. It would not be until April 1925 that the North Atlantic Conference, a cartel of the shipping companies operating on these routes, would formally introduce Tourist Third Cabin, but as far as the *Olympic* was concerned it meant that passengers travelling in this new class would be assigned either to the less attractive second-class or the best of

S. S. Fort St. George.
Photo by Courtesy of the Furness Bermuda Line.

ABOVE: *The SS* Fort St George.

the third-class accommodations, for a fee only slightly in excess of the standard third-class fare. In effect, it was the economy-plus of the 1920s.

COLLISION ON THE HUDSON

For ten weeks during the winter of 1923/24 the *Olympic* remained at Belfast, during which time further work was carried out on the sternpost. The positive news was that the bracing repairs carried out in August 1922 were holding, with only minor welding required just above the braces to satisfy the surveyor's requirements, and by 20 February the *Olympic* slipped effortlessly back into her regular routine for her first voyage of the season. However, barely one month later the *Olympic*'s stern would once again become the

focus of attention in a manner that few would have anticipated.

Shortly after 11am on 22 March 1924, Captain Howarth gave the order to reverse engines as the *Olympic* pulled away from Pier 59 and into the Hudson River. As soon as the bow had cleared the end of the pier, control of the vessel passed to Captain John Swainson, the New York river pilot, for a procedure that had been carried out safely and successfully on countless occasions. At the same time, the Furness Bermuda liner *Fort St George* was fast approaching from upstream. The *Fort St George* was no stranger to the Olympic class liners – in her previous guise as the Adelaide Steamship Company's *Wandilla*, she had gone alongside the *Britannic* at Mudros in October 1916 to deliver Adalbert Messany from Malta on the first stage of his infamous journey back to Austria – but on this occasion the rendezvous with the *Britannic*'s sibling would be less controlled. As the *Olympic*'s bow continued to swing towards downstream, Howarth noticed that the *Fort St George* was closing fast, although he judged that there was still sufficient space in the channel for the 7,785 GRT liner to pass under the ship's counter. Sadly, it was not to be; instead of passing astern, the *Fort St George*'s turn to starboard came too late and at precisely 11.12am the two vessels came into contact as the Furness Bermuda liner collided with the *Olympic*'s stern. Unable to return to the pier, Howarth had no option other than to anchor off Quarantine, near Staten Island, where a

diver was sent down to survey the damage. For the most part it seemed to be largely confined to some scarred plating beneath the *Olympic*'s counter, the inspection fortunately revealing no major structural damage; after a few adjustments to the steering gear, the *Olympic* was allowed to proceed. The *Fort St George*, on the other hand, had come off a lot worse, suffering a broken mainmast and major damage to lifeboats, decking and railings extending over 150 feet along her port side.

Despite the collision, the *Olympic*'s performance for the return trip would suggest

BELOW: *The* Olympic's *scarred stern plating following the collision with the* Fort St George.

ABOVE: *The Olympic class builder's model being prepared for display at the 1924 British Empire Exhibition, still incorporating the Britannic's enclosed forward Promenade and B deck window arrangements eight years after her loss.*

that the diver's initial prognosis had been correct, but inevitably the issue of who was at fault could only be resolved in the American court. In the end it would not be a rerun of the old *Olympic/Hawke* collision inquiry, with the American court ultimately finding in favour of the White Star Line some three years later. Unlike the previous case, the Furness Bermuda Line would have few grounds for appeal, with the court finding that the *Olympic* had given the correct signals (one long blast on the ship's whistle followed by three short blasts) before reversing into the river, that the *Fort St George* could have been closer to the distant New Jersey shoreline, and that she should have ported her helm sooner when Captain Francis decided to pass astern of the *Olympic*. The court also cited the *Fort St George*'s 'reckless' excessive

speed, made worse by the fact that some of the witnesses had even testified that the Bermuda liner almost seemed to be racing the RMSP's liner *Arcadian*, her rival on the Bermuda run. In his summing up, Judge Augustus Noble Hand had no doubt what he thought, citing the 'inexcusable neglect' aboard the *Fort St George* and also dismissing the Bermuda Line's claim that the *Olympic* had reversed too far out into the river.

After a four-day turnaround at Southampton, the *Olympic* was once again bound for New York on 3 April, her performance on that voyage, and indeed for the rest of the year, seeming to indicate that no long-term damage had been sustained in the collision. As ever, Captain Howarth found himself more concerned with on-board activities, such as the mysterious disappearance on the morning of 27 April of second-class passenger George Garizio, who had reportedly not slept in his bed the previous night. Enquiries revealed very little, other than that his dining companions had noticed that he seemed a bit quiet at dinner the previous evening, but with two searches of the ship proving fruitless Captain Howarth had no option but to list him in the log as 'missing'. Two voyages later there was another mysterious crew disappearance, when bedroom steward Arthur Paul failed to report for duty on the morning on 17 June. No one had noticed anything particularly unusual in his demeanour when he was last seen on duty the evening before, but when hands were called at 5am the following morning his bunk had not been slept in. The customary search was carried out, but no trace of Arthur Paul was ever seen again.

There were also the occasional instances of petty larceny, when on 14 June master-at-arms EA Coward, while making his rounds before going off duty for the night, came across a seaman named Connolly standing beside the opening at the top of No 4 hatch, the locking bar having been forced and the grating removed. Observing seaman W Shave standing below on one of the lower decks, Coward asked 'what the game was', to which Connolly replied that they were getting a trunk up. Coward sent for the bosun's mate to see if the two men did indeed have authority to be in the hold, only

for Connolly and Shave to suddenly change their story, this time claiming that they had permission from one of the butchers to retrieve a barrel from the hold to make a drum. It was only two days later, when they were hauled in front of Captain Howarth, that the two men would finally admit that they had no authority to be in the hold, after butcher B Kellaway had refused to tell the master-at-arms that he had given them permission to be there.

This voyage would be particularly notable for one other reason, as when the *Olympic* departed from New York she was carrying home the body of Lord Pirrie, her creator, who had died on board the SS *Ebro* on 7 June. Pirrie had travelled to Buenos Aires aboard the SS *Arlanza* on 21 March for a business trip to South America, inspecting ports and facilities in the region for future projects, before deciding to extend his trip for a vacation to Valparaíso and Antofagasta in Chile. It was while at Antofagasta that he caught a chill, but his determination to be taken up on deck to see the Panama Canal would ultimately be his undoing; he died aboard the SS *Ebro* while en route to New York. The *Ebro* reached New York just in time for Pirrie's embalmed body to be placed aboard the *Olympic* for her scheduled crossing, where it would lie in state in a first-class cabin on E deck. Upon arrival at Southampton on 20 June, Pirrie's body was taken to his Lea Park estate, near Godalming in Surrey, before being laid to rest in the Belfast City Cemetery three days later.

The social highlight of the year was unquestionably the *Olympic*'s departure from New York on 25 October. On board was none other than the Prince of Wales, returning to England after a ten-week holiday on what would turn out to be a particularly rough crossing, the news reports of the voyage recording that Edward was apparently unaffected by the rough weather and made good use of the squash court. He also showed particular interest in the wireless reports in the run-up to the British general election, which was not surprising as on the same day that the *Olympic* departed New York the *Daily Mail* had published the Zinoviev letter, alleging it to be a directive from Grigory Zinoviev, head of the Communist International in Moscow, to the Communist Party of Great Britain to say that the resumption of diplomatic relations by a Labour government would hasten the radicalisation of the British working class. The result of this apparent interference in British politics, although the letter was later proved to be a forgery, would massively undermine the Liberal vote; by the time the *Olympic* arrived back at Southampton on 31 October, Prime Minister Ramsey MacDonald's minority Labour government had been swept away in a landslide victory for Stanley Baldwin's Conservatives.

The remaining five voyages would not be so thrilling, but sadly Captain Howarth's tenure as skipper would end on a poignant note when, on 18 February 1925, he had to enter into the log the death of one-day-old Philip John Bélanger. Two days later the *Olympic* returned safely to Southampton at the end of his 18th voyage in the ship, where his successor, Captain William Marshall, would assume command.

On the whole, Marshall would also enjoy

ABOVE: *Lord and Lady Mountbatten on board the* Olympic *in 1925.*

a relatively uneventful year at the helm, recording only one further death in the ship's log that year – 11-month-old Jakia Domet, a third-class passenger who had succumbed to bronchopneumonia on 14 April 1925. Nor would the official introduction that same month of Tourist Third Cabin on the North Atlantic result in any major alterations to the ship's accommodations until her next major refit, but before long an old problem would once again return to haunt her as, one by one, numerous structural issues slowly began to creep up on the 14-year-old former White Star flagship.

CHAPTER NINETEEN

THE APPROACHING STORM

On 25 April 1925, after the *Olympic* had been placed in the floating dock at Southampton for a routine survey, Mr O Sullivan, the Board of Trade's senior ship surveyor, found himself being called that evening to examine a fracture in the upper arch of the stern frame. Without realising it, his inspection would highlight a longer running structural issue.

The survey itself revealed a number of loose rivets that Sullivan later noted 'called for serious consideration'. Fortunately, the bearing of the centre turbine shaft had not been affected by any potential movement or distortion of the frame and the aft hull plating also showed no signs of stress, meaning that the sternpost itself was still well supported. The lower arch also seemed to be unaffected, and with the 1922 sternpost repairs still in a satisfactory condition it was agreed that by renewing the loose rivets and fitting a $1^{1}/_{8}$-inch strap on either side of the arch, the repairs would suffice for the issue of a three-month certificate.

Based on conversations with chief engineer John Thearle, the consensus was that the problem most likely originated in November or December 1924, when water was found to be leaking into the aft peak tank after a number of vibrations had been felt. Neither occurrence was considered to be unusual, especially as

leakage in the aft peak tank was apparently regarded as fairly common in the larger vessels, but it was concerning enough for arrangements to be made to have the area inspected by divers after every crossing, and even to disengage the centre propeller altogether when the ship was in heavy weather. In the meantime, a plaster cast mould was made of the affected areas in preparation for more substantial work to be carried out when the ship was next due to be dry-docked, but with the seasonal weather set to improve and the temporary repairs completed, the *Olympic* was cleared for her scheduled departure on 30 April. For a while the repairs seemed to be holding, with further examinations at New York proving satisfactory, so when the ship returned to Southampton on 15 May the two stiffening strips remained structurally sound. Apart from a minor problem with a few slack rivets, there was nothing to prevent the ship sailing again on 20 May, but it would seem that even at this preliminary stage the White Star Line was thinking on the lines of a more radical and long-term fix. Although various options for strengthening the affected area continued to be discussed throughout the autumn, by November 1925 the decision had been taken to carry out a complete reconstruction of the stern.

On 14 January 1926 the *Olympic*, complete with a totally rebuilt stern, was finally ready to be removed from the dry dock, only for the ship's stem to suffer a fracture after striking a fender as she was undocking. The resulting damage to the forward starboard hull plates in M and N strakes meant that the forward 7 feet of the M strake plating would require cropping and part renewal, while the lower plate only needed welding, but although the repair was considered satisfactory by Mr F Daniel, another

senior ship surveyor at Southampton, as cracks had previously appeared on each side of the stem in the same strakes there was concern that the extent of the damage may have been exacerbated due to the bow plating in the area being fatigued by panting and other stresses. In the past, the *Olympic* had remained on the Board's Confidential List due to the issues with the sternpost and ongoing observation of the oil-fuel installation, but although Daniel was happy for the observation of the now reconstructed sternpost to be scaled back, focus instead shifted to the other end of the *Olympic*'s hull as the repairs to the forward shell plating were subjected to regular examination.

By 27 January the *Olympic* was ready to resume her place on the North Atlantic. As with Marshall's first year in command there

BELOW: *The* Olympic *in the floating dock at Southampton.*

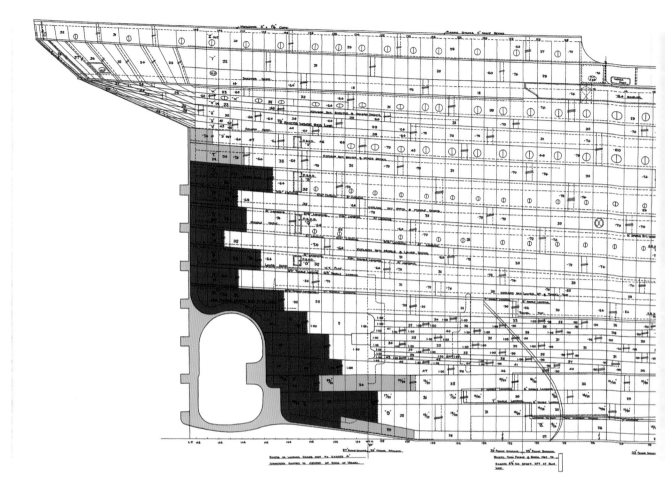

was little of concern to record, perhaps the most unusual entry in the log coming on 22 February, when a messenger in the purser's office named Leonard Payne was found to be defrauding the company. Having access to the ship's papers, Payne had decided to unilaterally improve his working conditions by awarding himself an unofficial £2 monthly pay increase in the ship's articles, but not surprisingly the purser became suspicious when he saw the books and Payne was subsequently 'removed from duty'. On the other hand, the voyage was memorable in one respect, when two days later a third-class passenger named Caroline Barsam gave birth to

a son in the ship's hospital. Mentions of births and deaths in any ship's log were not unusual – indeed, they were required by law – but in this case it was more noteworthy, if only because Valerie and Caroline Barsam, to celebrate the birth of their son, had christened him Olympic Valerie!

Issues of passengers being lost overboard continued to be rare, but perhaps the most dramatic example came at 6.04am on 24 May, when Toefile Rechleuicien, a 52-year-old housewife from Lithuania, fell overboard. As soon as the news reached the bridge, the engines were reversed in order to return to the

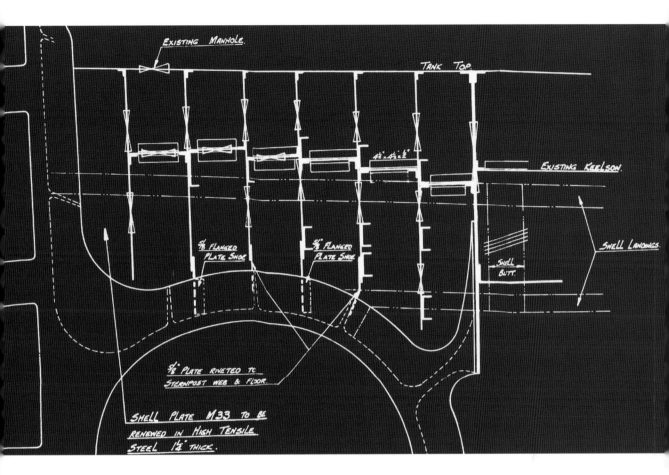

LEFT AND ABOVE: *The* Olympic's *new stern frame was built in three parts as opposed to the original two. Combined with an additional keelson, strengthening of the peak tank and thicker plating in the N and O strakes, the new structure added considerably to the stiffness of the stern. The red plates were replaced altogether, while those shaded in pink were removed and reused after the work had been completed.*

area as quickly as possible without having to make a large turn. After 15 minutes someone saw what they thought looked like a body and lifebuoy, but although the emergency cutter had been lowered within three minutes, sadly it would all be in vain. Twenty minutes later the boat returned without success and at 6.53am,

with little hope of finding the body, the *Olympic* continued on to New York.

Distress calls were also reassuringly rare, but at 9.18am on 16 September 1926, while 200 miles west of the Scilly Isles, Captain Marshall would find himself called to assist a vessel in distress. The ship in question was the Trieste-registered SS *Ellenia*, en route from Hampton Roads to London. The previous day she had been involved in a collision with the British steamer SS *Induna*, and evidently her condition was deteriorating. Within 12 minutes the *Ellenia* was in sight and at 9.52 Marshall slowed to half speed and stood by to

ABOVE: *Work on the new stern being carried out in the floating dock at Southampton.*

render assistance. A radio signal to the master of the *Ellenia* asking if he wished to abandon his ship was answered in the affirmative, but shortly afterwards another message arrived to say 'Now I do not abandon ship. Thank you.' Fourth Officer J Law was dispatched in one of the lifeboats to ask the captain of the stricken vessel if he needed assistance, and was back on board within 40 minutes, confirming that *Ellenia*'s captain did not wish to abandon ship but that he had requested a tow. With two French vessels already standing by, Marshall signalled *Ellenia*'s position to the nearby SS *Laguna*, which would be on the scene within an hour, before resuming an easterly course at 11.19am. Later they would learn that the *Ellenia* had actually sunk, but fortunately her crew had all been picked up by the French

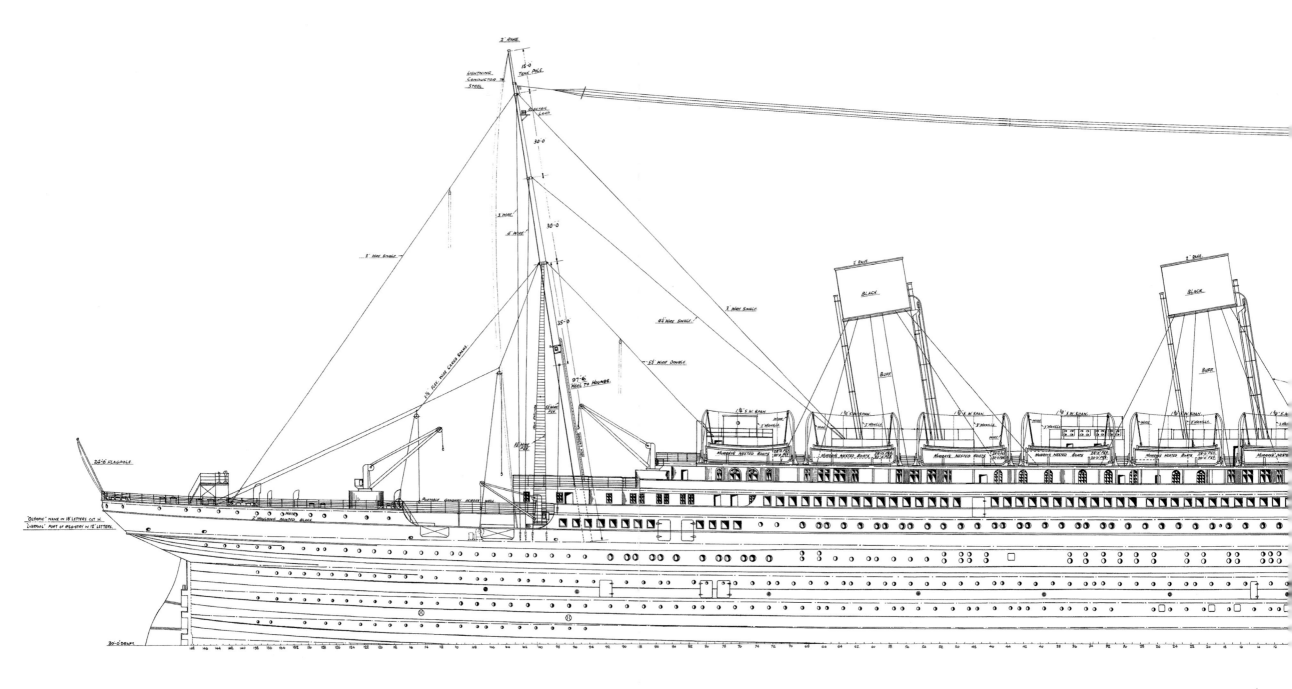

T.R.S.S. "OLYMPIC."

RIGGING PLAN.

Scale:- 1/16" = 1 FOOT.

fishing vessel *Petite Suzanne*.

The remainder of 1926 would bring less excitement, but it would not be a happy start to the new year when, on the afternoon of 1 January 1927, third-class passenger James Kipila died on board from pneumonia and heart failure. On the other hand, this particular New Year's Day would be something of an occasion for the British mercantile marine. Despite the drop in steerage passengers on the North Atlantic, the initial outlook in 1926 had been encouraging enough for Sir Frederick Lewis of Furness Withy & Co to open discussions with IMM, with a view to the purchase of their interest in the White Star Line. In truth, IMM had proved to be one of JP Morgan's less successful ventures, so much so that soon after the war the company had already been considering the sale of its foreign-held shipping concerns. A British consortium led by Lord Pirrie and Sir Owen Philipps' Royal Mail Steam Packet Company had even been on the verge of handing over the £27,000,000 asking price to finalise the transaction, before the deal was vetoed at the last minute by President Woodrow Wilson on the grounds that the sale was not in America's interest. Considering the subsequent American immigration restrictions this may well have been a blessing in disguise, but the dream of buying back the White Star Line for Britain had not gone away. The General Strike of 1926 may have persuaded Sir Frederick to shelve his plans to purchase the company, but Sir Owen Philipps, by now raised to the peerage as the 1st Baron Kylsant, quickly stepped into the void. The discussions continued and in November that year IMM agreed to the sale of their shares in

the Oceanic Steam Navigation Company for the sum of £7,000,000 plus interest – a price that many considered excessive, especially as IMM continued to retain the White Star agency in America. Nevertheless, on 1 January 1927 the White Star Line officially became a subsidiary of the Royal Mail Group; after almost 16 years in service, the *Olympic* was finally a British ship in every sense of the word.

In the meantime, for the *Olympic* it was very much a case of business as usual. The Southampton to New York service maintained by the *Olympic*, *Majestic* and *Homeric* remained largely unaltered, the only noticeable difference being the transfer of ownership of the *Nomadic* and *Traffic* to the Compagnie Cherbourgeoise de Transbordement, Paris, effectively farming out White Star's Cherbourg-based tendering operations to an independent company.

The year itself began in a relatively straightforward manner, with two uneventful voyages to New York, but by 16 March concerns at the Board of Trade regarding several structural issues were growing fast. The *Olympic*'s name had already been red-flagged on the Board's confidential list so that they could continue to observe the 1926 stern and bow repairs, but the prognosis was not encouraging. In early 1927 a number of slack rivets continued to be reported in the arch of the stern frame, indicating that there was still considerable vibration in the area, but while the bow repairs of January 1926 still held good, the discovery of two small cracks that had subsequently appeared on the port side, opposite the original fracture, meant that the bow remained a cause for concern. More serious

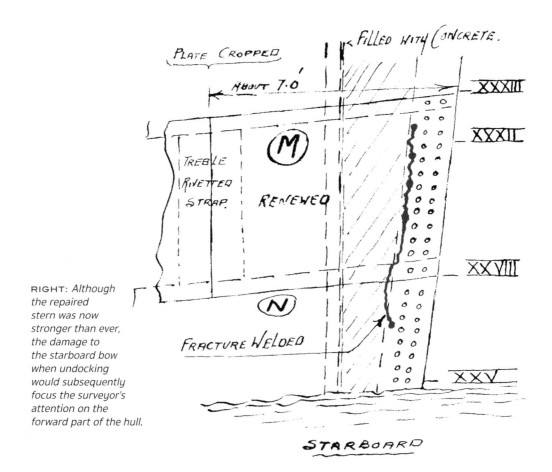

PLATE CROPPED

← FILLED WITH CONCRETE.

← ABOUT 7·0'

TREBLE RIVETTED STRAP.

(M)

RENEWED

(N)

FRACTURE WELDED

XXXIII

XXXII

XXVIII

XXV

STARBOARD

RIGHT: *Although the repaired stern was now stronger than ever, the damage to the starboard bow when undocking would subsequently focus the surveyor's attention on the forward part of the hull.*

was the appearance of six small cracks in the bridge deck sheer strake and doubler between the lower edge of the side scuttles to a small drainage hole immediately below, which in several cases extended to rivet holes in the shell plating and doubling. The most likely cause was put down to fatigue brought on by the reversal of high stresses in the affected areas, with the normal stresses being magnified by the narrow strip between the bottom of the scuttles and the plate landing. For the time being it was hoped that the fractures themselves would relieve the concentrated stresses, and that they would proceed no further, but either way the bridge deck was now being watched very closely.

By the end of the year the *Olympic*'s interior was also in need of an overhaul and on 17 December White Star finally proposed their first major internal alteration since the 1920 refit, dividing the second-class dining room in two to create a separate tourist dining saloon. However, it was not simply a question of running a soundproof dividing bulkhead down the middle. Such an arrangement would have resulted in dining space for only 174 tourist passengers, but while another 95 passengers could be seated if 12 cabins were removed on the port side, that option would only be practicable by installing a hinged watertight door into the bulkhead itself. This was the only major structural work carried out during the survey, although the ongoing observations of the bow reported that while previous repairs were satisfactory, an additional 12-inch fracture had now developed on the port side at the 38-foot mark. The stern frame rivets were for the most part holding, requiring only limited welding of the area, but while there was for the time being no extension of the existing fractures in the C deck shell, the affected areas still needed to be surface welded to prevent any unsightly rust marks from showing up beneath the white-painted area.

BELOW: *The modified second-class dining room was divided in two and extended on the port side to accommodate the Tourist passengers.*

THE LAST OF THE GOOD DAYS

The *Olympic*'s 1928 season on the North Atlantic proved on the whole to be a great success and by 7 September Captain Marshall had completed 11 round trips between Southampton and New York, the only casualty of the year being on his last westbound voyage when second-class passenger Antonina Swiatek died from cardiac disease. On 11 September 1928 it was the turn of Captain Walter Parker to take command, as Marshall was being transferred to the *Majestic*. Parker would later recall that Marshall became so emotional at the thought of leaving his ship after three and a half years at the helm that he offered to take the *Majestic* instead, to which Marshall replied, 'I suppose I ought to feel honoured. She is, after all, the largest ship in the

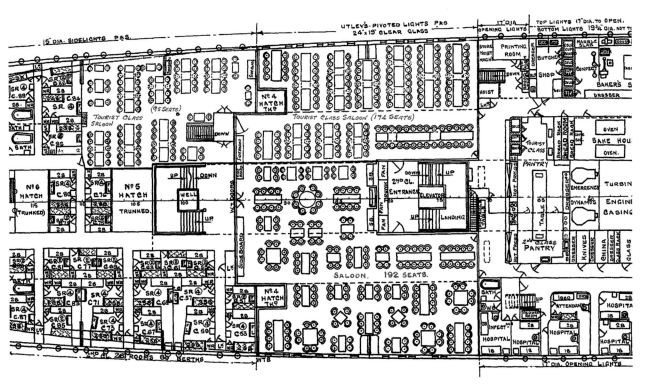

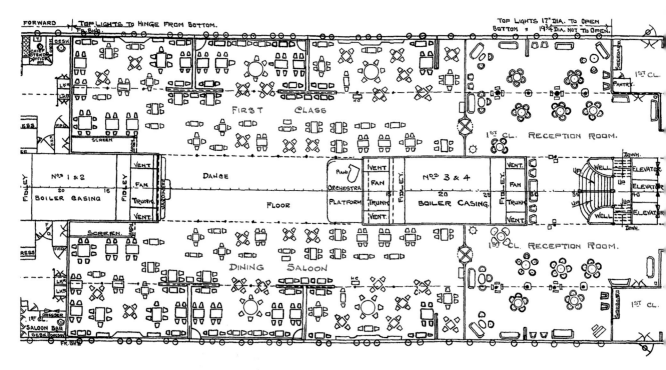

ABOVE: *By 1928 the* Olympic's *first-class dining room had also been remodelled to include a dance floor, a sign of the changing times.*

world, you know, Parker – but I am leaving the best to you, for all that.' In time, Parker would come to agree with him, but unfortunately his first two months in command would not be the happiest. Misfortune was to strike on his very first voyage when, on 25 September, Junior Assistant Second Engineer James Laidlaw died in the ship's hospital from blood poisoning due to a carbuncle on his knee. Two voyages later misfortune struck the crew yet again, when bosun's mate John Gravell was killed in hold 3 when he fell from the bridge deck to the mail room down on G deck while unshipping a ventilator.

Parker would complete five voyages before arriving back at Southampton at the end of the year on 28 December 1928, where the *Olympic* would undergo her next refit. On this occasion, however, the internal work would be a lot more

extensive. The dining room alterations carried out at the start of the year had more than proved their worth, so much so that, before the end of the year, second class on the North Atlantic had been largely superseded and merged with tourist third cabin into tourist class. As a result, the internal alterations would be further developed, this time with particular attention being given to the first-class accommodation.

By 13 February 1929 the transformation was complete and the *Olympic* returned to service for the new season, but the one thing that does not seem to have changed was the crew's luck, the jinx returning on 30 June 1929 when wireless operator Kevin Cowhey was

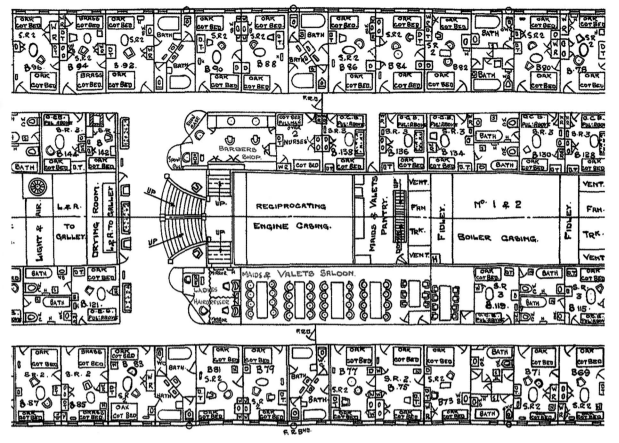

ABOVE: *The barber's shop on the port side would be augmented by a ladies' hairdresser to starboard.*

BELOW: *A throwback to Bruce Ismay's original concept of the larger cabins and suites on the* Titanic's *B deck, sixteen of the forward cabins on the* Olympic *were also enlarged.*

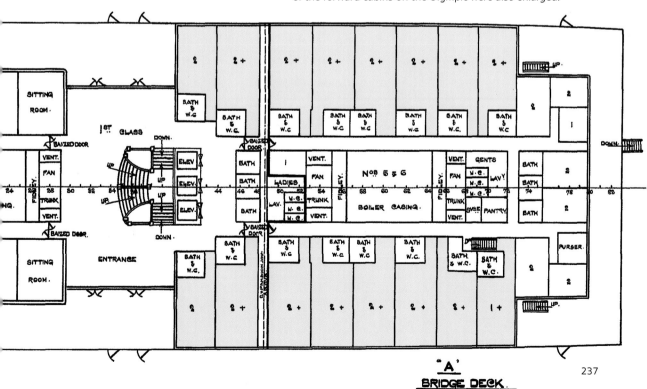

"A"
BRIDGE DECK

admitted to the ship's hospital with asthma and cardiac trouble, dying three days later. Even so, Parker's tenure of command was, on the whole, a happy one and as ever it would be events over which the White Star Line had no control that would cast their greatest shadow. However, few if any would have been prepared for what came on Thursday 24 October 1929, a day that would later become infamous as 'Black Thursday', when the Wall Street stock market plunged by an unimaginable 11 per cent.

It was not just the financial markets that were subject to turmoil. During the afternoon of 18 November 1929 the *Olympic* was in position 42° 12' N, 56° 56' W when a violent tremor caused the ship to vibrate almost continuously for two minutes. Captain Parker was in his chart room at the time, but the officers on watch confirmed that the ship had not been in collision with another vessel, while the possibility of a dropped propeller blade was quickly ruled out because the engines were still running smoothly. Apart from the loss of electrical lighting in the mail room, the ship was largely unaffected, although interestingly enough

BELOW: *Included in the first major refit after White Star was taken over by RMSP, the* Olympic's *staircase and reception room were stained in green to give the ageing decor a more modern feel.*

many of the passengers further aft in the ship's lounge had felt nothing while a film was being screened. Before long, the ship's wireless shed the necessary light on the mystery, when reports confirmed that there had been a huge undersea earthquake, which had even ruptured a dozen submarine telegraphic cables between Europe and America.

Two days later the *Olympic* arrived safely at New York, seemingly none the worse for the experience, but while the ship had safely weathered the turbulent waters of the Grand Banks, this would be nothing compared to the approaching financial storm. On 31 December

BELOW: *In April 1925 Imperial Airways inaugurated the concept of in-flight movies with a screening of First National's* The Lost World *during a flight from London to Paris. Before long the White Star Line followed suit, but the handling, shipping and housing of the film was extremely dangerous due to its highly flammable nitrate backing, which if ignited could not be extinguished because the combustion process generated its own oxygen.*

1929, Captain Walter Parker and the ship's chief engineer, John Thearle, who had been in the ship since she entered service, both reached the mandatory retirement age. Without realising it, both men had seen the last of the *Olympic*'s glory days.

CHAPTER TWENTY

THE HOUSE OF CARDS

On 2 January 1930, Captain Eustace White assumed the mantle of the *Olympic*'s latest commander, at a time when the future of the largest British-built ship was looking increasingly uncertain. Passenger traffic on the North Atlantic already bore little similarity to the peak years of almost 20 years earlier, while the financial carnage on Wall Street had instigated a massive decline of the American economy as the Great Depression took hold. Throughout the 1930s this year-on-year downward spiral would have a hugely detrimental effect on the number of passengers carried, as each of the shipping companies responded to the increasingly challenging market realities on the North Atlantic.

The stormy financial waters were also casting a giant shadow over Lord Kylsant's maritime ambitions. RMSP's purchase of the White Star Line had been only the first step of his master plan, as he continued to borrow millions to finance the ongoing expansion of his marine empire. In 1928 he had also purchased the Australian government's Commonwealth Line for £1,900,000 in the name of the White Star Line, before going on to spend a further £994,000 to buy out the Shaw, Savill & Albion Line, even though he already held a controlling interest in the company. There seemed to be no end to his optimism when in June of that year he placed a £3,500,000 order with Harland & Wolff, which he had also controlled since Lord Pirrie's death in 1924, for the *Oceanic*, a projected White Star liner of 60,000 tons. Beneath the surface, however, the foundations

of Kylsant's mercantile empire were already beginning to crack, so much so that by the autumn of 1929 work on the *Oceanic* had been suspended due to the lack of capital, while the Royal Mail Group struggled to repay the government loans advanced for the expansion of the fleet in the early twenties.

Nor was it simply the economic or financial issues that were casting an unwelcome shadow over the *Olympic*'s future. By the beginning of 1929, the ship's new stern frame – still only three years old – was already showing signs of considerable pitting, supposedly caused by an 'obscure electrochemical action', and by 1930 the pitting had increased to the point where the sternpost needed to be sheathed in white metal to protect it from any further deterioration. Unfortunately, the problems did not end there. In January 1931 another survey indicated that the cracks in the upper works of the bridge deck were starting to show serious signs of extension, similar to those that had been found six years earlier in the upper works of the *Leviathan* and *Majestic*, while the list of additional defects included in the surveyor's summary of 4 February included a strained girder at the fore end of funnel 2, along with fractured and slack rivets. The aft expansion joint at the forward end of the engine casing also had slack rivets in the deck girder, while some of the light plating forward of the casing was cracked. Immediately beneath the aft expansion joint, the deckhouse foundation plates and angles on each side were cracking, while the bridge structure had slack rivets in the P-Q landing of the shell plating at four butts on each side, and at one butt on the starboard side below the aft expansion joint. It all added up to quite a list, and a reasonably sure sign that all the riveting in this seam was starting to deteriorate amidships. For a time, White Star compromised with extensive welding and fitting doublers over the affected areas,

BELOW: *Detail of the nature of the cracks in the* Olympic's *hull.*

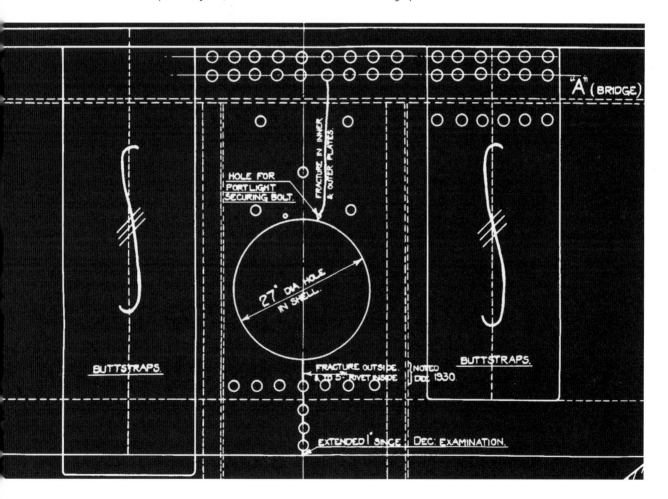

but the remedial work could only be regarded as temporary at best. More to the point, the structural issues were almost certainly being caused by working stresses, in which case it was likely that other areas of the strake were approaching their yield point and would soon follow suit, possibly even giving way altogether in rough weather once the other areas had been stiffened. Either way, the surveyors were not confident that the repairs would prove effective in the long term, so much so that instead of the usual 12-month passenger certificate being issued, a six-month certificate was instead issued in January 1931 to allow for a more extensive survey at the summer docking. Crucially, however, the mounting number of defects could no longer be looked upon simply as natural occurrences inherent in an ageing ship. One of the Board's internal memos from 9 January 1931 now regarded the problems more as symptoms of questionable design:

> '*I here point out that that these three vessels are the largest vessels at present afloat and their construction can only be regarded as to have been experimental. The builders were working with unknown factors, but in the light of our experience with those three ships it can now be seen that there were serious defects in their design which ought to have been foreseen.*'

The analysis of the structural issues also had intriguing overtones for new Cunarder Yard No 534 (ultimately to be named *Queen Mary*), the keel having been laid barely one month earlier on the Clyde. The scantlings had already been approved by Lloyd's Register and submitted to the Board of Trade for approval, but based on what had transpired in the *Olympic* the Board was suddenly concerned by the approved combination of materials in the side plating of the upper works of the new vessel. Dr James Montgomerie, Lloyd's Principal Surveyor for Scotland, shared these concerns and arranged to inspect the *Olympic* at Southampton on 27 January, accompanied by Cunard marine architect George Paterson; clearly the visit would prove worthwhile, with a subsequent handwritten note in the Board of Trade records confirming that the surveyor's observations had been able to secure improvements in the design of the new vessel.

While that was good news for Cunard, the outlook for the White Star Line was less upbeat. In December 1929 the United States liner *Leviathan* had suffered similar structural issues, which had resulted in three months of extensive repair work at an estimated cost of £300,000, but while the *Olympic*'s bridge deck shell plating was now showing structural failures 'of equal seriousness but of a different character', the cost of rebuilding the affected areas was still likely to be in the region of £100,000. For a 20-year-old vessel in an uncertain economic environment, this looked like an increasingly questionable investment; even if it was viable, the company's financial position was dire. By October 1929 Kylsant's over-expansion had all but exhausted RMSP's reserves, prompting a government audit that had revealed the widespread manipulation of resources between its constituent parts. It would signal the end

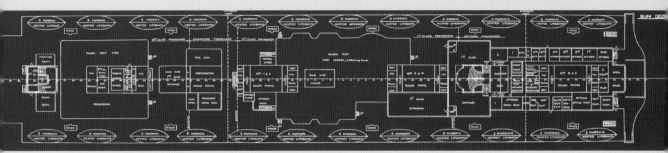

for Lord Kylsant's ambitions and in September 1931 he would also be convicted and sentenced to 12 months in prison for publishing misleading statements in the 1928 RMSP debenture stock issue.

In 1932 the bankrupt Royal Mail Steam Packet Company was reconstituted into the Royal Mail Line Ltd, but for the White Star

ABOVE: *The final configuration of the* Olympic's *boat deck, with an additional radio room and machine room located aft.*

BELOW: *The* Olympic *and* Berengaria *dominating Southampton's Ocean Dock in 1932.*

ships were sold for £500,000 to the newly formed Aberdeen and Commonwealth Line, resulting in a cumulative loss to the White Star Line of £1,487,807.

But this is to anticipate events. Throughout 1931 the *Olympic*, under the command of Captain Edgar Trant, had stood up well to the conditions at sea, so much so that when the repairs were examined in July of that year and found to be in good condition, the ship's passenger certificate was duly extended for a further six months. More importantly, at the next survey the repairs carried out during the previous winter were still holding, so on 23 February 1932 the annual load line and passenger certificate was granted for the usual 12-month period. However, this would be the last of the good news.

On 14 October 1932 the *Olympic* returned to Southampton where, later that day, a routine inspection revealed cracks in the reciprocating engine bedplates and part of the crank shaft. At first it was thought that these cracks had resulted from the defects in the topsides, primarily because fractured casings of this nature were usually associated with the longitudinal working of the hull structure, but in the end no positive link could be traced, other than that both issues probably resulted

Line the financial writing was also on the wall. Kylsant's acquisition of the Commonwealth and Shaw, Savill lines, both purchases having been made in the name of White Star Line Ltd, had all but broken the company, with the Oceanic Steam Navigation Company reporting its first ever financial loss in 1930. Things might have been different had it not been for the world financial crisis, but the Depression had changed everything and by the end of 1932 White Star was unable to maintain their repayment schedule. When the Australian government refused to extend the payments due from the company, on 8 March 1933 the Commonwealth

from a sequence of heavy-weather voyages during the winter of 1926/27. Either way, the problem was serious enough that not only was the scheduled voyage of 19 October cancelled, but also the remainder of the ship's 1932 season; instead, the *Olympic* would spend four months undergoing major repairs to the engine bedplates, along with extensive re-riveting beneath the engine thrust blocks. But perhaps the most telling piece of the Board's correspondence on the growing list of defects in White Star's former flagship comes on 9 November 1932, noting that the White Star Line had taken the decision to limit the *Olympic*'s service speed to 21 knots in order to mitigate the stresses to which the hull was subjected. On 1 March 1933 the *Olympic* finally returned to service for what would be her 225th voyage, still under the watchful eye of the Board of Trade surveyors who, for the time being, were more than happy with the engine repairs, noting that during the engine trials, 'Everything went very satisfactorily, there being practically no movement of the bed plates'. Chief Engineer

Charles McKimm was even more impressed, noting that he had never known the engines and thrust blocks to be so free from movement.

Meanwhile, the future remained uncertain. White Star's enforced sale of the Commonwealth Line vessels had left the company teetering on the abyss of financial oblivion, and in an attempt to salvage something from the financial scrap heap, in the autumn of 1933 Colonel Frank Bustard, the company's passenger traffic manager, approached Joseph Bruce Ismay, now long retired from the company, in the hope that he would be able to put together a rescue plan. Ismay agreed to meet with Bustard to discuss the possibilities, but it was too little too late. When the White Star Line recorded its third successive annual trading loss later that year, the UK Government Treasury was finally forced to step in.

BELOW: *The* Olympic *secured in Berth 43 at Southampton. In the distance lies the three-funnelled Canadian Pacific liner* Empress of Britain.

WHITE STAR LINE.

TRIPLE-SCREW R.M.S. "OLYMPIC,"
46,439 TONS,
THE LARGEST BRITISH STEAMER,
PASSING AMBROSE CHANNEL LIGHTSHIP.

The financial problems were not unique to the White Star Line. Cunard was also in serious financial trouble in the early thirties, so much so that in December 1931 they had been forced to halt construction on Yard No 534 in Glasgow. Neville Chamberlain, then Chancellor of the Exchequer, was in a position to assist, but the Treasury could not contemplate a situation whereby it would be seen to be backing two commercial rivals in an increasingly limited market. The only way the Cunard and White Star Lines could both be given government support was for the two companies to agree to a merger, in return for which the British government would guarantee a loan of up to £9,500,000, not only covering the working capital of the new company but also enabling work to resume on 534 at the John Brown shipyard. On 30 December 1933 the boards of the two former

ABOVE: *This 1930s postcard perfectly illustrates the apparent vulnerability of an anchored 600-ton lightship to a moving liner of the* Olympic's *size.*

rival companies met to agree terms and on 28 March 1934 the North Atlantic Shipping Bill was given the Royal Assent. On 10 May 1934 Cunard White Star Ltd was registered, with the former White Star Line interests controlling 38 per cent of the new company and contributing ten ships to the new fleet, although by the end of the year the *Adriatic*, *Albertic* and *Calgaric* had all been sold for scrap.

THE BEGINNING OF THE END

Meanwhile, the *Olympic*'s long-term future seemed uncertain at best, and to further complicate matters less than a week after

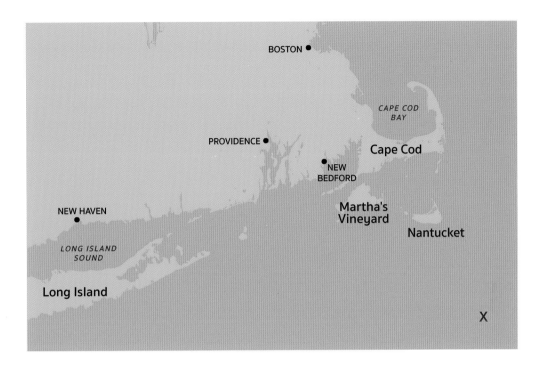

ABOVE: *The location of the Nantucket light ship collision, 15 May 1934.*

the formation of the new company she would once again be making the headlines for all the wrong reasons. On the morning of Tuesday 15 May 1934, under the command of Captain John Binks, the *Olympic* was south of Cape Cod and inbound for New York. Because of heavy fog, Binks had been on almost continuous watch for 30 hours, and by 10.50am the ship was nearing the Nantucket lightship (*LV-117*), near the south-east extent of the Nantucket shoals. If the visibility outside was minimal, the situation in the *Olympic*'s wireless room was equally uncertain, as radio operator Frank Clark struggled to keep contact with the lightship's radio beacon, receiving the last transmission at 10.56am before losing the signal altogether.

Two minutes later, the officers on the bridge heard the lightship's foghorn in the distance as the *Olympic*'s speed was reduced to 10 knots, although due to the distortion caused by the fog it was impossible to be sure of the exact bearing from which the sound had come. Clark was immediately ordered to get another fix on the lightship, but he could get no response; the only thing of which he could be certain was that, based on the strength of the previous signal, they were within 30 miles.

In the meantime, aboard the *LV-117* Captain George Braithwaite was relaxing in his cabin, buried in a good novel, wireless operator John Perry was in his radio cabin and first mate Clifton E Mosher was on watch topside. Suddenly, the huge frame of the 52,310-ton *Olympic* materialised out of the fog on the lightship's port side, probably no more than a

247

few hundred yards distant. Despite the poor visibility, Mosher was in no doubt about what he could see, calling out 'The *Olympic* is upon us!' as he sounded the emergency bell to warn the members of the crew below. The sudden activity on the *Olympic*'s bridge was no less frantic. At 11.06am, *LV-117*'s red-painted hull suddenly emerged from the fog directly ahead as Captain Binks ordered the engines to full astern, but already it was too late; seconds later, the *Olympic* ploughed into the port side of the anchored lightship. Mosher recalled the collision as being 'like a hard push and a terrific shaking, a crunching and grinding', but either way the momentum of the *Olympic*, even though she was by this time making only 3 or 4 knots, was not going to be arrested by the 630-ton lightship. Perry recalled barely having

time to get out on deck before being forced to swim for his life, while oiler Robert Laurent commented, 'It all happened so quickly, you had no chance to panic. We all had our life preservers and it was a good thing that we did.'

Within six minutes of coming to a complete stop, the *Olympic*'s two emergency boats had been sent away to rescue any survivors, but with the fog rendering an extensive search all but impossible, at 11.27am boat 4, equipped with its own engine and wireless, was lowered to continue the search further afield. In the meantime, Captain Binks dropped anchor to await the return of the rescue parties,

BELOW: *The four Nantucket lightship survivors photographed in the* Olympic*'s forward main entrance.*

as he continued to sound the ship's whistle periodically so that the emergency boats had a bearing to return to the ship. By the time the three boats returned, four survivors had been rescued and three bodies had been recovered, but at 12.29pm, with no further hope of finding *LV-117*'s four missing crewmen, the *Olympic* resumed her heading for New York.

The *Olympic* arrived in port the following morning, seemingly little worse for wear other than the scarred paintwork on her stem. The inquiry opened at the New York Custom House on 17 May, but although in this case there could be little doubt that the *Olympic* was at fault, the parallels with 1912 remained. The *Titanic* had been accused of steaming too fast in the vicinity of ice, yet it had emerged during the inquiries that it was a not uncommon practice of many captains on the North Atlantic to do just that. This time, John Binks was the White Star skipper under scrutiny, but it soon became apparent that his actions were by no means unusual either, with other liners regularly passing close to the lightship and at high speed, including the SS *Paris*, which had passed within a few hundred yards of the lightship only a few hours before the collision. Four months previously, the SS *Washington* had been involved in a less serious glancing collision with the *LV-117*, but while the damage in that case was limited to the radio antenna being carried away and minor damage to some hull plates, near misses were such a common occurrence that, barely a month before the fatal collision, radio operator John Perry had commented to friends, 'Someday we are just going to get it head on, and that will be the finish. One of those big liners will just ride

through us one of these days.' The inquiry also highlighted another weakness in the system. Although navigation by 'riding the beam' was frowned upon for what were now all too obvious safety reasons, liners had nevertheless been having difficulty in picking up the transmissions from the Cape Cod and Pollock Rip lightships for nearly a year before the collision, making it more difficult to triangulate their position. Frank Clark would even testify that he had lost contact with *LV-117* ten minutes before the collision, but that his radio equipment was not malfunctioning because he was still able to pick up other beacons.

Shortly after midnight on 18 May the *Olympic* was allowed to depart as scheduled, Cunard White Star having accepted liability for the collision. The legal discussions would continue into January 1936, not because the company was trying to wriggle off the legal hook but rather to dispel any allegations of negligent navigation and to agree upon an acceptable level of damages. In that respect they would ultimately be successful, with the original damages of $500,000 eventually reduced to $325,000.

The *Olympic*'s next arrival at New York on 5 June would be less eventful, but nonetheless significant as it would mark the last occasion on which she would dock at Pier 59. The amalgamation of the two companies meant that henceforth the Cunard White Star Line's New York terminal would be based at Cunard's terminal, but her maiden arrival at Pier 54 would also be memorable for other reasons when no sooner had the *Olympic* docked at her new western terminal on 26 June than

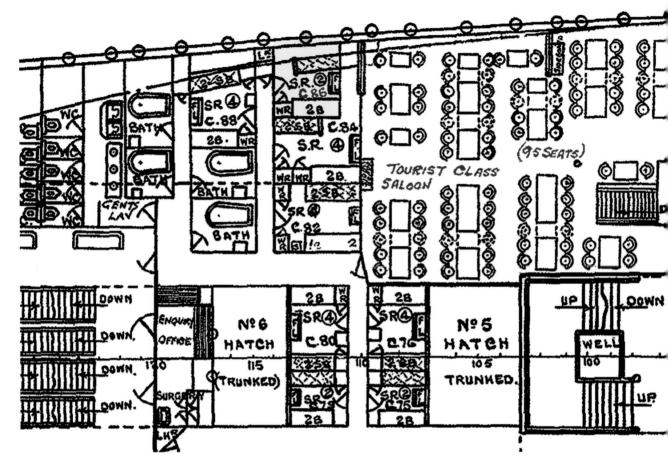

the New York police went aboard to examine a potential crime scene. In this case it was cabin C86, in which Yugoslavian national Captain Ivan Poderjay had travelled during the *Olympic*'s 22 December voyage to Southampton. Poderjay was being investigated for the disappearance of New York lawyer Agnes Tufverson, whom he had married bigamously earlier that month. Agnes, according to Captain John H Ayres of the New York Missing Persons Bureau, had last been seen with Poderjay at her apartment on 20 December 1933, coincidentally the same day that Poderjay was alleged to have purchased a strong tranquilliser and 200 razor blades, along with a large steamer trunk the following day.

ABOVE: *Ivan Poderjay's cabin on the* Olympic, *with the 20-inch porthole through which Agnes Tufverson's body could have been ejected while at sea.*

When sailing for England aboard the *Olympic*, he had taken with him six pieces of hand luggage and four large trunks, one of which he kept in his cabin, and when the Austrian police later searched Poderjay's flat in Vienna they found a trunk containing Agnes's clothing. He was immediately arrested and extradited to America to stand trial, but without a body and considering the circumstantial nature of the available evidence, in the end Poderjay could only be found guilty of perjury and bigamy.

He would still go on to serve five years at New York's Auburn Prison before being extradited back to Yugoslavia in 1940, but as for Agnes Tufverson, nothing more would ever be seen of her.

Sadly, the *Olympic*'s future was looking only marginally more secure. The reality was that ships of her ilk were no longer financially viable, perhaps best illustrated by the fact that when she had collided with the Nantucket lightship there were fewer than 200 passengers on board. To be fair, the reduced numbers were not unique to the *Olympic*, but there was little room for sentiment in the cold economic realities of the Depression. Even the legendary *Mauretania* had been withdrawn from service in October 1934, and it came as no surprise when, on 25 January 1935, it was announced that the *Olympic* would be going the same way at the end of her spring schedule. Captain Reginald Peel, formerly of the Cunard liner *Alaunia*, would command the ship on what would be her final five voyages, which were for the most part uneventful, with only the penultimate voyage marred by the death of Third Butcher James Macey in a New York hospital on 15 March from an abscess on the brain. Twelve days later the *Olympic* would depart from Southampton on what would be her 257th and final round trip to New York, carrying with her an intriguing ghost from the past, in this case Able Seaman Fred Fleet, the man who on a cold April night 23 years earlier had served as the lookout on the *Titanic*.

By 12 April the *Olympic* was once again back at Southampton, where speculation abounded as to her future. There is evidence to suggest that in early 1935 Cunard White Star had been contemplating the option of using the ship for cruising, but by the spring it was clear that the company had no practicable use for her in the foreseeable future. Two months later, as she languished at the Western Dock's berth 108 – 2 miles upstream from her customary berth in the Ocean Dock – there were even discussions of a possible sale to a syndicate proposing the use of the ship as a floating hotel on the French Riviera. In the end, it all came to nothing. On 1 July the *Mauretania* departed Southampton on her final voyage to the scrapyard at Rosyth and when the *Olympic* was opened to potential buyers on 20 August there was no longer any doubt that she would soon follow suit. Even at this late stage, rumours abounded of a return to service, not to mention the less likely possibility of being sold to the Italian government for service as a trooper for their Abyssinia campaign, but it was not to be. The following month it was announced that the *Olympic* had been sold for £97,500 to Sir John Jarvis, High Sheriff of Surrey and, from November 1935, also Conservative MP for Guildford, who through his 'Surrey Fund' had set about alleviating unemployment in Jarrow, one of the areas worst hit by the Depression. The closure of the Palmers' Shipbuilding & Iron Company in 1933 had resulted in a devastating impact on Jarrow, but through Jarvis's efforts the yard had been partially reopened, this time focusing more on ship breaking than shipbuilding. The old engine shop would even be converted into a steel foundry, where the process of recycling the steel from both the *Olympic* and later the *Berengaria* would take place.

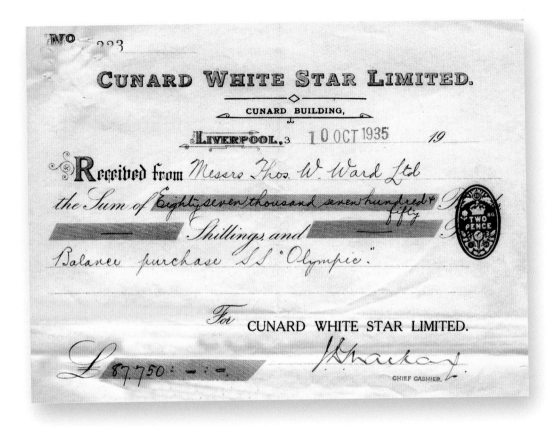

NO 223

CUNARD WHITE STAR LIMITED.

CUNARD BUILDING,

LIVERPOOL, 3. 10 OCT 1935 19

Received from *Messrs Thos. W. Ward Ltd*

the Sum of *Eighty seven thousand seven hundred & fifty*

Shillings and

Balance purchase SS "Olympic."

TWO PENCE

For CUNARD WHITE STAR LIMITED.

£ 87.750 : — : —.

CHIEF CASHIER.

ABOVE: *Receipt for the outstanding balance on the purchase of the* Olympic *by Thomas Ward Ltd, received the day before the ship departed on her final voyage to the breaker's yard at Jarrow.*

At 4.12pm on 11 October 1935, under the command of Captain Peter Vaughan, the old White Star flagship departed from Southampton for positively her final time. On board was a single passenger – the South Shields river pilot who would guide the *Olympic* to her final port of call at Palmer's Yard on the Tyne. Passing the Ocean Dock, where the *Majestic* and *Homeric* were both secured, she then headed south along Southampton Water for one last time as speedboats from Hubert Scott-Paine's British Power Boat Company at Hythe provided a guard of honour until the ship passed the Isle of Wight and headed east into the English Channel. By the evening of Saturday 12 October the *Olympic* was anchored off the Northumbrian coast, but it would not be until the following

afternoon's flood tide that the ship would be able to complete the final stage of the voyage up the Tyne. By 4.45pm the *Olympic* was finally secured in Palmer's Yard, and not a moment too soon as within half an hour the tide had already dropped enough for the ship's tired hull to be settling on the riverbed.

The coming days would see the final stripping of the once mighty corpse, when on Tuesday 5 November the London auctioneers Knight, Frank & Rutley began the ten-day process of auctioning off the ship's fittings, by now neatly divided into 4,456 lots. Once the hull had

Vessel	OLYMPIC		Dismantled at	INVERKEITHING x JARROW		N.H.P.		
Tonnage	Gross 46.439 Nett 20,994		Length O.A.	852'·5		Date of Arrival	Sept 1935	
Type	LINER		Beam	92'·5		Date Commenced	25 9. 35	
Draft on Arrival	Fwd. 31'6" Aft 31'9	JARROW INV. 16'6" 18'0"	Lt. Displacement			Date Completed	30 · 5 · 47	

OUT-TURN			Av. per Ton Depot	Realizations			% Out-Turn on G.R.T.	Demolition Costs		Cost per Ton		Remarks
Material	Weight			£	s.	d.		Service	Total Cost	£ s. d.	£ s. d.	
Steel Scrap	2549	4 2						Wages				Via Jarrow.
Cast Iron	2968	17 2						Oxygen				
Re-Rolling								Gases				£97,500 @ Southampton - left 5'6 11/Oct/35
Tubes								Cranage				Sir J. Jarvis Bt.
Rounds and Shafting	3412	3 -						Consumable Tools				£09230/5.
Anchors and Cable								Carriage or Freight				
Plates								Harbour Dues, Pilotage				
Armour								Towage, etc.				
Machinery	33	12 2						Rubbish Cartage				
Timber, Fitments, etc.	1504	17 3						Sundry Expenses				
Copper	267	19 -						Total Aggregate				
Gun Metal	271	16 1						Remuneration				
Yellow Metal	463	11 -						Selling Commission				
Lead and Zinc	185	17 -						Total Cost				
Total	3441	18 2										
Coal											20 /1.	
Fuel Oil												
Ballast												
Rubbish	3275	10 1										
Total	3769	8 3										

Remarks table:

MATERIAL	AT JARROW	AT INVERKEITHING	TOTAL
	11/10/35	20/9/37	
COPPER	194 12 1	73 6 3	267 19 -
GUNMETAL	189 13 2	82 2 3	271 16 1
YELLOW METAL Ec	325 10 -	138 1 -	463 11 -
LEAD & ZINC	131 19 3	53 17 1	185 17 -
MACHINERY	8 13 3	24 18 3	33 12 2
CAST SCRAP	1783 11 -	1185 6 2	2968 17 2
GENERAL SCRAP	13,343 12 2	12005 12 -	25,349 4 2
USABLE	2361 11 3	1110 11 1	3472 3 -
TIMBER ETC	1375 11 3	129 6 -	1504 17 3
	19,615 1 1	14,802 17 1	34,417 18 2
RUBBISH ETC	2600 9 -	675 1 1	3275 10 1
	22,215 10 1	15,477 18 2	37,693 8 3

VESSEL	OLYMPIC	Gross or Disp. Tonnage	46.439	DEPOT	INVERKEITHING	Date Delivered	Sept 1935.	TYPE	LINER

been stripped bare, the dismantling process could finally begin in earnest, and although the numbers employed were nowhere near as great as they were in the shipyard's heyday, the process would still keep many hundreds of people gainfully employed for almost two years until, on 19 September 1937, what remained of the hull would be towed for final demolition to the Thomas Ward ship-breaking facility at Inverkeithing.

In an interesting twist of fate, it is a curious coincidence that the *Olympic*'s last journey would end at almost the same time as that of one of her creators. Lord Pirrie had died in 1924, but perhaps the images of the *Olympic*'s dismantled hull being towed unceremoniously north to Inverkeithing would ultimately prove

ABOVE: *Ward's out-turn records for the* Olympic *between 1935 and 1947, itemising the materials salvaged or scrapped from the ship.*

too much for Joseph Bruce Ismay, the man whose business acumen had led to her conception 30 years earlier. Within a month he suffered a stroke at his Mayfair home in London, dying on 17 October 1937. Unlike Pirrie's headstone in Belfast, Ismay's grave at Putney Vale contains no reference to his illustrious shipping background. Perhaps the last words on the ship herself should be reserved for Captain Bertram Fox Hayes, the man who had commanded the *Olympic* for six years between 1915 and 1921: 'The finest ship in my estimation that has ever been built or ever will be.'

THE OLYMPIC CLASS IN RETROSPECT

It's been almost 90 years since the *Olympic*'s final journey to the breaker's yard, yet the Olympic class liners, as well as and the White Star Line, continue to cast a huge shadow over the public imagination. It may be that no one will ever be able to truly say that they will be forgotten, so what is this mysterious fascination that the *Olympic*, *Titanic* and *Britannic* continue to exert?

LEFT: Saved from the Titanic, *the first known* Titanic *movie released only one month after the disaster.*

Inevitably, it starts and will almost certainly end with the *Titanic*. The disaster that befell the ship took the lives of over 1,500 people and, as a result, things on the North Atlantic would never be the same again. In practical terms, this meant increased watertight compartmentalisation, lifeboat capacity for everyone on board, round-the-clock radio watches, the first international conference for the Safety of Life at Sea in 1913 and the establishment of the International Ice Patrol in 1914 to help ensure safe navigation in the North Atlantic and Arctic regions. These factors, more than anything, are part of the *Titanic*'s enduring legacy, albeit achieved at a terrible cost.

The *Titanic* has also attained an almost mythical role in popular culture, stimulated in no small part by the public's insatiable fascination in the immediate aftermath of the disaster. On 14 May 1912, barely one month after the sinking, the Eclair Film Company of New Jersey released *Saved from the Titanic*, a ten-minute one-reeler featuring the American actress Dorothy Gibson, who had not only escaped from the *Titanic* in the first lifeboat to be lowered but also wore the same clothing in the film that she had worn on the ship. Three months later it was the turn of the Continental Kunstfilm company in Berlin to release *In Nacht und Eis*, which for added realism had filmed sequences aboard the German liner *Kaiserin Auguste Victoria* at Cuxhaven. Fortunately for White Star, the film industry of 1912 was incapable of maintaining a sustained supply of *Titanic* movies, and as public interest in the disaster dwindled, the British shipping world endeavoured to move on following one of its darkest hours.

To a certain extent they were successful, assisted in no small part by the more widespread and even more traumatic memories of the Great War of 1914–18, but the fate of the *Titanic* still retained an almost mythical quality, which was always going to be fertile ground for the entertainment industry. The reality is that during the inter-war years the *Titanic* no longer belonged solely to the White Star Line, as one by one the filmmakers stamped their individual marks on the story, inevitably focusing more on the dramatic potential than

ABOVE: In Nacht und Eis *was filmed in the months immediately following the sinking of the* Titanic, *and fortunately it still survives to this day.*

any great need for historical accuracy. British International Pictures' 1929 movie *Atlantic*, a film based on Ernest Raymond's play *The Berg*, told the story of the fictional SS *Atlantic*, a liner that sinks after colliding with an iceberg, and it caused enough concern for the White Star management that attempts were even made to have the production blocked for fear of the damage it might do to the reputation not only of the company, but to British shipping as a whole. Raymond's play was undoubtedly based on the *Titanic*, with some of the events and dialogue bearing a tangible resemblance to events on the night the *Titanic* sank, but fearful of being accused of censorship the Board of Trade declined to take any action – not that they had the power to interfere anyway. In the end, the White Star Line had to content themselves with an offer from the producers to project notices in the theatres to the effect that it was no longer possible for such a disaster to happen, as all British liners now carried lifeboats for everyone on board.

Ten years later it was the turn of the Americans to raise the unwelcome spectre of another cinematic *Titanic* movie. David O Selznick's *Titanic* was also intended to be his first in partnership with British director Alfred Hitchcock, but despite Hitchcock's supposedly 'thoroughly British outlook', it too led to official representations being sent to American ambassador Joseph Kennedy in an attempt to bring pressure on Selznick International Pictures to reconsider. In truth, the British government had no power whatsoever to exert any real pressure on a foreign-made film, but in the end commercial pressures would scuttle SIP's *Titanic* project. Selznick was already heavily committed to *Gone with the Wind* and having also purchased the screen rights to Daphne du Maurier's *Rebecca*, it left the studio with little financial room for manoeuvre. As a result, Hitchcock's first film for Selznick would instead be *Rebecca*, while America's belated entry into the Second World War in December 1941 would ultimately put paid to any chance

of the *Titanic* film ever going into production. Bearing in mind that at one stage Selznick had even been contemplating the notion of buying the laid-up SS *Leviathan* and sinking her in front of the cameras, it is intriguing to speculate how Hitchcock might have handled the project had it ever gone into production, but it was not to be.

With the whole world in flames, it would be natural to assume that from 1940 onwards the *Titanic* would not be at the forefront of anyone's thoughts for the foreseeable future, yet it is at this time that what is perhaps the most intriguing cinematic version of the disaster went into production. Following the fall of France in June 1940, Joseph Goebbels, the German Reichminister for Public Enlightenment and Propaganda, was on the lookout for any conceivable way to attack Great Britain, which stubbornly refused to come to terms with Germany. The *Titanic* story seemed to provide the perfect opportunity, as Goebbels contemplated a production effectively depicting the British ruling class as a corrupt elite. 'Sir' Bruce Ismay, the movie's principal villain, would be the perfect tool for Goebbels' masterpiece, with the German *Titanic* effectively portraying a microcosm of British society – albeit one as seen by the Nazis.

The director tasked with creating Goebbels' *Titanic* was Herbert Selpin, who brought with him screenwriter Walter Zerlett-Olfenius, with whom he had a long-standing creative partnership. In addition to the elaborate sets at the Tobis Studios at Johannisthal (also known as the Jofa Studios), a 20-foot model of the *Titanic* was specially constructed for the sinking sequences to be filmed on the Scharmützelsee to the east

of Berlin, so that the film lights would be less likely to provide an easy target for the Allied bombers. The largest and most expensive prop of all would be Hamburg South America's liner *Cap Arcona*, then serving as an accommodation ship at Gotenhafen (now Gdynia) in occupied Poland.

With a budget of almost four million Reichmarks, filming commenced at Tobis on 23 February 1942, but it was not until 29 April that Selpin was finally headed for Gotenhafen to begin filming sequences on the *Cap Arcona*. By this time, however, the production was already plagued with problems. Already behind schedule, technical issues with the model had created further delays and progress at Gotenhafen was further hampered by inebriated officers who clearly had an eye for

ABOVE: *Walter Zerlett-Olfenius, the screenwriter on Herbert Selpin's* Titanic *movie who in 1942 would turn on his long time friend and betray him to the Nazis.*

the pretty young actresses that were suddenly swarming all over the base. To address the problem, Selpin called a crisis meeting at the Grand Hotel, where his after-dinner rant against not only the officers of the Kriegsmarine but also the entire German war effort, proved too much for Zerlett-Olfenius, a committed Nazi who had been sent ahead to sort out any issues before Selpin arrived. In many ways Selpin and Zerlett-Olfenius had often been looked upon as a bit of an odd couple with completely different characters, but while in the past their relationship seemed to have been constructive, Selpin's outburst had proved too much for

Zerlett. Piqued by the open rebuke, the errant scriptwriter felt he had no option but to report Selpin's disloyalty to Hans Hinkel, the head of the film department in Berlin. Not only that, but he fully understood the implications of what he was about to do when he confessed to Fritz Maurischat, the film's art director, 'I have become my best friend's grave digger.'

At the end of July, Selpin was summoned to Berlin. The evidence seems to suggest that at first Goebbels wanted to brush the matter under the carpet and offer Selpin a chance to recant his heresies, but while a simple apology would probably have sufficed, for some unaccountable reason Selpin declined to take the opportunity; instead, he admitted not only to the charges but also that he still meant every word. As a result, Goebbels saw little option other than to have Selpin arrested and taken to the Alexanderplatz police headquarters, where he would await his trial. What happened next remains a mystery. Selpin was officially informed that evening of his expulsion from the Reichskulturkammer (Reich Chamber of Culture), effectively ending his career as a film director, but it was not until the following morning that he was found dead in his cell, hanged with his own suspenders. Was it murder or suicide? The understandable tendency is to want to blame Goebbels, but his private diary states that Selpin had committed suicide in his prison cell, adding almost scornfully that it would probably have been the verdict of the court anyway. The truth of what really happened will never be known, but while the Reichminister may not have had any direct involvement in Selpin's death, the possibility of an overly zealous Gestapo officer doing the deed cannot be ruled out.

The unenviable task of completing the film fell to director Werner Klingler, but in the end it would all be for nothing. Principal photography finally completed in October and on 17 December 1942 Ewald von Demandowsky, head of production at Tobis Films and also Reichsfilmdramaturg (adviser for dramatic films) at the Ministry of Culture, gave Goebbels a private screening of the movie in Berlin. Unfortunately, it was not at all what the Reichminister had hoped for, writing in his diary that night: 'I don't like the end. It needs to be changed completely.'

So what had gone wrong? The simple answer is that by the end of 1942 the complexion of the war had changed completely when compared to the military situation in the summer of 1940. A triumphant Germany was no longer on the verge of invading Britain, while the combination of the German Sixth Army being encircled at Stalingrad and the Allied strategic bombing campaign on the German cities was taking a heavy toll on the morale of the civilian population. The tables had been turned so completely that even the depiction of Sir Bruce Ismay, heedlessly driving the *Titanic* towards its doom, might have been interpreted as an equally powerful allegory for Hitler and Germany. Goebbels saw little prospect of being able to release the film in Germany until the military situation improved, so instead *Titanic*, complete with its new ending, premiered in Paris in November 1943, in an attempt to recoup at least some of the film's huge financial outlay.

Unfortunately for Goebbels, his ambitions for Tobis's *Titanic* film would never be realised;

following Germany's unconditional surrender in May 1945, the entire output of the Nazi film industry was effectively put into cold storage until the victorious Allies could decide what to do with it. Interestingly, though, *Titanic* did have an afterlife of sorts when the Russians released the film in East Germany in April 1950. Even more intriguingly, the Russian censors evidently saw no need to make any cuts to the original film, reasoning that Goebbels' depiction of the British ruling class worked just as well as a depiction of the unacceptable face of capitalism. In the British sector, the film would not be so warmly received by the occupying powers, and when it was eventually released, all the anti-British sequences were cut from the final version.

Not surprisingly, Herbert Selpin's *Titanic* film would never be released in the UK or America, so leaving an open field for the American and British filmmakers. First to develop their own *Titanic* project would be Twentieth Century Fox in 1953. Directed by Jean Negulesco, Fox's *Titanic* starred Hollywood screen idols Barbara Stanwyck – at one time the highest paid actress in Hollywood – and Clifton Webb, and while lacking in any real historical authenticity, the production remains stylish and well made. For historical accuracy, however, the Rank Organisation's *A Night to Remember*, released five years later, probably remains *the* definitive *Titanic* movie. Perhaps this should come as no surprise as the film's producer, William MacQuitty, the son of James MacQuitty, a former managing director of the *Belfast*

BELOW: *The film crew pose in front of the model specially built for Lew Grade's 1980* Raise the Titanic. *At 55 feet it still remains the largest model of the* Titanic *ever built.*

Telegraph, had been at the Harland & Wolff shipyard on 31 May 1911 to witness the actual launch of the *Titanic*. The spectacle must have had a huge impact on young William, who 46 years later would purchase the screen rights to Walter Lord's book and begin filming the story of the *Titanic*'s last night at Pinewood Studios. Despite the faithfulness to both the set design and the historical detail, however, *A Night to Remember*, while still being one of the top 20 movies at the 1959 UK box office, would only be a moderate financial success, but the film has left an enduring legacy in the *Titanic* world with many still regarding this film as the most faithful screen version of the story.

It would be another 20 years before filmmakers were once again ready to tackle the subject of the *Titanic* on celluloid, and interestingly this time they seemed to be approaching the story from completely different angles. In 1979 two films would go into production, with *S.O.S Titanic* being produced for Thorn EMI by Lord Bernard Delfont, while his brother, Lord Lew Grade, had been in the pre-production phase of *Raise the Titanic* at ITC Films for almost three years. Once again, the *Titanic* was making film history, with *S.O.S. Titanic* having the distinction of being one of the first productions to be composed for two different formats in order to satisfy the technical requirements for both a 1.85:1 aspect ratio theatrical release and the 1.33:1 ratio for a two-part television mini-series. *Raise the Titanic*, on the other hand, would make cinematic history for all the wrong reasons, as the scale of the model resulted in a production budget spiralling out of control, not to mention a script that had been through so many drafts that the finished film bore little or no similarity to the original 1976 novel written by Clive Cussler. When *Raise the Titanic* was released in the summer of 1980, the box office takings were less than stellar, some estimates putting its eventual financial loss at well over $30,000,000. For Grade himself, it was the beginning of the end for his ambitions as a Hollywood mogul, and within two years he had been ousted from ITC. It would not be the end of Grade's career – indeed, he would continue to work in the entertainment business until his death in 1998 – and despite it all, Lew Grade left us with one of the most memorable *Titanic* quotes when he said: '*Raise the Titanic*? My God, it would have been cheaper to lower the Atlantic.'

RENAISSANCE

For 73 years, the *Titanic* had remained largely in the domain of the filmmakers, but all that would change at 12.48am on 1 September 1985, when a co-American/French expedition to locate the wreck led by Dr Robert D Ballard of the Woods Hole Oceanographic Institution and Jean-Louis Michel of IFREMER (the French Institute for Research and Exploration of the

TOP RIGHT: *The rusticles on the* Titanic *are slowly eating away at the wreck, to the point where one day it will collapse under its own weight.*

RIGHT: *Captain Smith's bathtub on the* Titanic, *photographed in 2005. The roof of the officers' deck house in this area has since collapsed.*

Sea) observed images of unidentified wreckage at the bottom of the North Atlantic. Within minutes, the unmistakeable outline of an upended Scotch marine boiler appeared on the screen, confirmation if it were needed that the *Titanic*'s resting place had finally been found. At a stroke, the *Titanic* was no longer just a mythical entity. Within hours the news had gone around the world, closely followed by the pictures, but while the location of the wreck had the potential to answer many of the questions about what really happened that night, thoughts in some quarters were turning to salvage the moment the discovery had been announced. Divisions among the explorers also started to come to the surface within weeks of

the wreck's discovery, and by the time Ballard returned to the *Titanic* the following year to carry out a more detailed imaging of the wreck site, those differences between Woods Hole and IFREMER had become a complete schism. Any hopes of the wreck being protected ultimately came to naught when, despite the 1986 American RMS Titanic Maritime Memorial Act, the following year IFREMER, in partnership with Titanic Ventures, a consortium of American investors, returned to the site to carry out the first salvage activities on the wreck.

BELOW: *The enormous* Titanic *film set at Rosarito in Mexico, specially constructed for James Cameron's 1997 movie.*

Article 149 of the United Nations Convention on the Law of the Sea (UNCLOS), which deals with the issue of wrecks located in international waters beyond the jurisdiction of any nation, states that 'All objects of an archaeological and historical nature found in the Area shall be preserved or disposed of for the benefit of mankind as a whole, particular regard being paid to the preferential rights of the State or country of origin, or the State of cultural origin, or the State of historical and archaeological origin.' This meant that until an internationally protected area had been established, the wreck of the *Titanic* was effectively a legitimate target for any individuals or organisations with the technical ability and funding to carry out such activities. Admiralty law also acknowledged the exclusive rights of those individuals to carry out salvage work, provided they had the capacity to prudently and effectively perform salvage operations, and as a result RMS Titanic, Inc, having been granted American salvor-in-possession status on 7 June 1994 by the US District Court for the Eastern District of Virginia, has now conducted eight expeditions to the wreck site, resulting in the recovery of over 5,500 artefacts from the seabed. This legal status has not always sufficed to prevent others accessing the site for reasons other than commercial salvage, as was clearly demonstrated when film director James Cameron, without the permission of RMS Titanic Inc, visited the wreck to film pre-production sequences for his 1997 *Titanic* movie.

Since 1987, the *Titanic* has also become a virtual battleground between those who advocate retrievals from the site and those who look upon such activities as little more than grave robbery. As a result, the wreck has had a huge impact on the laws of marine salvage and international collaboration, not to mention intellectual property rights, but more recently a stronger international structure for the preservation of the wreck site has taken shape. In April 2012, the centenary of the sinking, the wreck of the *Titanic* became eligible for protection under the terms of the UNESCO Convention on the Protection of the Underwater Cultural Heritage, while on 18 November 2019 the 2003 international *Agreement concerning the Shipwrecked Vessel RMS Titanic* came into force when the treaty was finally ratified by the American government. Under this agreement, any salvage by UK- or US-based companies or entities will require the permission of both countries, provided there is a justifiable educational or cultural reason.

With the *Britannic*, it is very different. When the wreck was located by Jacques Cousteau in November 1975, there was nothing like the hysteria that occurred when the *Titanic* was found nearly ten years later. After Cousteau's exploration of the wreck in the summer of 1976, the *Britannic* quickly returned to a state of relative obscurity at the bottom of the Kea Channel, where she would remain undisturbed until Bob Ballard returned to the site in August 1995 to commemorate the tenth anniversary of the discovery of the *Titanic* wreck by exploring her sister ship. Inevitably, the resulting headlines alerted the world of technical diving to the prize lying at the bottom of the Kea Channel and in the ensuing years the *Britannic* has become the ultimate wreck that any self-respecting technical diver plans

to put on their 'bucket list'. In the *Britannic's* case, however, the situation is more controlled, with the wreck having a UK owner and the fact that she lies comfortably within the boundaries of Greek territorial waters combining to ensure that any archaeological activities are carried out correctly and in conjunction with the Greek cultural authorities.

It is curious that two near identical wrecks in two very different environments, both biologically and legally, seem to have taken on an extraordinary impact in the world of diving, marine salvage and film-making, while many *Titanic* devotees mourn the fact that little now

ABOVE: *The wreck of the HMHS* Britannic *photographed from a submersible in 2014.*

remains of the *Olympic*, which after completing 24 years of successful commercial service was unceremoniously scrapped at Jarrow. Despite the fact that she was the first and undeniably the most successful ship of the class, there are now only a handful of scattered remains, largely throughout the north-east of England, most notably the oak panelling of the ship's former lounge at the White Swan Hotel in Alnwick. The *Olympic* as a physical entity is long gone, yet

ABOVE: *Where it all began. The old Harland & Wolff shipyard is now the home of the Titanic Belfast visitors' centre and the Titanic Hotel.*

it is curious that some believe that because the *Titanic* and *Britannic* are still recognisably intact, they have in some way had a much kinder fate. Odd though that thinking might be, while the two wrecks do remain recognisable for now, the process of deterioration began as soon as they settled on the seabed and as such it is inevitable that they must one day collapse. It has never been a question of if the two wrecks would collapse, but simply one of when; the *Britannic* seems to be winning the race in terms of longevity, but even there the clock is undeniably ticking.

For the time being, the *Titanic* and *Britannic* continue to serve as tangible reminders to feed the growing public fascination in all three Olympic class vessels. For so long overshadowed by the tragedy of the *Titanic* and the accident of history that occurred on the night of 14/15 April 1912, the *Olympic* and *Britannic* are now also firmly established in the saga of the once mighty White Star Line, and it will be many years – if ever – before we hear the last of the *Titanic* and her sisters...

BIBLIOGRAPHY AND SOURCES

BOOKS
Anderson, Roy *White Star* (T Stephenson & Sons, 1964)
Ballard, Dr Robert D *The Discovery of the Titanic* (Hodder & Stoughton 1987)
Beaumont, John CH *The British Mercantile Marine during the War* (Gay & Hancock, 1919)
Beaumont, John CH *Ships and People* (Geoffrey Bles, 926)
Chirnside, Mark *RMS Olympic: Titanic's Sister* (The History Press, 2015)
Eaton, John P & Haas, Charles A *Titanic: Triumph and Tragedy* (Patrick Stephens, 1986)
Fleming, John A *The Last Voyage of His Majesty's Hospital Ship Britannic* (Wordsmith Publications, 1998)
Hutchings, David F & de Kerbrech, Richard P *RMS Titanic: 1909–12 (Olympic Class)* (Haynes Publishing, 2011)
Jessop, Violet *Titanic Survivor* (Sheridan House, 1997)
Lord, Walter *A Night to Remember* (Longmans Green & Co, 1956)
Lord, Walter *The Night Lives On* (Viking, 1987)
Louden-Brown, Paul *The White Star Line* (Titanic Historical Society, 2001)
Lynch, Don & Marschall, Ken *Titanic: An Illustrated History* (Hodder & Stoughton, 1992)
McCluskie, Tom *Anatomy of the Titanic* (PRC Publishing, 1998)
McCluskie, Tom *Titanic & Her Sisters Olympic & Britannic* (PRC Publishing, 1998)
Mills, Simon *HMHS Britannic: The Last Titan* (Shipping Books Press, 1992)
Mills, Simon *RMS Olympic: The Old Reliable* (Shipping Books Press, 1993)
Mills, Simon *The Titanic in Pictures* (Wordsmith Publications, 1995)
Mills, Simon *Hostage to Fortune: The Dramatic Story of the Last Olympian, HMHS Britannic*
    (Wordsmith Publications, 2002)
Mills, Simon *Exploring the Britannic* (Adlard Coles/Bloomsbury Publishing, 2019)
Mills, Simon *The Unseen Britannic* (The History Press, Revised Edition 2020)
Moss, Michael & Hume, John R *Shipbuilders to the World: 125 Years of Harland & Wolff, Belfast 1861–1986*
    (Blackstaff Press, 1986)
Oldham, Wilton J *The Ismay Line* (Journal of Commerce, Liverpool, 1961)

SOURCES
Engineering (27 February 1914)
The Shipbuilder (February 1914)
The Titanic Commutator (Journal of the Titanic Historical Society)
Public Record Office of Northern Ireland (PRONI)
UK National Archives

PICTURE CREDITS

Andrey Alekseev: 187
Beaverbrook Collection of War Art, Canadian War
    Museum (Accession No.: CWM 19710261): 165
Cyril Codus: 18–19, 50–1, 80–1, 118–19, 148–9,
    190–1
Lionel Codus: 42, 76 (top)
Alasdair Fairbairn: 148
John Fleming Jr.: 153, 159, 170, 171, 180 (right)
Getty Images: 1, 6, 8, 13 (right), 35, 36, 48, 51 (top),
    56, 57, 102, 103, 106, 107, 112, 130, 211, 213,
    214, 227, 229, 238, 243 (bottom), 245, 248
Ronald Goodman: 151
Harland & Wolff: 22, 23, 24, 25, 26, 28, 30–1, 47, 49,
    52, 59, 66, 67, 75 (bottom), 79, 94–5, 108 (top),
    110, 113, 114, 116–17, 117 (bottom), 124, 125,
    128, 144, 200, 201, 202, 204, 206, 208, 209,
    216–17, 221, 230, 231, 235, 236, 237, 241,
    243 (top), 250
Peter Lamont: 262

Lone Wolf Media: 260
Margaret Meehan: 61, 180 (left)
Marine Technology Special Collection, Newcastle
    University: 252, 253
Jonathan Mitchell: 150, 152, 168, 176, 181
Jeff Paynter: 259
Peter Pearce: 65, 196, 224, 232
Vasilije Ristović: 43, 87, 91, 100
Bill Smith: 4
Parks Stephenson: 74 (bottom), 94 (bottom)
Titanic Historical Society, Inc.: 173
U-Group: 264
US Library of Congress: 60, 82, 101
Vintage Digital Revival/HFX Studios – Tom Lynskey,
    Levi Rourke, Matthew DeWinkeleer: 37, 92, 122, 123,
    126
Vintage Digital Revival/HFX Studios – Tom Lynskey,
    Levi Rourke, Kyle Hudak, Matthew DeWinkeleer:
    119 (top), 120, 145, 146, 147, 166, 178, 183 (top)

INDEX

C

Caesarea, HMT 186
Café Parisien 75, 111, 126
Calgaric, SS 246
Californian, SS 88, 90, 97, 102
Calshot Spit Buoy 63
Cameron, James 263
Cameron, Robert 127
Canada 164, 192, 199
Canadian Expeditionary Force 163
Canadian Field Hospital 157
Canadian government 163
Canadian Pacific Line 217
Canadian, SS 138
Canute Road 66
Cap Arcona, SS 257
Cape Cod 97, 247
Cape Cod lightship 249
Cape Race 90
Cape Town 162
Cape Verde Islands 162
Carlisle, Alexander Montgomery 20, 33, 43–44, 93, 102–3, 111
Carlton, Thomas 207
Carmania, SS 9
Caronia, SS 9, 86, 88
Carpathia, SS 97, 102
Carrickfergus 78
Carruthers, Francis 77, 78, 109
Carter, William 99
Cedric, SS 20, 138, 148, 205, 220
Celtic, SS 20, 137, 138, 191, 205
Chamberlain, Neville 246
Chaplin, Charlie 215
Cherbourg 48, 50, 52–4, 57, 84, 85, 214, 215
Cherry, Richard (Rt Hon Lord Justice) 72
Churchill, Sidney 155
Clark, Frank (Radio Operator) 247, 249
Clarke, Maurice (Captain) 82, 86, 104, 105, 107
Clyde (river) 9, 134, 135, 199, 242
Cochrane, HMS 105
Coffey, John (Fireman) 85
Colombus, SS 207
Commonwealth Line 240, 244, 245
Communist International 227
Compagnie Cherbourgeoise de Transbordement 233
Compagnie Générale Transatlantique (CGT) 8
Concanon, Henry (Colonel) 149
Conelly, J (Lookout) 171
Conference for the Safety of Life at Sea (1913) 254
Confidential List 229, 233
Connolly (Seaman) 226
Conscription 164
Constantine (King) 185
Continental Kunstfilm 255
Convention on the Protection of the Underwater Cultural Heritage 263
Conyngham, USS 194
Corner, The 88
Costley, William (Senior 7th Engineer) 133

Cottam, Harold (Radio Operator) 97
Cotter, Joseph 164
Cousteau, Jacques (Commander) 263
Coward, EA (Master-at-Arms) 226
Cowes 156, 159, 167, 168
Cowhey, Kevin (Wireless Operator) 236–8
Cunard Line 8, 9, 14, 61, 97, 113, 133, 138–9, 140, 167, 205, 207, 212, 217, 242, 246, 251
Cunard White Star Ltd 246, 249, 251
Cunningham, Michael (Steward) 133
Cussler, Clive 260
Cuthbertson, John (Private) 172
Cuxhaven 255

D

Daily Mail 227
Daly, Eugene 85
Dampier, Cecil (Captain, RN) 135–6
Daniel, F 229
Danzig 207
Dardanelles 163
Darlington Forge Company 23
Dartmouth Hospital 189
David, Hugh (Captain) 220, 221
Davis, USS 194–5
Davison, Frederick 213
Dawpool 38
Delfont, Bernard (Lord) 260
Demandowsky, Ewald von 258
Des Moines, USS 155
Design D 16
Deutschland, SS 10
Devonport Flotilla 195
Dickinson, John 71
Dillingham Immigration Restriction Act 212
Director of Transports 141
Dixon, Arthur (Steward) 211
Dobbin, James 49–50
Domet, Jakia 227
Dominion Line 7
Donovan, James 163
Doro Passage 171
Dover Castle, HMHS 159
Dowse, Elizabeth (Matron) 168, 172, 175, 182
Drake Battalion, Royal Naval Division 154
Drapetsona Cemetery 185
Duff Gordon, Lucille (Lady) 85, 96
Duff Gordon, Cosmo (Sir) 85, 97
Duke of Argyll, SS 49
Duncan, HMS 184, 185
Dunluce Castle, HMHS 157, 169
Dyke, Harry (Assistant Commander) 151, 175, 181

E

Eastleigh Hospital 190
Ebro, SS 226
Eclair Film Company 255
Edinburgh Castle, SS 44
Edward (Prince of Wales) 227
Egypt 188
Egypt Point 64

Egypt, HMHS 151, 152, 157
Ellenia, SS 231–2
Ellis Island 215
Emmwise, Iris 132
Engelhardt collapsible lifeboats 43, 93, 99
Engineering magazine 114, 118
English Channel 57, 194, 199, 218, 252
Ermine, RFA 186
Essequibo, HMHS 155, 156
Euboea 171
Europe 12, 52, 212, 222, 239

F

Fairbanks, Douglas 215
Fearnhead, T (Captain, RAMC) 178
Ferdinando, Prince of Udine 192
Fielding, Gordon (Fifth Officer) 172, 175, 176, 180–1
Flamborough Head 9
Fleet, Frederick (Lookout) 90, 251
Fleetwood 49
Fleming, Rev John 171, 173, 180
Fleming, Percy 132
Fleming, Robert (Chief Engineer) 181
Foresight HMS 183
Formosa, HMHS 155, 157
Fort St George, SS 223–5
Fournet, Dartige du (Admiral) 142
Foxhound, HMS 183, 184, 185, 186
Francatelli, Laura 97
France 50, 52, 133, 134, 144, 157, 166, 189, 256
Francis (Captain) 225
Frankfurt, SS 97
Franklin, Benjamin (Surgeon General) 158
Franklin, Phillip 193
French Riviera 251
Furmston-Evans, Cyril (Radio Operator) 90, 97
Furness Bermuda Line 225
Furness Withy & Company 233
Further Exploits of Sexton Blake, The 197
Fury, HMS 136

G

Galbraith, Thomas (Lieutenant, RN) 135–6
Gale (Captain) 83
Galeka, HMHS 169
Gallic, SS 52–3
Gallipoli 138, 144, 154, 156, 160, 162, 167
Garizio, George 226
Garland, Ada (Nurse) 173
Garland, John (Doctor, RAMC) 143
Gaumont British Productions 197, 199
General Strike 233
Geneva Convention 191
George V (King) 56
German Government 149, 189
German High Command 191
German High Seas Fleet 166
Germany 7, 10, 133, 144, 167, 191,

ACKNOWLEDGEMENTS

This book has probably been longer in development than any other on which I have previously worked, so many names and faces may have undoubtedly disappeared into the fog of time. Hopefully I will get the opportunity to correct any omissions in future editions of this book, but in the meantime the following list of friends and colleagues who have given help and advice over the years will suffice, with thanks in particular to Mark Chirnside, Alasdair Fairbairn, John Fleming Jr, Ronald Goodman, David Hutchings, Ed and Karen Kamuda, Richard de Kerbrech, Paul Louden-Brown, Ken Marschall, Tom McCluskie, David McVeigh, Margaret and Mary Meehan, Michail Michailakis, Angus and Jonathan Mitchell and Parks Stephenson. Thanks are also due to Jonathan Eyers, my editor at Adlard Coles/Bloomsbury Publishing, who first asked me to write this book, helped to source many of the images and whenever I made a request nearly always said 'yes', and to Louise Turpin for the engaging design of this book.